Confucianism
and
Christianity

T0374900

Confucianism and Christianity

A Comparative Study of Jen and Agape

XINZHONG YAO

sussex
ACADEMIC
PRESS
Brighton • Chicago • Toronto

First published in 1996, reprinted 1977 and 2017, in Great Britain by
SUSSEX ACADEMIC PRESS
P.O. Box 139
Eastbourne BN24 9BP

Distributed in North America by
SUSSEX ACADEMIC PRESS
Independent Publishers Group
814 N Franklin St, Chicago, IL 60610, USA

British Library Cataloguing in Publication Data
A CIP catalogue record for this book is available from the British Library.

Paperback ISBN 978-1-898723-76-9

Typeset & designed by Sussex Academic Press, Brighton & Eastbourne.
Printed and bound by CPI Group (UK) Ltd, Croydon, CR0 4YY

Contents

Acknowledgements

On a sunny day in May 1991, I made my first visit to Lampeter via Oxford. Although at that time I had no idea that I would settle down here for so many years, I was attracted by the beautiful scenery around the campus as well as by the warm welcome from the staff of the Department of Theology and Religious Studies. Three months later, I came to Wales from Canterbury where I had just finished my post-doctoral research sponsored by the British Council, and started my new career, being located in the Department of Philosophy with the status of Visiting Fellow. Since then until 1994, when I was appointed as a full-time lecturer in Chinese Religion and Ethics at Lampeter, I had been teaching both for St David's University College and for the University of Wales College of Cardiff. During this period, my teaching and research received full support from the head of the Department of Theology and Religious Studies at Lampeter and the head of the Department of Theology and Religious Studies in Cardiff. I was constantly encouraged by colleagues from these two departments and the Department of Philosophy at Lampeter, and my ideas were positively responded to by the students who attended my lectures. This support and encouragement enabled me to carry on with my research in the area of comparative studies between Confucianism and Christianity, and contributed to the completion of the book which I am presenting to the reader.

As far as the content of this book is concerned, I am deeply grateful to Professor D. P. Davies and Professor Peter Baelz for their reading of, and their comments on, the script. Their knowledge and untiring efforts have improved the quality of my writing and helped clarify my own ideas, especially about Christian discourses on love. There are many others who have provided substantial help to my writing and study in this or that way. Among them, Professor Paul Badham, Professor John Bowker, Dr David Cockburn, the late Professor P. B. Hinchliff, Professor Humphrey Palmer and Emeritus Professor Cyril Williams must be acknowledged for their patient reading of this or that part of the script; most of their comments have been incorporated into this book.

My writing benefited from the award of a Visiting Scholarship at St John's College, Oxford, 1994. I would also like to thank the Spalding Trust for its constant support.

Several parts of this book have been published in journals. Among them, 'Jesus and Confucius: A Comparison' (*The Scottish Journal of Religious Studies*, vol. 16, no. 1, 1995, pp. 37–50) is an adapted version of part of chapter 2; and 'Jen, Love and Universality: Three Arguments concerning Jen in Confucianism' (*Asian Philosophy*, vol. 5, no. 2, 1995, pp. 181–95) is part of chapter 6. I thank the editors of these journals for their publication of the above mentioned articles and permission to reprint these articles as parts of this book.

The book was revised in the summer of 1997 for the current paperback edition.

Xinzhong Yao

1

Introduction

For one hundred years or so, the comparative study of different traditions in different parts of the world has been an urgent task, not only for anthropologists and sociologists, but also for philosophers, theologians and historians. As the world becomes increasingly smaller, in terms of travel and communication, more and more people are realizing that we have entered an age in which each of the world's religions, great or small, has encountered or is encountering others. The world of religion is no longer viewed as composed of different religious blocks, but as a single block with a multi-framed structure. However, as well as interdependence and co-existence between different traditions, clashes and conflicts resulting from religious diversity and exclusiveness continue, sometimes more fiercely than before. As we approach the millennium, the search for effective ways to enable different religious systems to co-exist peacefully in mutual complementarity has emerged as a necessary condition for economic development, social progress, human prosperity and even survival.

USES AND MISUSES OF A COMPARATIVE STUDY OF RELIGIONS

The combination of diversity and interdependence in the religious world calls for comparative studies of religion. The possibility of a comparative study of religion arises out of the nature of the human expression of religious vision. Human beings have developed different views of the world and the beyond. At first glance, these views diverge from each other. However, most scholars believe that beneath these views lies some shared vision, which provides a ground for a comparative study of religion. Such a positive philosophy of the religious nature of human beings suggests that, just as tributaries come together to form a single river, so different religious expressions may be integrated into a single comprehensive enterprise, to which individual religions will make their own specific contributions. It maintains that various races, nations and peoples share a fundamental religious framework and that, despite their different approaches, they are moving towards the same, or at least a similar, spiritual goal. It is on this presumption that people explore the possibilities of a comparative approach to the study of world religions and proclaim that a unity of religions in the world will be achieved in the near future.

Other scholars, however, hold a different opinion. For them, religions are essentially divergent rather than convergent. Between religions there is little room for communication, even less for mutual complementarity. For this reason, they take up a negative attitude to the comparative study of religion: religious values belong to the realm of subjectivity, and it is therefore impossible to evaluate different religious views because there is no equivalent in this field to the laws which operate in the field of science and which command universal assent. Influenced by philosophical positivism, some scholars insist that the comparative study of religion can be fruitful only in the area of anthropological or sociological studies, but not in the area of philosophical or religious studies. The former are descriptive disciplines, the latter are normative. As descriptions, sociological or anthropological studies of religion will certainly add to our knowledge of various world cultures and traditions, but a normative approach will bring nothing but confusion and chaos. They argue that harmony in the world of religion cannot be created by 'philosophical imagination'. It can come only from recognizing what religions are. Diversity is the nature of human religiosity, and this nature prevents any attempt to harmonize different faiths and bring them together.

Although, generally speaking, these two different opinions concerning the possibility of comparative studies of religion have their own specific merits, both fall short of the truth. On the one hand, there is no compelling evidence that diversity of human religiosity prevents us from comparing different faiths and religious views. It is open to us to press on with a comparative study of religion, not only in the fields of sociology and anthropology, but also in those of philosophy, ethics and religious studies. It is indeed true that most forms of human religion tend to be exclusive. However, this tendency should not be taken as an excuse for refusing to open one's eyes to other faiths, nor for failing to reflect on their differences and similarities in philosophical terms. The interaction of the modern world is breaking down the fences between different traditions, and the history of religions has shown that the co-existence of religions must begin with the awareness and admission of the existence of other faiths. Neglect of other faiths brings misunderstanding, misunderstanding breeds hostility, and hostility develops into war and destruction. Such war and destruction as are caused by hostility between faiths are contrary to the essence of religion, which is to find ways to eternity and lasting happiness by creating harmony and peace in a disharmonious world. To create peace and harmony in the world, we have to reduce hostility and misunderstanding between different traditions. To reduce hostility and misunderstanding, we have to initiate dialogue between different faiths.[1] To initiate dialogue, we have to undertake comparative studies of the theories and practices of different religions, so that this dialogue may be meaningful and productive.

On the other hand, we must admit that, in recognizing the difficulties and problems inherent in the comparative study of religion, the negative view is at least partly right even though we do not agree with its rejection of such a study. With this insight, we can avoid repeating the mistakes frequently made in this field. By showing too much enthusiasm, for example, some scholars tend to oversimplify their subjects in making their comparisons. According to David Little and Sumner B. Twiss, there are three major misuses of the comparative study of religion:

> First, the attempt to typify 'whole religious traditions', like Christianity, Buddhism, and Islam, and then to compare them with each other in broad terms, is liable to gross oversimplification. Such an approach ignores and obscures the complex and intricate variations and divergences within each tradition and thus distorts, rather than clarifies, religious phenomena. Second, the comparative study of religion has often been undertaken for apologetic purposes, either overt or covert, and that calls into question the objectivity of the results. Third, attempts have been made, on the basis of comparative study, to derive theories which purport to explain the origin and development of religion.[2]

To guard against these misuses, we must always have in mind the diversity of the human expressions of religious vision and refuse to be deluded either by a simplistic approach or by a superficial overview. A proper attitude towards the comparison of religions is to combine a positive belief in the continuity of human nature and the value of a comparative approach with caution in comparing any two specific forms of human tradition.

Success in a comparative study of religion will come only when the study is carried out on the basis of a consistent principle of impartiality. In practice, it always seems easier to base a comparison on one's own religious beliefs. There is nothing wrong in this approach. The problem is that this approach often leads people to making judgements in favour of their own religious background. In this kind of comparative study, whatever conclusions are drawn at the end of research, they are often variant forms of the claim that one religion is superior to another, or is itself unique.[3] The promotion of one religion at the expense of others, or the prescriptive suggestion that 'other religions *should learn* from this one', proves not only speculative but also counter-productive. It reduces the value of a comparative study, not because it is permeated with one's own religious belief, but because it violates the principle of a comparative study and allows prejudice to overrule impartiality. Comparison of this kind turns out to be of little theoretical value and of even less practical use, because it will immediately evoke opposition from other religious traditions, so that it is regarded more as a provocative challenge than as the conclusion of scientific research.

A qualified comparison between religions must be based on the principle of impartiality. The principle of impartiality does not preclude the religious commitment of a researcher, nor does it separate one's personal values from the value of making a comparison. There was a time when the end of absolute objectivity was pursued, and the subject and object were completely separated. To be correct one had to observe things as they were in isolation, not allowing any personal values to come into one's interpretation of what was observed. However, such mechanical 'objectivity' has long been abandoned. Hermeneutical theory has moved beyond the liberal or enlightenment idea of objectivity and come to the realization that there is no value-free interpretation. To do a piece of research is to establish a relationship between the observed and the observer, or between the interpretee and the interpreter. A reliable interpretation of religions must therefore be based on an open-ended, listening, critical and appreciative dialogue.

Understood as such, the principle of impartiality pursues its goal in the process of observing and interpreting. There is no 'perfect' religion which is exempt from criticism, nor is there a totally 'objective' standard available. An impartial comparison does not mean that one should never make any judgement or criticism over this or that tradition; nor does it imply that one should always place oneself exactly midway between two religions which one intends to compare. It is the principle that one should apply the same criteria to both sides from beginning to end. It insists that a religious tradition must be respected, but it also allows one to reject something within the classical writings or traditional practices of any religion that is inconsistent with the principle of human religiosity, and therefore it enables one to make evaluative judgements in due course and after careful consideration. Without such judgements of pros and cons, advantages and disadvantages, a study would be shallow and superficial. However, the principle of impartiality restrains one from making arbitrary, partial and inconsistent judgements, and consequently one's own values and commitments are also subject to examination. Such an understanding of the process of open and self-critical reflection is the most important element of the principle of impartiality and therefore is a prerequisite for any successful comparison of religions.

LOOKING FOR SIMILARITIES BETWEEN RELIGIONS

A proper comparison of religions is engaged in three tasks: looking for similarities, discovering differences and, because of overlap and mutual involvement, examining similarities in differences and differences in similarities.

A comparative study must first search for similarities between religions, which is a starting-point for any comparison. To compare two essentially different things makes no sense and is a waste of time. In this author's opinion, however, there are no two completely different religions in this world, and it is always possible to find, here or there, some similarities between any two forms of religious expression. The question is how to find and evaluate them. There are basically two ways of looking for similarities between religions. One is to examine their phenomenological frameworks; the other is to examine their structures.

Although the religious world is pluralistic and multi-dimensional, its phenomenological framework is clear. As far as space is concerned, there are world religions that are practised throughout the world, and regional religions that are practised in specific parts of the world or among particular groups of people or nations. As far as time is concerned, there are traditional religions that are based mainly on the historical recordings of original beliefs and practices, and reformed or new religious movements that come into being either by a transformation of old beliefs and rituals or by the creation of new ones. As far as the nature of religion is concerned, there are unitary religions that adhere to a single belief and practice and exclude the basic elements from any other tradition, and syncretistic religions that are formed by drawing upon and harmonizing different beliefs, rituals and ethics. From such a phenomenological description, we can at once find out whether or not there exist *prima facie* similarities between two religions: for example, whether they are world religions or regional ones; whether they have the potentiality to universalize their teachings or are confined to their own origins; whether they are more traditionally orientated or have been more adapted to the modern world; whether they are syncretic towards other religious beliefs or are more fundamentalistic in keeping their own dogma. The discovery of such similarities is interesting. However, it is insufficient to be the basis of a piece of academic research. At its best, it is the beginning of a sociological or anthropological study. In order to find more essential common characteristics between different traditions, we have to examine in greater detail the structural features of those traditions that we intend to compare.

By structural features we mean those features of a religion that reflect inner structure and corresponding functions. The analysis of religious structure is related to the definition of religion. It is important to have a clear idea of what a religion is before attempting to compare religions. This approach does have its critics. Max Weber saw in this approach a danger that 'factual religion' would be replaced by 'imagined religion'. For him, a proper definition of religion is not possible at the start of the investigation. He believes, on the contrary, that 'Definitions [of religion] can be attempted, if at all, only at the conclusion of the study'.[4] It is our view, however, that without a proper understanding of what a religion is, research would have no starting point. Although it is difficult to give a satisfactory and straightforward definition, it is nonetheless desirable to make the simple statement that a religion is concerned both with a way to overcome the limitations of life and with a search thereby for life's ultimate meaning. To overcome life's limitations, a religion must extend its view from the temporal to the eternal; to find life's ultimate meaning, it must examine the dual relationship between

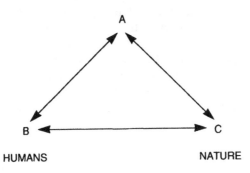

Figure 1.1

human beings and the finite world, and between humans and the Infinite, the first providing the context in which the ultimate meaning is sought, the second showing how the limitations of life must be overcome if one wants to reach the ultimate and unlimited. Therefore, in the religious world, human beings do not exist in isolation. They exist not only in relationship with one another, and in relationships between the individual and the community, but also in relationships between humans and the Transcendent, and between humans and Nature. The Transcendent, Humans and Nature are thus three cornerstones of the basic structure of a religious building.

An investigation of the inner structure of a religion can become very complicated. However, a simple pattern for understanding it could be a triangle, the three points of which, A, B and C, represent respectively the Transcendent, Humans and Nature. The structure and functions of a religion are then to be found in the mutual relations between these three points (see figure 1.1).

Any mature religion has a structure based on these three points, whatever form each of these points may take. The relationships between each of the three points and the other two give rise to three aspects of religious theory and practice, clearly distinguishable but closely related to each other. The first aspect focuses on Point A and the relationships originating from Point A and extending *to* Point B and Point C. Because they originate from Point A, and because Point A represents the Transcendent, these relationships are often known as the 'transcendental' aspect of a religion. 'Transcendental discourse' is different from theological doctrine. The latter, in its literal and common usage in Christianity, Judaism and Islam, means discourse about God. However, there are other religions which do not talk about such a God or gods. Thus, the transcendental discourse of a religion refers to theoretical reflection on the Unlimited, or Infinite, and his/her/its creative relation to human beings and to the natural world. The focus of the transcendental aspect of a religion is on the Transcendent, which may assume almost any form:

> It may be a quality (for example, wisdom, love), a relation (for example, harmony, unity), a particular natural entity (sun, earth, sky, river, animal, and so on), a particular human individual or group (such as a king, the dead), nature as a whole (that is, Nature), a pure form or realm of pure form (for example, Good, Truth, All Ideas), pure being (such as One, Being Itself, Ground of Being), or transcendent active being (such as Allah, Yahweh, God).[5]

Therefore, while we may agree that not every form of world religions has a conception of God, most have a transcendental aspect, whether focusing on salvation through the power or being that is outside humanity, or emphasizing human self-transformation. Generally speaking, the typical form of the Transcendent in world religions is a super-natural and super-human power or force or personality, in which Transcendent Being or Power is believed to control human affairs and destiny and to decide the evolutionary course of nature. According to this kind of transcendental principle, human beings and nature are essentially dependent on the Transcendent.

The second aspect of the structure of a religion focuses on Point B and on the relationships originating from Point B and extending *to* Points A and C. Point B represents human beings, and the relationships initiated by humans may be called the 'religious' aspect of a religion. The term 'religion' may be used either in a broad or a narrow sense. In its broad sense, a religion is constituted by all the relationships between religious subjects and objects, and by all the religious theories and practices connected with transcending the limitations of life and searching for life's ultimate meaning. However, in its narrow sense, as used here, it refers mainly to one of the three aspects found within a religious structure: the relationships of humans as religious subjects with the Transcendent and Nature as religious objects, and their efforts to find the ultimate meaning of life through communicating with the Infinite and through harmonizing life with its material conditions. In developing these relationships, they invent and promote special beliefs, emotions, worship, rituals, behaviour and life-styles. Since the focus of this aspect is on the relationship of humans as religious subject *to* the Transcendent as religious object, it is distinct from the transcendental discourse, which focuses on the religious object and its relationship *to* humans. The typical form of religious expression is faith. Faith is an attitude and orientation towards the Transcendent. The question that concerns a comparative study of religion is not whether faith is true or idolatrous, as Paul Tillich suggests,[6] but whether it is properly functional or malfunctional. A properly functional faith establishes communication between the religious subject and the religious object, while a malfunctional faith blocks or breaks this communication, so that the religious subject cannot attain to the Transcendent. When this happens, the religious aspect of a religion degenerates and is overshadowed either by its transcendental dimension or by its ethical dimension, which is another aspect of religious structure.

Humans exist not only in their relationships with the Transcendent, through which they receive or seek for the ultimate meaning of life, but also in their relationships among themselves and with Nature, in which they develop meaning in daily life. These relationships and activities make up the third aspect of religious structure: the ethical aspect, which focuses on Point B and its relationship with Point A and Point C. The search for the ultimate meaning of life must be carried out in awareness of human nature and activity, and the ethical aspect of religion is an extension of the transcendental discourse and religious aspects. In terms of the triangle, ethics is religious because human nature and behaviour are interpreted in the light of their relationship with the transcendental. The action-guiding function of morality does not contain its legitimacy in itself, but in its commitment to the religious ultimate. Therefore, what differentiates religious ethics from philosophical or anthropological ethics is the fact that it is based on the transcendental value of moral rules and moral perceptions. Its authority, through communication between the human and the sacred, is provided by the latter; its environmental awareness is promoted, in the course of the search for the ultimate meaning of life, by the realization that nature and humanity are partners rather than competitors;[7] and its aim, by way of moral effort, is to discover the ultimate meaning of life

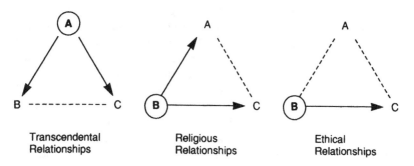

Figure 1.2

and to overcome its limitations rather than to give a rational justification of one's actions and motives. Due to the variety of expression of human relationships with the Transcendent and with one another, the line between a religious and a purely rational ethics is sometimes difficult to draw. Within the framework of religious traditions, however, an ethic often falls into one of the following categories: an ethic that is subordinate to theology, and an ethic that is itself identified with transcendental discourse. In the former, ethics is taken only as a secondary means to the transcendental goal, while in the latter, ethics is regarded as the only way to transcendence. These two kinds of ethics will be discussed when we come to compare Christian ethics and Confucian ethics.

The three aspects of a religion, the transcendental dimension, the religious dimension and the ethical dimension, are thus formed respectively by the relationship extending *from* the Transcendent (A) to Humans (B) and to Nature (C), by the relationship extending *from* Humans to the Transcendent and to Nature, and by the relationship extending *from* humans to other humans and to nature (see figure 1.2).

Generally speaking, any religious system includes within itself these three aspects, and any of its central concepts has these three dimensions. By distinguishing each aspect from the others, a comparative study no longer presents a confused amalgam of two religions, but a comparison of corresponding aspects: for example, of the transcendental discourse of one religion with the transcendental discourse of the other. Among these three distinct aspects, the fewest similarities between two different types of religion are found in the conception and expression of the Transcendent. Although, as we have said, every religion possesses a transcendental aspect, this does not mean that it necessarily has a theology focused on God or God's creation. We must take into account the different images of the Transcendent and the diverse approaches to transcendence presented in different traditions. More similarities can be found in the religious aspect, that is, in the human pursuit of transcendence, aspirations for the eternal and worship of the ultimate. Faith may be directed to different objects, and rituals and symbols may vary from one tradition to another, but their underlying principles have much in common: transcending the temporal and attaining to the eternal. When we enter the field of the ethical – involving an individual's attitudes towards himself, his fellowmen and his environment, as well as human relationships in society, and the rules, principles and disciplines set up to guide social behaviour – we find the greatest number of similarities between different types of religion, even though their transcendental foundations and religious orientations may be far apart. From the Buddhist 'Five Prohibitions' to the Judaic 'Ten Commandments' (except for the theological items), from Christian '*agape* as neighbour-love' to the Confucian '*jen* as loving all', we find a common condemnation of selfishness, egoism and indifference to others' suffering, and a common praise of sincerity, altruism and idealism. However, even in this area, the 'similar' should not be understood as the 'same'. The forms of moral discipline, the idea of 'perfection' and its constituent virtues, and the functions of virtues, are sufficiently different from one religion to another to make them distinct, not only as regards the substance of ethical values, but also as regards the forms and function of moral norms, rules and institutions.

Similarities between religions exist not only in their corresponding aspects – such as the transcendental discourse of this religion and the transcendental discourse of that religion – but also in the ways all these three aspects combine. The three aspects of a religion interdepend and interact in this or that way, from which the dynamic character of a religion emerges. The interdependence and interaction of the three aspects underlie all forms of religion, and their ways are more or less similar. In their interdependence, the transcendental consideration is always decisive and lays the basis for the other two aspects, which are regarded as its extension or application. In their interaction, however, the religious and ethical aspects of a religion are not passive and completely pre-determined

by their transcendental principle. On the one hand, they can moti-
vate transcendental search and deepen human understanding of its
underlying idea. On the other, they can apply the underlying principle to practical issues and cultivate conscience, sense of responsibility and piety of faith, so that the transcendental principle is no
longer outside and beyond human beings, but within and among
them.

MAKING DISTINCTIONS BETWEEN RELIGIONS

In a comparative study of religion, similarities and differences must
be held together. No two religions are completely different, nor
are any two religions totally the same. The similarities between
two religious traditions must be placed against the background of
their differences. In one sense, their differences are more important
for a comparative study than their similarities, because it is these
differences that have led to two *different* traditions. If we do not
pay enough attention to the differences, our comparison will go
awry, producing no more than an artificially unitary framework of
two religions that are obviously different in their origins, doctrines
and principles. In religion, similarities are based on the common
nature of human beings, while differences reflect diverse expressions of human civilization, culture and tradition. Different cultures,
different ways of life, and even different languages give rise to
different expressions of religious belief and create different forms of
world-view. The divergencies between religions, which contribute
one of the important reasons for undertaking a comparative study,
present a real difficulty for pursuing the goal of harmonizing
existing religions. Some scholars thus tend to believe that these
divergencies have produced a gap too wide to be bridged by any
comparative approach. We may well regret their pessimism, but
we must acknowledge that it is dangerous to identify religious
expressions in one religion with apparently similar expressions in
another, without careful comparison and proper criticism.

This danger requires us to make clear distinctions between religions. Theologians, philosophers and anthropologists have argued
in many ways that there are distinct groups of religions in the world.
For example, in order to explore the 'historically grounded and
phenomenologically *dynamic typology of religion*'[8] in the world, Hans
Küng distinguishes 'three existing great religion river systems'.

According to him, the first great river system is of Semitic origin and of prophetic character, and is composed of the 'three Abrahamic religions', Judaism, Christianity and Islam. In this system, the common feature is a 'piety of belief'. The second is of Indian origin and is characterized by its mysticism. Jainism, Buddhism and Hinduism belong to this system and centre their teaching on the idea that everything is one and that the ultimate goal is to be integrated into this mystical One. The third great river system is of Chinese origin and revolves around the perfect ideal of the sage, giving rise to a system of religions of wisdom. In this system, the wisdom of Confucian sages and Taoist masters leads people to salvation.[9]

Hans Küng's typology of religions is a useful attempt to distinguish between existing religions in the world, especially in relation to their geographical and historical features. However, as he himself admits, it is easy to develop a stereotype such as that the similarities in different systems of religion as well as the differences within the same system are obscured. For example, in prophetic religions there is also a strong element of wisdom, as well as a tendency towards mysticism. Again, the central principle in religions of wisdom often overlaps with the central principle in religions of mysticism. With its preference for geography and history and its inadequacy for distinguishing different types of religion, this typology of the world religions is obviously unsuitable for our purpose – a comparison between Christianity and Confucianism. What we now need is a pattern which can be used to present essential and structural differences between religions, while disregarding the phenomenal variety of origin and geography. To establish a typology of this sort, we will return to the triangle of religious structure. Every form of religious expression must have three points, and therefore three aspects, if it is to constitute a structural entity. However, the emphasis in different religions is different. These different emphases lead to different relationships, and these, in turn, constitute different religious structures. These differences in religious relationships and structures enable us to divide the world religions into three archetypes, each revealing a distinguishing feature by focusing on one of the triangle's three points, from which all relationships, whether between humans or between humans and their transcendence develop (see figure 1.3).

The first type of religion is that which is developed around Point A. It is characterized by its reliance on the Transcendent, so that the Transcendent is understood as Theistic Being, active and personal.

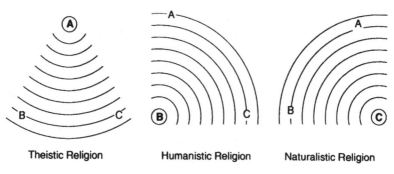

Theistic Religion   Humanistic Religion   Naturalistic Religion

Figure 1.3

Therefore, this kind of religion may well be called 'theocentric religion', in which Theistic Being, either singular or plural, is both the starting point and the end of all relationships. As the centre of religion, Theistic Being is the source of all meaningful relationships; or more precisely, the meaning and value of all relationships are those projected by Theistic Being, and humans and nature are related to Theistic Being through his creation and omnipresent grace. As the transcendent power of religion, Theistic Being alone is the initiator and mover of human transcendence. Dependent on Theistic Being, Point B (Humans) and Point C (Nature) gain their position and value in the universe from divine existence and creation. Human hope for transcendence can be realized only by the theistic grace that engages the human heart. Human attitudes to each other and to the natural world are based on the need to imitate the character of the Theistic Being. Because theistic religion emphasizes the divine, it also stresses the importance of the human response to divine grace. Therefore, a theistic religion does not deny the responsibility of humans for their own existence and activity. However, it insists that this responsibility is generated by Theistic Being and rooted in his care for humans. Without Theistic Being's initiation, humans can do nothing meaningful. Nature and natural beings are taken as signs of theistic creation and have no independent position in the whole system. A typically theocentric religion is Judaism, in which God is the beginning and end of all life. Other religions, like Christianity and Islam, share many characteristics of its theory and practice.

The second type of religion is humanistic, in which B (humans) occupies the central position and human transcendence is taken as fulfilling humanity. What is meant by humanistic religion needs to be defined, since the term humanism has acquired a technical connotation suggesting a school of philosophy in the eighteenth and nineteenth centuries. Humanism as used here, however, indicates a tradition that is in contrast to theism which searches for salvation in the divine source. Thus, a humanistic religion maintains that human beings can and will attain transcendence by fulfilling humanity in their nature or heart. In this kind of tradition, the process of human transcendence is regarded as one of self-cultivation by one's own efforts in ethics and politics, which are matters not merely of moral but also of transcendental significance. The Transcendent may be taken sometimes in the sense of Theistic Power or even acknowledged and reverenced in the form of divine authority or administration. However, in contrast to theocentric religion, in which any relationship must have its ultimate source in its creation by the Theistic Being, the relationships of a humanistic religion start with human beings and are projected by the fulfilment of humanity. Its structure finds its balance at Point B. The Transcendent is essentially internalized as embodied in human nature, and humans attain transcendence in fulfilling this nature. The internalization of the Transcendent produces a spirituality which distinguishes it from that of a typical theocentric religion. Within the framework of a humanistic religion the Transcendent is understood in concepts constructed *by* human intelligence rather than given by revelation; unity between it/him and the human world is emphasized more than their separation; the maintenance of this unity is generally regarded as a human duty rather than as the task of a Messiah empowered with divine authority; and the function of the Transcendent lies more in the expression of universal laws or principles than in the expression of personal will, so that it does not engage directly with human affairs but works indirectly through human activity. Consequently, transcendence is more a process of moral activity than an endowment from divinity. A humanistic religion aims at human transcendence, but it rejects the view that transcendence is primarily initiated by theistic Being. It takes human transcendence as human perfection, in which the limitation of life is broken through and the ultimate meaning of life found. It maintains that human nature is the same as the nature of the Transcendent and that therefore temporal and secular human beings are able to transform and promote themselves to the level of eternity and sacredness. Confucianism, especially neo-Confucianism, is the classical representation of this kind of religion.[10] While Christianity possesses a clear tendency towards a humanistic religion, since it assumes that Jesus Christ, who is its centre and focus, is at the same time truly God and truly Man, it is basically a theistic religion, because the Transcendent is equated with God, God and divine grace are taken as the centre of its spirituality, and human transcendence is possible only through divine grace.[11] Some modern Christian theologians argue that there are significant humanistic factors in Christianity, such as the emphasis on Jesus as a moral teacher, on Christ as a human model, or on salvation as the *human* response to Jesus' call. We admit that these teachings are part of Christian doctrine. However, we shall argue that they are based on the fact that it is God, through Jesus Christ, who offers the possibility of human salvation, and that therefore, Christianity, basically and essentially, is a theocentric rather than a humanistic tradition.

The third type of religion is naturalistic, in which Point C (nature or natural law) occupies the central position. Both the Transcendent and human beings are viewed as parts of nature or as products of natural process. Only by following nature can human beings attain transcendence. Some forms of naturalistic religion may believe in the superiority of a theistic being. However, in the last analysis, the function and role of this being give way to those of natural laws. Other forms of naturalistic religion may emphasize human engagement in the evolutionary process of nature. However, this engagement does not justify human superiority over nature. Rather, human value is achieved in being part of nature and human transcendence is possible only because of the underlying power of nature. Taoism, especially early or classical Taoism, is an exact exemplar of this type of religion, in which Tao, the Way of Nature, is taken as both creator and warrant of human and theistic beings. Buddhism, in the theory of some schools, may be regarded as a naturalistic religion; but as a popular faith, especially in Pure Land Buddhism with its devotion to Amitabha, it may be regarded as a theocentric religion. The natural theology that became popular in Europe in the seventeenth and eighteenth centuries may be regarded as a compromise between naturalistic religion and theocentric religion.

This typology of the world's religions reveals clear differences of religious structure and relationship. However, we must not over-emphasize such demarcation and so give an impression that there exists a 'pure' theocentric religion, or a 'pure' humanistic religion, or a 'pure' naturalistic religion. Admittedly, each type has its own specific characteristics and can thereby be distinguished from the others. However, none of them is absolutely exclusive of the others. The three forms of religious expression frequently overlap. There are humanistic factors in a theocentric religion, and theistic factors in a humanistic religion. For example, while Confucianism is normally taken to be a humanistic religion, it shows a strong theistic colour in respect of its concept of *Tian*, when *Tian* is interpreted as the supreme Lord, or Sovereign in Heaven, especially in the early stage of its development. Again, while Christianity is a theocentric religion, because its centre and focus is God and it insists that God alone makes human salvation possible, nonetheless it possesses many humanistic features, because it emphasizes that human engagement in transcendence is also necessary. Therefore, when we compare two different religions, we should not only separate them into their types, for example, one as a 'theocentric religion' and another as a 'humanistic religion', but we should also attend to the ways in which they overlap, paying attention, for example, to the humanistic elements in theocentric religion and to the theistic elements in humanistic religion. That is what we have stressed above: we must take into account the differences in similarities and the similarities in differences.

This study is essentially about two types of religion: Christianity as a theocentric religion and Confucianism as a humanistic religion. The analysis and comparison of the theocentric and humanistic elements in Christianity and Confucianism will be the central theme of this thesis. Neither Confucianism nor Christianity exists in only one form. In so far as they are different types, a comparison between them will be of value for our knowledge, not only of differences in religious manifestation but also of differences in basic human religiosity. In so far as either of them includes aspects of the other, an analysis of their similarities in difference and of their differences in similarity will be of even greater value for our understanding of human nature and human culture.

PURPOSE AND OUTLINE OF THIS COMPARATIVE STUDY

Before we proceed with our exploration of these two traditions, we must consider the best way of undertaking a comparative study between them. On the one hand, it must be based on factual description; on the other, a comparison for the sake of comparison, though valuable for increasing our knowledge, is unlikely to produce conclusions useful either for a historical survey or for a theoretical analysis. To achieve our primary purpose, we must adopt a variety of approaches, so that we may be able to penetrate the various levels of each religion and understand their concepts, principles and spirituality, and in this way obtain an appreciation of their differences and similarities.

This is an extremely complicated project and must be dealt with carefully. When discussing how to progress in learning, *the Doctrine of the Mean* outlines five ways: studying extensively; making inquiries accurately; reflecting carefully; discriminating clearly; and practising earnestly.[12] We may adapt these five methods to suggest five steps in a systematic and comparative study of Confucianism and Christianity. Studying is the first step. A religion can be said to be a compound of beliefs, emotions, rituals, sacred writings, forms of worship, rules, behaviour, attitudes and ways of life. Only through extensive study, especially of its basic classics, fundamental doctrine, propagated virtues, and ideal personalities, will it be possible for us to understand the essential character of the theories and practices of a religion, and to prepare the ground for a comparison. If, however, we intend to compare two traditions, or two key concepts of different traditions, it is not enough simply to study them. What we should do next is to make inquiries about anything that is not clear to us. It is obvious that there must be many grey points in religious doctrine, either because of its history or because of its theoretical obscurity. Leaving them unexplored could produce misunderstanding of the religion in question. Inquiries should be directed to the classical writings or to the commentaries which are abundant in most traditional religions. Further, both study and enquiry need reflection. Study and reflection are two sides of the same process. 'Study without thinking remains in confusion, while thinking without study will be in peril' (*Analects*, II, 15). Only when studying, enquiring and reflecting go hand in hand can we clearly grasp the similarities and differences between the two religions. From this knowledge we are naturally led to the next step, that of establishing the true relationship between the religions. To establish this relationship, we must first carefully distinguish them and only then relate them. The greatest danger at this point is to make merely subjective assertions. Compared with other subjects, a comparative study of religion is especially open to bias and partiality, devaluing one religion in favour of the other, according to one's own preference rather than one's substantial research. To avoid this bias, it is necessary for us to apply the principle of impartiality in all our judgements, consistently and equally to both sides. Finally, we have to extend our research to those issues that are practically urgent, drawing out conclusions which will help people to deal with inter-faith conflicts, reduce misunderstanding, and thereby make a contribution to a more harmonious and peaceful life.

Having outlined guiding lines, proper processes and basic approaches, we are now in a better position to speak of a specific comparison between Confucianism and Christianity, in respect of their central principles. Although these two traditions did not formally encounter each other until the end of the sixteenth century, they have since then had close contacts, especially in the East Asian countries of China, Japan, Korea and Vietnam, which were at that time Confucian states or states with a strong Confucian tradition. Their contacts continue in modern times and provide new grounds for a comparative study. On the one hand, Christianity is entering and spreading in these countries. For example, in China the number of new Christians is increasing.[13] On the other, Confucianism has survived the impact of Western culture and communist revolution and is being revived as a motive force for modernization. We are repeatedly reminded that East Asia has in the last 30 years become a booming and fast growing area. Some scholars claim that 'the new patterns of behaviour in these rapidly modernizing societies are undergoing modification that can only be understood with reference to the ancient Confucian heritage', so that 'Confucianism is in no way a religion of the past, but rather a living, *contemporary spiritual power* that influences people directly or indirectly'.[14] Tu Wei-ming argues that Confucianism is moving towards a third epoch, in view of the extraordinary revitalization of Confucianism in the last few decades. He also suggests that the new creativity of Confucianism is not simply confined to the East Asian cultures but also offers a positive response to universal and perennial human problems and concerns.[15] Contacts and exchanges between Confucianism and Christianity are leading not only to confrontation but also to new opportunities for mutual understanding and interaction. How far can they be said to share a common transcendental orientation? To what extent are they working harmoniously within the context of the whole human religious enterprise? To what degree do they share a common ethic which can be taken as a resource for the whole of humanity? To answer these questions, something more

than political and economic endeavour is called for. There is also
a need for an appropriately rigorous and systematic analysis.

In undertaking such a task, it is unrealistic to hope to cover all
aspects of these two traditions, not least because of the limitations
of available space and time. Facing us are two great traditions,
each of which can be traced to an ancient origin, each of which
has been subject to a continuing process of change, and each of
which contains various schools, sects and dimensions. This makes
an overall comparison difficult, if not impossible. When Marshall
Hodgson wrote a multi-volume work on Islam, he concluded from
his own experience that 'a serious exploration of any religious
tradition in its several dimensions could consume more than one
life, and it is not to be expected that many persons can genuinely
explore two'.[16] This warning must be taken seriously before any
comparative project is pursued.

There are many approaches to carrying out a specific comparison
of Confucianism and Christianity. For example, we might compare
them in respect of their institutions, belief systems, or religious
practices. Or again, we might undertake a philosophical investigation of the logic by which they have developed their own
intellectual systems, temporarily disregarding expressions of popular faith and religious behaviour. There has been intense interest in
both these approaches. From the debates between earlier Christian
missionaries and Confucian scholars to the contemporary academic
researches of Chinese and Western scholars, advances have been
made which increase mutual understanding and, to some extent,
lead to the mutual encouragement of both traditions. Our study,
building on the achievements of previous research, aims at a specific goal in comparing two single concepts in the two religions,
namely, *agape* in Christianity and *jen*[17] in Confucianism. This task
is both simple and complex. It is simple, because it is limited to a
comparison of two concepts, and thus has a more specific goal than
most other kinds of comparative study. It is complex, because these
two concepts are not pure notions, precepts or philosophical terms,
but focal points of the religions to which they belong. To understand
them, we have to have an adequate knowledge of their background,
and have to explore their origin, development and functions. Anders
Nygren puts it in this way: 'The comparative study of different
religions does not consist merely in the collection of data concerning
rituals and beliefs; its true aim is to seek the underlying ideas which
alone give meaning and coherence to the external facts.'[18] *Jen* and

agape are, respectively, just such underlying ideas in Confucianism and Christianity. Without *agape*, there would be no such religion as Christianity, so that Christianity can be said to be a religion of *agape*; without *jen*, Confucianism would not be the Chinese tradition as we know it, so that Confucianism may be described as a system with *jen* as its centre.

What is meant by *jen* and *agape*, what positions they have had in their respective religions, and what contrasts there are between *jen* and *agape* will be discussed in due course. For the moment, we may be content with the suggestion that they are the life and soul of their own religious traditions, and that the similarities and dissimilarities between Christianity as a theocentric religion and Confucianism as a humanistic religion are revealed more vividly in a comparison of *jen* and *agape* than in any other studies. While *agape* can be translated in English as 'love', it is in fact more than love, in that it defines the relationship between Christians and their God, and between Christians and their neighbours. While *jen* in Chinese is not the translation of 'love', it is in fact essentially love, both ethical and religious, in that it defines the relationship between Confucians and their transcendental pursuit, between Confucians and their ideal, and between Confucians and their fellow human beings. In the fact that in one sense they both signify 'love', but more than 'love' in another, we have found the starting-point of our comparative study. However, what we intend to do is not just to interpret *jen* and *agape* in this or that way. We will examine them in their own traditions, compare them in their contrasts and relate them in their similarities.

Since *agape* and *jen* are each at the centre of their religions, the central thread running through the doctrines and essential characteristics of their traditions, in order to explore their significance we must first survey the two religions themselves. Confucianism grew up in the soil of Chinese culture and is rooted in a long tradition existing even before Confucius. However, it was Confucius who inherited and moulded this tradition into a systematic doctrine, and so prepared for its further development and transformation later. Is this tradition religious? This question was asked in the past and is still asked today. It is the task of the first section of chapter 2 to examine the religious dimensions of Confucianism, so that the proposition we have made in the introduction that it is a humanistic religion may be firmly established. Christianity evolved from Israelite tradition, first as a radical sect and then as an independent movement. In order to trace its origin and development, we must first examine its doctrine in the light of Israelite tradition, and evaluate the contributions made by Jesus and his followers. This will be the content of the second section. As we have already said, the central difference between Confucianism and Christianity, in respect of principle, is that the former is a humanistic and the latter essentially a theocentric religion. However, this distinction must be analysed in greater detail. Is it applicable throughout the two traditions? What form does it take in other aspects of the traditions that is important for our understanding of the divergences and convergence between *jen* and *agape*? Does Confucianism, while essentially a humanistic religion, also possess theistic elements? What is the significance for our comparison of *jen* and *agape*? To answer these questions, a comparison between Confucius and Jesus, the masters and supposed founders of these two traditions, becomes necessary, and this will be attempted in the last section of chapter 2.

Our topic proper will formally begin in chapter 3, where the historical development and evolutionary stages of these two key concepts will be examined, including their origin, position and functions. From this examination we shall see that, although there is a wide gap between these two concepts, they have a similar function in the human pursuit of the ideal and the eternal. In chapters 4–6 we shall examine in detail *jen* and *agape*, making it clear what is differentiated and what is shared between Christian spirituality and Confucian spirituality. Chapter 4 will look at the first contrast between *jen* as humanity and *agape* as divinity. As the principle of a humanistic tradition, *jen* is identified with humanity, by which transcendence is defined. For most Confucians, the Transcendent is in humanity and there is no transcendence outside human own existence and activity. As the principle of a theistic tradition, *agape* is essentially God's grace, manifested in creation, covenant and love for his creatures. For most Christians, transcendence is God's salvation. Different as they are, *jen* and *agape* are nevertheless similar in that they bring forth a 'new people'. This theme will be examined in the last section of this chapter. Chapter 5 devotes itself to the examination of Christian and Confucian ways to transcendence in terms of *jen* and *agape*. In looking for the way to transcendence, Confucians identified *jen* with virtue, while in searching for the possibility of human transcendence, Christians believe that humans are powerless on their own and must respond to God's love. However, even in this contrast, similarities and differences between *jen* and *agape* remain. In one sense, both *jen* and *agape* can be said to be virtues, and in another sense they are not simply virtues. *Jen* and *agape* are superior to virtue and are the root from which the virtues grow. They give meaning to the virtues from different origins. *Jen* derives from its human origin, and therefore in Confucianism the virtues are essentially forms of human goodness and *jen* is essentially a spirit of humanity; while *agape* derives from its theistic origin, and therefore Christian virtues are based on theistic virtues. Since *jen* and *agape* are both taken as the way to transcendence, they contain within themselves a similar tension between inner will and outer command. One of the most important meanings of *jen* in Confucianism is in its relationship to *li*, the moral or natural laws, while a fundamental aspect of *agape* in Christianity is its relationship to God's calling. Just as *jen* in Confucianism comes into being in its incorporation of natural law, *agape* in Christianity comes into being in its readiness to respond to the calling of God. The tension between autonomy and obedience exists in both Confucian spirituality and Christian spirituality, although their forms and their solutions to this tension are different. The difference between humanistic *jen* and theistic *agape* is also revealed in human relationships. Thus chapter 6 is designed to consider the universality of love both in Confucianism and in Christianity. Love is the deepest meaning of *jen* in Confucianism, fulfilling all other meanings. Contrary to the popular opinion that *jen* as love is subject to family structure and is thus a limited disposition, we shall see that Confucian love is universally applicable and extends the idea of brotherhood to all creatures in the cosmos. *Agape* signifies neighbour-love, where the neighbour is anybody in need whom we encounter, but it is sometimes said to be human love and to include mutual affection, selfless consideration of others and compassion for the suffering. Whatever meanings *jen* and *agape* have acquired, both refer to the relationship between one person and another, between the particular and the universal, between limited life and unlimited life. Their value lies in the fact that they point to a transcendental way for limited and finite being: in love the limited will identify with the unlimited, the material will identify with the spiritual, and the temporal will identify with the eternal. Chapter 7 is an attempt to summarize what we have done in previous chapters in comparing *jen* and *agape*: they are central to two different, yet related, kinds of spirituality: humanistic spirituality and theistic spirituality. Humanistic spirituality takes fulfilled humanity as transcendence and ethical growth as the way to transcendence, while theistic spirituality finds in divine grace the source and resource of spiritual development and therefore takes human response to God's calling as the only way to attaining to the ultimate goal. Consequently, humanistic spirituality uses the language of ethics to express its transcendental goal and the way to transcendence, while theistic spirituality uses theological language to define its transcendental ideal and its way to salvation. However, the differences between the two kinds of spirituality are far more complex than we had presumed, while their similarities are far more profound than we had imagined. A comparative study of them has a much wider application and greater practical value for a consideration of the West and China in terms of their history, culture, politics and ways of life. Although these aspects are beyond our present research, they are raised as questions for further study.

2

Confucianism and Christianity

Once upon a time there was a frog who lived in a well. His life was peaceful, without fear of competition or danger of attack from rivals. He was content with this life-style and wanted never to leave his dwelling-place, as he knew of no other circumstances than his own. For him, the world was his well, and the sky was only a little circle which his view from the bottom of the well revealed to him. He would have lived like this until he died, had not another frog come to his well one day and told him that the world was much bigger than his well and the sky was much more extensive than the circle of the well's opening. This comparison disturbed his peaceful life and disrupted his previous harmony. Ashamed of his ignorance and arrogance, he determined to learn a lesson from his isolated life and to get to know more about the world.

This ancient Chinese parable reminds us that the world is so great that we should not confine ourselves to our own living quarters, nor turn a blind eye to its other parts. The same is true of the religious world. People who have created their own forms of religious expression tend to rely on their own view of the world and to be ignorant or suspicious of others. Confucians, for hundreds of years, believed that they were the only persons who had discovered the truth about the world. Their main native rivals, Taoists and Buddhists, in order to maintain their existence, had to reconcile themselves to the basic principles of Confucianism. In this way, Confucians built up a strong confidence that their teaching was *the* Truth, and that the Confucian Way was universally applicable. However, when they were told that other people, who represented another tradition and who were later backed by advanced economic and military power, had come to compete with them and to try to exert the same, if not greater, influence, they were deeply disturbed. Their spirit of syncretism disappeared as their authority was challenged, and they tried by every means to drive the newcomer out of their domain. However, whatever attitude they held to this 'foreign' religion, history brought the two traditions together. As soon as the other 'frog' came in, this 'frog' was forced to come out of his well and to enter a much wider and broader world, where life was full of challenges and dangers as well as new opportunities.

It is not our purpose to explore the whole tradition of Confucianism, nor to examine that of Christianity. The nature, position, function and value of these two traditions have been discussed for centuries. What we intend to do in this chapter is to present a brief but clear outline of both Confucian and Christian traditions to prepare for our comparison between *jen* and *agape* in the following chapters.

CONFUCIUS AND CONFUCIANISM

'Confucius' is a Latinization of Kung Futzu.[1] Kung Futzu or Kung Tzu, Master Kung, is a reverent title for Kung Chiu or Kung Chung Ni (551–479 BCE). The age in which Confucius lived and taught was one of great social change, called the period of the Spring and Autumn (770–476 BCE). In this period, the authentic power of the royal house of the Chou dynasty (1121–249 BCE) was declining and that of the princes of the feudal states was rising. Military wars between states and political intrigues within states were intensified by weak kings, ambitious princes and greedy officials. The old social order was being destroyed and a new one was yet to be set up, while the people were left in endless suffering and misery. Confucius, unable to bear this chaos, aimed to save the world from destruction and 'to bring peace to the old, to have trust in friends and to cherish the young' (*Analects*, V, 26). In order to do so, he saw just and benevolent government as one of the most important preconditions. For him, good government should be based not on cruel punishment, but on moral virtues. Good government comes from good rulers, and a good ruler 'who governs the state by his virtue is like the pole star which stays at its own position while all the other stars revolve around it' (II, 1). An efficient way of securing 'governing by virtue' was by performing rites and ceremonies correctly. This not only enabled the performer to remain in a state of sincerity and loyalty, but also set up models for other people and therefore led them to cultivate the virtues and habits of good behaviour. In developing his thought, Confucius pondered the meaning of tradition and promoted the culture of old times. Although he aimed at reforming the government and rebuilding the social order, he was also highly committed to the ancient ways of the previous dynasties, which he described as the Great Way of the Golden Age, an embodiment of goodness and harmony. While much of his attention was devoted to politics, good government was for him only a means of creating a new people by encouraging them to cultivate their virtue and become *chun-tzu*, true gentlemen or persons of virtue. At that time, *chun-tzu* referred either to persons in authority or to persons of moral excellence. The emphasis of this term in Confucius' mind was on the latter, so that it became a recognizable personality achieved by a determined will, cultivated virtues and a consistent habit of good behaviour rather than by family kinship and clan connections. A *chun-tzu*, who was full of sincerity in relation to his world and full of harmony in relation to his true self, would in turn be the most suitable person to do administrative work.

However noble his ideal, Confucius could not carry it out in that violent age, and had to leave his home state (Lu) for other states, in the hope that his words would be heard, his politics practised and his ideal actualized somewhere else. For thirteen years, he and his disciples travelled from one state to another. At last, when he realized that there was no hope of achieving his goal, he returned to the State of Lu and devoted the rest of his life to teaching disciples and editing ancient classics. In this way he expected his disciples and followers to carry out his wishes and hand on his teachings to later generations.

Confucius was born into a declining aristocratic family and his father died when he was very young.[2] The humbleness of his living conditions and the nobility of his ancestry were perhaps two of the main factors which led him to the path of learning. This learning, however, was not only of ordinary knowledge, but also of the ancient ideal – the Great Way *(tao)*, which was taken as what he lived for: 'One would die in the evening without regret if he had heard *tao* in the morning' (IV, 8). In this sense, *tao*, the Way, is the truth of the world and the principle of the universe, by which one is able to transcend one's limitation and find the ultimate meaning of life. The learning of such a Way requires painstaking effort. He said of himself that he set his heart on learning when fifteen years old, and that by the age of thirty he had achieved a measure of success.

Ten years later, he reached a higher stage, when he was no longer confused and distracted by the trivial affairs of life, such as riches or poverty, nobility or meanness, life or death. By the age of fifty, he believed that he had understood the Mandate of *Tian* (Heaven) and could now distinguish and relate the Heavenly Way and the human ways. After two more decades, at the age of seventy, he had reached the peak of this learning, so that he could do everything according to his own heart's desire but without deviating, even slightly, from the *tao* (II, 4). This is interpreted that he had at last reached full maturity in faith, in emotion, in judgement and in behaviour, and that his self had been completely integrated with the universal order and spirit of the cosmos, namely, he had attained transcendence.

Confucius understood himself as a 'transmitter but not a maker', and a person of virtue 'faithfully devoted to learning the ancient classics' (*Analects*, Book VII, 1). However, while the importance of Confucius in transmitting the tradition and the great Way of the Golden Age is fully appreciated, this self-description has been considered merely a mask of the humility of this great master. In the area of learning, he is regarded not only as a transmitter but also as a creator. Traditionally, he has been credited with editing most of the important classics of Confucianism. For example, he is believed to have selected 305 poems from more than 3,000 pieces to make up *Shi Ching* (or the *Book of Poetry*), and to have written *Chun Chiu* (or the *Spring and Autumn Annals*). Whether or not this accreditation was historically correct is open to debate. In fact, from the Han dynasties (206 BCE–220 CE) down to today, arguments about the authorship and editorship of these classics have frequently broken out between Confucians and other schools, among Confucian scholars themselves, and between modern Chinese scholars and Western scholars. Some of them have lent their firm support to this tradition,[3] while others have taken a negative view of it.[4]

The most authentic source for our knowledge of Confucius and his teaching is a book called *Lun Yu*, 'the selected or recorded sayings', or in its more familiar English title in the West, the *Analects of Confucius*. The *Analects* consists of twenty books and nearly five hundred chapters. There is little logical connection between the books, nor can any historical relationship be detected from their order, each book being titled with the first two characters of its first chapter. The recorders of these sayings are generally regarded as disciples or students of the disciples of Confucius, while the editors lived much later: it took about one hundred years after the death of Confucius to incorporate the previous recordings into a book. What we today read as the *Analects* basically came from an edition in the first century BCE by a Confucian scholar of the former Han dynasty (206 BCE–24 CE), Chang Yu, who harmonized several editions current in his time and compiled from them a textbook.[5]

Confucius was only one scholar among many, or a master of learning, when he was alive. However, some time after his death he was given a number of honorific titles by princes and officials. It is said that, in the second year after his death, the prince of Lu turned his house into a temple, where sacrifice was made to him.[6] Having set up the Han dynasty (206 BCE), the first emperors of the former Han dynasty seem to have modified the hostile attitude to Confucianism taken by the Chin dynasty (221–206 BCE), and it is believed that in 195 BCE the founder (Kao Tsu) of the Han dynasty visited the tomb of Confucius and offered the greatest sacrifice, *Tai Lao*, consisting of three domestic animals: an ox, a sheep and a pig. During the Han dynasty, scholars paid their respect to Confucius in a religious manner, and reiterated Confucian principles in the language of mysticism. This religious mysticism altered the character of Confucius himself as well as of his teaching. During the time of Emperor Wu (reigned from 141 to 87 BCE) of the Han dynasty, Confucius was promoted to a position of pre-eminence, and Confucianism became the state ideology. In 8 BCE, a hereditary fief was given to Confucius' descendants, to make it possible for them to sacrifice both to Confucius and to their forefathers of the Shang dynasty. In the first year of the common era, an emperor repaired the Temple of Confucius at Confucius' home town, and revered him as 'Duke Ni'. In 59 CE, Emperor Ming of the late Han Dynasty (25–220 CE), who was also responsible for formally introducing Buddhism from India to China, ordered sacrifices to Confucius to be offered in all schools and a complete code of sacrificial ritual to be drawn up for worship. In 657 Confucius began to be worshipped as 'the perfect Sage, the ancient Teacher', and from then on this title remained until the beginning of this century. In each centre of learning, in each city, town and even village, a temple of culture (Confucius was regarded as the promoter, transmitter and patron god of culture) was dedicated to him, in which students, scholars, officers, and royal members gathered and paid their homage at every important festival.

Although Confucius played a decisive role in forming Confucian tradition, Confucianism should be treated more as a tradition which is rooted in Chinese culture than a school which was formed by Confucius. Therefore, on the one hand, we can accept that Confucianism, as a school, started with Confucius. On the other hand, however, we note that this school did not launch a new movement. A long and rich tradition had existed long before Confucius, and Confucius and his followers developed this tradition into a way of life, both practical and theoretical. In this sense, 'Confucianism' is a misleading translation of that which is referred to as '*ju chia*', '*ju chiao*' and '*kung chiao*' in China. The term '*ju*' in '*ju chia*' and '*ju chiao*' refers to the members of an ancient class who were well known for their knowledge of '*li*' (propriety, rituals and rites) and professionalism in the cultic ceremonies. Later, this word was extended to refer generally to scholar-officials of the Confucian tradition, who were devoted to learning and/or who participated in government at various levels. '*Chia*' means a structure of family–home, and thus a group of people who have the same or similar ideals and pursuits and who relate to one another in a way similar to that of family members. From the original meaning of 'educating' and 'instructing' a child, *chiao* is modified to refer to the doctrine of a tradition or a group of people which honours a single tradition and observes the same rituals. In this usage, '*chiao*' has gained a meaning similar to 'religion' in English. By '*ju chia*' or '*ju chiao*' is meant a school of literati, or scholars, or learned people, who adhere to the ancient tradition and who devote themselves to the study and interpretation of its classics and carrying out the ideal embodied in those classics. '*Kung Chiao*', an expression which appeared much later and is used much less frequently than the other two, refers to a school, a tradition or a religion which was promoted, explored, transmitted and interpreted by Confucius.

Just as in Christianity there is a relationship of continuity between the Old Testament and the New Testament, similarly the connection between the pre-Confucius tradition and the teaching of Confucius and his followers is strong, whatever role we believe Confucius played in its transmission and however much we believe he contributed to it. There are abundant materials in the *Analects* which tell us how a Confucian should treat this tradition and how determined Confucius himself was to carry it forward. This is a tradition which is preserved mainly in the Confucian 'Five Classics', the *Book of Poetry*, the *Book of History*, the *Book of Changes*, the *Book of Rites*, and the *Spring and Autumn Annals*. These five classics are concerned with different subject matter: from poems to rituals, from divination to moral rules, from history to myths. Underlying these different topics, however, are several common principles, which are inherited and developed by Confucius and Confucians, and are recognized as the core of Confucian doctrine.

The first principle of this heritage is that of the unity between *Tian*[7] (Heaven) and human beings. *Tian*, though understood by some of the later Confucian schools as a natural reality, has a very strong spiritual connotation and in most parts of these classics is revealed as the highest spiritual power or being. Therefore, the unity between *Tian* and human beings refers not only to a harmonious state of the world, and a harmonious relation between nature and culture, but also to a continuous relationship between spirit and matter, between mind and body and between the sacred and the secular. In this way Confucianism developed its characteristics of spirituality: the Transcendent and humans are harmoniously related, are mutually affected and mutually interact; human transcendence can be attained only through their own moral efforts, which are manifested in the areas of politics, religion and ethics; and sage-kings are necessary in the process of human transcendence. We read that the Shang people believed that their God (*Shang Ti*, Lord on High) could be consulted only by their kings, and that God's blessings could reach the people only through sage-kings.[8] When the Chou people won over the Shang dynasty, on the one hand they inherited the ideas of the sage-kingship, and on the other they gradually developed the religious awareness that the supreme God (*Tian*) must be both righteous and universal. *Tian* could confer his decree on a righteous king to govern the world, and could take away the mandate from an unworthy king. With this religious consciousness, the Chou people strongly believed that the prosperity or decline of the state, and the welfare of the people, depended totally upon whether or not their king was worthy of *Tian*'s decree. The ruin of the former dynasties, the Hsia (21st–16th century BCE) and the Shang, was believed to have been the result of *Tian*'s disfavour, because the last kings of these dynasties were so debauched and cruel that the people made their complaint to *Tian*. 'Heaven [*Tian*] had compassion on the people of the four quarters'[9] and withdrew his favouring decree from these kings, and this led to their collapse. However, by contrast with the notion of the Transcendent in the Shang dynasty, who was said to destroy a state directly himself, the Decree of *Tian* was carried out indirectly, through the moral virtues of the sovereign and through the will of the people. 'Heaven [*Tian*] loves the people, and the sovereign should reverently carry out (this mind) of Heaven [*Tian*].'[10] It was this teaching that became the basic principle of Confucianism.

The second principle is that of the unity between the ancestor and the descendant. Many scholars have observed that ancestral worship is the root of all religions. Family occupies a central position in Chinese culture. For a Confucian, it is one's greatest duty to make regular sacrifices to one's ancestors, and it is also the greatest honour to glorify one's ancestry. The religious motive for the Shang and Chou peoples to make sacrifices to their ancestors, according to the description in the *Book of History* and the *Book of Poetry*, was two-fold: the one was concerned with the dead, in the hope that the deceased would continue to live in a manner similar to the life-style they had on earth, and assuring them that their contribution to the family enterprise was remembered and carried on, so that the ancestors could rest in peace; the other was concerned with the living, in the hope that the descendants would obtain from their departed ancestors blessings and help in overcoming difficulties and avoiding disasters. To consult the spirits of the dead, to worship the ancestors and to praise the great achievements of the ancients, were practices given prominent emphasis in these classics. Ancestors were believed to be not only alive but also powerful in determining the destiny and welfare of the living community. If not provided with proper sacrifices, and if not informed periodically about the state of the family's affairs, ancestors would be upset and might return to punish their descendants. Confucius, who believed that the intimate relationship between the ancestor and the descendant was the foundation of religion, politics and ethics, accepted and developed this tradition, stressing that descendants should give three years to mourning for their deceased parents and should treat their ancestors as if they were still alive. Furthermore, he stressed the importance of *hsiao* (filial piety or filial love), and used this concept to characterize not only the proper rituals of sacrifice to the ancestors but also the proper attitude and behaviour towards living parents.[11] Later Confucians further developed and propagated this idea, so that filial piety acquired a high profile on the Confucian agenda and became an effective leverage in correcting social disorder, and a way to human transcendence.

The third principle of this heritage is that of the unity between the sage and the common people. If Hans Küng is correct when he says that Chinese religion is of a 'sage' character, he must mean by this that Chinese religion is a way of life instructed by transcendental persons, or 'sages'. According to the Confucian view, emphasis should not be given to a dualist opposition between the human world and the spiritual world, or between paradise and hell, but to the evolutionary contrast between the civilized and the barbarian, the cultivated and the uncultivated, and the morally developed and the morally deprived. Life as a whole is a developing process from the latter to the former, in which the instruction of sages is necessary. Sages, by their wisdom and virtues, have already understood the Way of Heaven and the Way of the ancients, which are the model for the ways of humans and the ways of the present. For Confucians, instruction of this kind is not limited to intellectual matters, but covers a wide range of cultural concerns. Confucius took a person who 'gave extensively to the common people and brought benefits to the multitude' (VI, 28) to be a sage. For him, a sage not only brings material benefit to people but also educates them by his virtues. The two sides are integrated into one character in a sage and are fulfilled in the unity between sage and common people. While the sage was always ready to instruct the people, the importance of the unity between sage and common people was not confined to this one-way flow. There was also a kind of flow from people to sage, that is, a sage must listen to people's voice and understand their needs, because people's wish is also the will of *Tian*. This two-way flow proves that between sage and common people there is no unbridgeable gulf. By learning and practice, it should be possible for everyone to attain sagehood. This theoretically optimistic view, though often counter-balanced by opposite opinions, provided an ideal that was most attractive for Confucians and led them to cultivate their moral personality and to study the classics unremittingly. They, like their Master, advocated 'love' (*jen*) as the highest good, the person of virtue (*chun-tzu*) as the ideal personality, and self-cultivation (*hsiu shen*) as the way to transcendence, transmitting Confucian tradition from one generation to another.

Should such a tradition as Confucianism be treated as a religion? This question has become a highly controversial issue since Christianity came to China. The definitions which have been given to Confucianism vary so greatly that they seem to refer to completely different things. Among these various definitions, there are three which are directly related to our discussion. First, there is the traditional and most popular definition of Confucianism as a system of morality or ethics. This is the definition favoured by many prominent scholars. For them, 'What is called in the West "Confucianism" is not a religion, but the traditional view of life and code of manner of the Chinese gentry for two thousand years';[12] Confucianism should be viewed only as 'a set of behavioural patterns';[13] and Confucius is a teacher of morals and 'it is considered wrong therefore to class his doctrine as a religion'.[14] From these remarks it would be natural to conclude that Confucianism does not constitute a religious synthesis relating human beings to God, but only an ethical system relating human beings to their fellows. Nor, on this view, should Confucius be treated as the founder of a religion, but as a teacher of morals, who proclaimed his moral ideal to the common people. Secondly, we have the definition of Confucianism as a socio-political system. Scholars who uphold this view argue that Confucius concentrated on political affairs, and that his overriding aim was to help set up a benevolent government, to bring peace to states and to promote the welfare of the people. What he himself intended was not to be a Saviour for the suffering people, or a Messiah for the coming heavenly kingdom, but to correct the disorder of the world and to rectify the mismanagement of the administration. It was important that one should cultivate an integrated character and that one should exert one's moral influence in transforming society. The close relationship between practising Confucius' teaching and administering a state was further strengthened by the methods of selecting civil servants and other officials which involved examining either a candidate's knowledge of the Confucian classics or his achievement in the Confucian cultivation of virtues. The traditional society, with its institutions, constitution, structure and guiding principle, was based on Confucianism, and Confucians not only put into practice the political ideal of the Confucian masters, but also took part in political organization, exercising power and administering the whole country. Since a large number of Confucians served as government officials, Confucian organization was connected with government bureaucracy and therefore was taken as something completely different from religious institutions or priesthood. Thirdly, we find an argument that Confucianism is basically a tradition associated with a school of scholars, or literati, who devoted themselves to the interpretation of the Confucian classics. These classics were regarded as 'sacred writings', as textbooks for education and as sources of a virtuous life. However, students of these classics were not aiming at salvation: they pursued learning either because it offered an entrance to an official career, or because it was considered to be an effective means of self-cultivation. On these grounds, it is said that Confucianism is a school of philosophy, or an orthodox ideology, rather than a religion.

We have no reason to deny the truth embodied in each of these three definitions. They reveal important aspects of Confucianism and throw light on its long and complex tradition. However, they fall short of covering the whole of Confucianism. Each of them defines one strand of Confucianism and by neglecting the fact that Confucianism is a much richer and deeper phenomenon, they provide us with only a partial and inadequate description. In fact, it serves no useful purpose to differentiate between philosophy, politics and religion in the Chinese tradition. To the ancient Chinese, the religious point of view was not so different from the philosophical or political point of view that it had to be named by a different term. Ninian Smart correctly objects to the popular Western assumption that three 'religions' existed in China and insists that they are but three parts of 'a single functioning system'. This objection could have provided him with a higher vantage point from which to obtain an overall view of the characteristics of the Chinese tradition, had he continued to explore its wholeness. However, in dealing with Confucianism, he misleadingly tries to separate its 'religion' from its 'thought', and uses 'Confucianism' to refer to the official cult and 'Confucian thought' to refer to the philosophical reflections from the time of Confucius.[15] In trying to separate the religious side from the philosophical side, he reduces much of his previous insight in his dealing with a tradition very different from that prevailing in Europe.

Some contemporary scholars have noticed the wholeness of the Chinese tradition and tend to use general terms to define or describe Confucianism which blur the distinctions created by Western classifications. John Bowker, for example, suggests that it would be appropriate to call Confucianism 'a system of *information process*'.[16] Tu Weiming thinks that 'Confucianism may be regarded as a *language* of moral community flowing from a universal moral value'. While De Vos prefers 'a system of thought', Peter Bol is more disposed to say that 'Confucianism is a notion created in the West to define and discuss a *phenomenon* that existed in the past'.[17] These general terms are certainly useful in avoiding looking at the Chinese tradition with an European eye, and they are of special value for understanding Confucianism as a comprehensive unity. However, our present purpose is not to find a suitable label for Confucianism in general, but to explore its religious characteristics. To this end, we have to leave the matter of general terminology for more specific considerations of what religion is.

There is no one definition that can be universally agreed upon. What 'religion' means for a Confucian is different from what it means to a Christian.[18] If we come to understand this difference, it will cause little surprise that the strongest objection to the idea that Confucianism is a religion comes from the Chinese side, especially from those who have had a good Confucian background. One of the most important reasons for their reluctance to accept this idea comes from the derogatory implications of the term 'tsung chiao (religion)'. Whereas in English the term 'religion' often carries, along with its descriptive meanings, a commendatory implication of 'devotion, fidelity or faithfulness, conscientiousness, pious affection or attachment',[19] its counterpart in Chinese used to be connected with superstition. A religion is usually regarded as a superstructure which consists of superstitions, dogmas, rituals and institutions both by ancient Confucians and by modern scholars who have a strong preference for Confucianism.[20] When Matteo Ricci observed several hundred years ago that 'the things of religion were not greatly appreciated',[21] what he meant by this was that the superstitious things were not appreciated at all in the circle of scholar-officials. Most of them preferred to use the term 'chia (school)', or 'tao (the Way)', rather than 'chiao (religion)' to refer to Taoism, Buddhism and Confucianism proper, because the latter usage of the term 'chiao' carried the meaning of 'superstition' and seemed to have lost its earlier meaning of 'education' and 'teaching', thus becoming degraded. This attitude to religion remained when Confucian scholars compared Confucianism with Christianity. The purpose of those who argued for Confucianism as a religion and of those who argued that it was not a religion was the same: to provide Confucianism with a foundation which enabled it to be the equivalent to the *state* religion in Western countries.

In order to demonstrate the characteristics of Confucianism as a religious tradition, it will be a good start to think of several aspects essential for the main religions in the world. Under the term 'religion', for example, the *Oxford English Dictionary* gives six sub-descriptions, such as a state of life, a monastic order, an action or a conduct, a belief or faith.[22] Ninian Smart gives six dimensions of a religion: doctrinal, mythical, ethical, ritual, experiential and social.[23] Of these dimensions, three are of great value in identifying the characteristics of Confucianism as a religion: a system of beliefs, an organized institution, and a system of rituals, in which Confucianism shares many elements with Christianity but parts from it at the most crucial points.

As far as belief is concerned, two questions should be asked. The first is whether or not there is a system of belief in Confucianism. If the answer is yes, then the second is, what these beliefs are. De Vos correctly points out that 'a system of thought can be considered a religion only if something is held sacred within this system'. However, he mistakenly concludes that, since in Confucianism one has to look to some source other than the supernatural for the embodiment of the sacred, it is impossible to identify it as a religion.[24] The Confucian source of the sacred is both within humanity and outside humanity, or more precisely, is in the unity between humanity and the Transcendent. Most Confucians do not like to talk about spirits, death and the world beyond. Instead, they concentrate on society, life and this world. However, we should not conclude that there are no spiritual elements in the system of Confucian belief. The spirits, especially those of departed ancestors, were viewed as guarantors and protectors of living human beings, and the living were regarded as supporters and assistants of the departed. The Confucian temple, which was set up as early as the beginning of the Han dynasty, became the centre of the Confucian tradition. Confucius, his parents, his main disciples and all great Confucians were looked upon as objects of Confucian veneration, and the greatest sacrifice was annually offered to Confucius himself. These facts undoubtedly reveal a belief in the spiritual world and a tradition of worshipping the spirits, and there is sufficient evidence to prove that the whole of Confucian doctrine is based on three beliefs: (1) belief in *Tian* (Heaven) as a divine order or as Supreme Lord, to whom or which individual Confucians devote themselves entirely and sincerely; (2) belief in human destiny, the course of which depends upon *Tian*; (3) belief in the laws of *Tian*, which can be known through divination, observation and the teachings of the sage.

Thus, if we define a religion by its transcendental dimension, either humanistic or theistic, and if we are convinced that Confucianism is not totally without this dimension, then we may perhaps conclude that Confucianism is a religion. However, there is still another difficulty to face, namely, how to explain the contradictions within its own literature. As soon as we open the *Analects* of Confucius, we are puzzled by its two opinions, apparently opposing each other over the same issue. On the one hand, Confucius required that service to ancestors should be given as if they were alive, and sacrifice to spiritual beings should be performed as if these beings were in front of us (III, 12). This seems to suggest that he admitted the existence of the other world, and considered service to ancestral spirits to be the most important part of human duty. On the other hand, when asked about serving spiritual beings and about death, he replied, 'If you are not yet able to serve human beings, how can you serve spiritual beings? If you do not yet understand life, how can you understand death?' (XI, 12). When his disciple asked what wisdom was, he taught him that wisdom was to 'devote yourself earnestly to man's duties, and respect spiritual beings, but keep them at a distance.'[25] This seems to suggest an opposite attitude. However, it appears to be a contradiction only if we think of it within the framework of a theistic religion. The contradiction will disappear as soon as we set it in the light of a humanistic religion.

A humanistic religion is a form of religion which takes the world as a unity of human beings and spirits or Spirit. While it does not deny the existence and importance of the Transcendent, it does insist that the human world and the spiritual world, this life and that life, are inseparable. Further, their unity can be understood only from the point of view of this world and this life – that is, from the point of view of human endeavour to transcend the limitation of life – in contrast to a theistic religion, which insists that their true relation can be revealed only by God and through God's grace. In this way, a humanistic religion moves the religious focus from the grace of the divine Spirit to the nature of humans, and from the life to come to the present life. It understands the world from *within* the world, not from outside the world, and thus renders the secular sacred. While it agrees with theistic religions that this world is not perfect and needs changing, it insists that human salvation is to be achieved, not by theistic power alone, but mainly from within, that is, through the self-transformation of human beings themselves. Transcendental power is understood more in the eternal and imperative law than in anthropomorphic being. Therefore the emphasis of transcendence in Confucius was laid on the fulfilment of the Mandate of Heaven, rather than personal salvation. The Mandate of Heaven is not only the source of righteousness but also the root of authority so that a true gentleman would stand in awe of it. To fulfil this mandate, the first thing is to understand it, which Confucius said he achieved when he was fifty years old. To understand the Mandate is not to search for it somewhere other than in human existence and activity. To know the Mandate of Heaven is to understand human nature and virtues, because human virtues are produced by it.[26] In this way, transcendence was transformed from the salvation from the world that was essential for shamanism in ancient times to human self-transformation that became the primary principle of Confucianism. The fundamental beliefs in *Tian*, in destiny and in the natural law are harmonized with, or identified with, confidence in human endeavour. The secular contains the sacred, and the secular is the way to the sacred. On the one hand, humans cannot change their destiny at will, because destiny is in the hands of *Tian*. On the other, it is human responsibility to fulfil this destiny by learning and practising what *Tian* decrees. Since what *Tian* decrees is not different from what the Way and virtues require, to perform the latter is thus to serve the former.

A system of institutions is generally regarded as another feature of a religion. A humanistic religion has its own characteristic institutions. Some scholars have concluded that 'if religion is interpreted as an organized system, then Confucianism is definitely not a religion. It has no priesthood, no church, no bible, no creed, no conversion, and no fixed system of gods. It has no interest in either theology or mythology.'[27] This approach is fallacious because it takes the pattern of Christian institution and generalizes it as a universal model to which all other types are subject. How it is possible to say that a tradition which functioned as the state orthodoxy of political, religious and ethical power in nearly two thousand years has no institution. It is true that it does not have an organization similar to that which is common in theistic religions. However, religious institutions can be of various forms; it is not necessary that all religions adopt the same form. A humanistic religion assumes a non-theistic institution, with its focus on human relationships. For example, in place of the professional priesthood in theistic religions, it had a vast system of scholar-officials with different ranks or orders. In this system, at the top, it was believed, was the emperor – the son of Heaven, who was taken as the mediator between *Tian* and the nation, ruling the country on behalf of *Tian*. At the bottom were millions of followers and students who accepted and were ready to carry out the Confucian way. In between was the political bureaucracy, composed of high and low scholar officials who performed administrative, sacrificial and moral duties. In their positions they were expected to promote the Confucian ideal and observe the Confucian disciplines. When they were not in office or when, willingly or reluctantly, they withdrew from administration, they were expected to practise the Confucian Way themselves and to teach their students in the Confucian 'church', that is, the schools.[28] Although they did not consciously set up an organization – their relationships were not the same as those of Christians, and 'there is no Confucian community that one may join, analogous to a church, shrine or synagogue'[29] – they nevertheless had their organizational principles and codes of conducts. One becomes a Confucian by learning as well as by faith in the Confucian Way. In this sense, the claim that 'everybody is an anonymous Confucian' is a misunderstanding. We can agree with the claim that 'everybody is a potential Confucian', but this must be understood in the sense that one becomes an actual Confucian only when one accepts the Confucian ideal, learns its classics and practises self-cultivation according to its principles. In this unorganized 'organization', these non-ordained 'teachers' devoted themselves to studying, propagating and preaching Confucian ideas, and this became the decisive factor which caused Confucianism to be promoted from one of several schools to a position of state ideology and so to maintain its dominant position as the state ideology for about two thousand years.

John Bowker has examined the world's religions in their function as 'ways through limitation' or 'route-finding activities'.[30] These ways or activities, in the practices of most traditions, have crystallized as religious rituals. Therefore the characteristics of a religion can be clearly identified by the form and contents of its rituals. In this aspect, Confucianism both shared with other pre-eminent religions and also had its own character. Confucianism inherited the Shang and the Chou ceremonies of religious performance and developed them into a system of elaborate rituals composed of three levels or parts, in which the moral and educational significance was emphasised more than anything else. The highest and most complicated rituals were performed during the royal sacrifices to *Tian*, the source of harmony and righteousness; to Confucius, the Sage and teacher of ten thousand generations; and to ancestors, the supporters and protectors of the living. The intermediate rituals were observed in such cases as sacrifices to the spirits of mountains and rivers, to the coming of spring and the ending of autumn, and in thanksgiving for all the spirits who had helped in keeping a harmonious and happy life in the world, the state, communities and families. At the lowest level there were the elaborate rituals of everyday life, from the rites of passage to the routines of family duties, from celebratory ceremonies in communities to customary greetings between individuals. These rituals were not only recorded in Confucian classics, but were also sincerely observed, at least in the scholars' own families. The strict performance of these rituals was believed to be necessary to ensure harmony, happiness and prosperity for the state, the land and the people.

Confucian rituals also reveal the characteristics of a humanistic religion. First, these rituals were not only ceremonies, but also ways to express human piety. Confucius taught that it was important to observe the ancient rituals strictly, but even more important to have a sincere heart and a pious spirit (III, 3). Therefore, when he was seriously ill and was reminded of the need to pray to the spirits, he first asked whether there was such a thing as prayer, and then said 'my praying has been for a long time'.[31] For him, prayer was an attitude of heart, a direction of the whole of life rather than a specific observance. Therefore, the life he had endeavoured to live in accordance with Heavenly Principle, in pursuit of goodness and in training others, was itself a form of prayer more effective than a particular ritual, even at the time of approaching death. Further, Confucius insisted that rituals were not the only means by which a person could communicate with the spiritual world, nor could they atone for the wrongdoing a person has done. If a person has intently put himself against *Tian*, namely, being immoral, then mere praying can do nothing exempting him from wrong (*Analects*, III, 13). Furthermore, the Confucian emphasis in their conception of rituals is always on the human side and rituals are endowed with great value for education, self-cultivation and political ideal. *Li* in Confucian contexts is never taken exclusively as rituals. It is also moral code and propriety. On the one hand, it is knowledge that humans have to learn to behave like humans. For this reason, Confucius said that 'one who has not learnt *li* cannot take one's stand [in human community]' (XVI, 13). On the other hand, *li* is activity in which people must take part to be good. To be a *chun Tzu* – the person of virtue – one must put *li* into practice by observing it (XV, 18), by which is meant to live on it and live for it. To observe *li* and to live on *li* are believed to be of great significance for politics, so much so that all people in the world would come to follow someone who has done so sincerely (XII, 1).

In summary, Confucianism is a religion – not a theistic religion, but a humanistic religion. Confucian spirituality is characterized by its humanizing religious matters in three ways. One is to moralize religious faith and practice. This characteristic of Confucianism is understood by Chung-ying Cheng as the fourth type of world religious thinking. For him, a religion is a specific experience of the ultimate and the total reality. Confucian experience of this ultimate and total is that

> in which the moral consciousness of the human person becomes a specific manifestation of the human person's consciousness of the ultimate and the total, and the consciousness of the ultimate and the total in the human person becomes also a specific moral fulfilment of the human person's nature and its ultimate goodness. Furthermore, morality is where the relation of the individual to the ultimate and the total and its significance are realized simultaneously.[32]

On the other hand, this feature of Confucianism is obviously misunderstood by Max Weber. Weber believed that to moralize a religion was to rationalize it; but he overlooked the possibility that moralization might be more than a rational process. When morality and religion are integrated, the moral sense becomes a religious attitude, while religious faith becomes a moral quality. To be moral in a humanistic religion is the same as to be religious in a theistic religion, because morality is what one should believe and perform in seeking salvation. The whole universe is moralized as a unity, in which human beings are governed by the moral principles of the universe. In neo-Confucianism, the transcendent power of the early Chinese history, *Tian*, was more frequently addressed as the Principle of Heaven. So, to have faith in *Tian* is to follow the moral principles of the universe. This moralization of *Tian* does not, as Weber suggested, eradicate 'all the residues of religious anchorage' within Confucianism.[33] Rather, it provides Confucianism with a specific religious character.

The second characteristic is to politicize the religious process of salvation. Since the focus of religion is moved from theistic divinity to humanistic sacredness, and since *Tian* is always assumed to be concerned with the well-being of humans, it is natural for Confucianism to give much more attention to political affairs than does a theistic religion. Correspondingly, the ultimate aim of the religious enterprise is transformed from salvation *from* the world – reaching the eternal by God's raising the temporal – to salvation *in* the world – reaching eternity through humans themselves transforming the temporal. To save the world is to save people, and to save people is to correct chaos and to re-establish a harmonious order in the state. Rodney L. Taylor, who believes that 'It is time for Confucianism to assume its rightful place amongst the major religious traditions of East Asian cultures and, in turn, the religious traditions of the world', singles out two core elements if a tradition is to be called religious: first, it must identify a religious authority or absolute; secondly, it must prescribe a relationship with what is defined as the absolute, in which the movement of individuals toward the absolute is a process of transformation. In Confucianism, the absolute is *Tian*, or the principle of *Tian*, and the best way in which individuals can be related to it is manifested in the sage as a transformed person.[34] The sage, in the words of Confucius, is the sage-king, who in his virtue has been one with the *Tao* of Heaven, and who is at the centre of the world by bringing peace and harmony to it. A theistic religion may affirm the affairs and order of this world, but this affirmation serves the ultimate goal: preparing for the coming Kingdom, while a humanistic tradition identifies the ultimate goal with the perfection of humanity in the orderly world. In this sense, Confucianism may be said to be 'a sociopolitical doctrine having religious qualities',[35] in contrast to a theistic religion that is 'a theological doctrine with sociopolitical qualities'.

The third characteristic of Confucian spirituality is that it is based on the structure of the family. While we recognize that Confucian scholar-officials were extremely important for the propagation of Confucianism, we should not neglect the other factor, that is, that the deeper social foundation for Confucianism was the family. The family provided everybody not only with a 'church', where the members of the family were linked to the traditional practices and rituals which Confucians had propagated, but also with a sense of continuity, an essential for any religion, whatever form it assumes. In a theistic religion like Christianity, it is the creation of humans in the image of God, and the death and resurrection of humans in and with Jesus Christ, that gives them a sense of continuity, so that they belong to eternity even when living in the world of time. In Confucianism, however, the sense of eternity lies not with the individual life, but with the collective life of human beings.

The eternal can be achieved by the continuity of the family. The Confucian family is composed of a chain connecting ancestors and their descendants. In the family, each generation is treated as a necessary link in this chain, and every work is a contribution to the huge enterprise initiated by the ancestors and developed by their successors. By performing one's duties in the family, one obtains a sense of responsibility and identity as an individual. Thus, as an individual, one may pass away. However, as a member of a family, one lives as long as the family exists. Therefore, it is not only a moral duty but also a religious mission for Confucians to regulate family relationships, to educate family members and to perform family rituals.

CHRISTIAN DOCTRINE AND ITS DEVELOPMENT

Thousands of miles westward from the valley of the Yellow River, the birthplace and domain of Confucianism, we come to another centre of the world's religions, the Jordan Valley, which was the origin of a religious stream comprising Judaism, Christianity and Islam. Nearly five centuries after Confucius' death, in Judaea in Palestine, Jesus of Nazareth came onto the stage of the world's religions. Since then, Christianity, named after Christ, 'the anointed One', a title attributed to Jesus by his followers, gradually developed, from a teaching to a movement, from a movement to a religion. Finally, by conquering first Europe and then almost one-quarter of the whole world's population, it emerged as one of the most significant religions in human history.

Christianity as a faith began with the life and teaching of Jesus, a wandering Jewish preacher, who was executed around 30 CE. Our present knowledge about him comes mainly from the four gospels of the New Testament of the Bible. However, the earliest of these gospels was not written until about 35 to 40 years after Jesus died. The gospels were based on earlier oral tradition, previous texts and prevailing theological interpretation at the time when they were written or edited. The New Testament, as we now have it, was not finally fixed until the Council of Carthage in the year 400. Whatever role it played in recording the historical events concerning Jesus and his disciples, it became the primary source and authority for Christian faith, principles and ideals.

The 'gospels' ('good news') have been attributed respectively to

Matthew, Mark, Luke and John, the first and the last of whom were Jesus' disciples, the second and third early converts. Other writings in the New Testament include the Acts of the Apostles, a history of the early church; the letters of some of the early church leaders; and the Book of Revelation. In these writings, Jesus is described as the Messiah, or Christ, who preached the good news of God's coming kingdom and pointed the way to eternal life instead of the way to death and destruction. It was believed that Jesus came to bring the gospel to the people, to reconcile human beings to God, and to awaken the indifferent by healing the sick, feeding the hungry and denouncing the hypocrisy of the established priesthood. Jesus urged people to repent of their sin, because the Kingdom of God was coming. It was said that his audience was so astonished by his teaching that they even forgot the need for food. Jesus' followers came mainly from the poor and lower classes, even from the socially and religiously outcast, which was reflected in his teaching when he said: 'it is not the healthy who need a doctor, but the sick . . . I have not come to call the righteous, but sinners' (Matthew 9:12–13). By these means, Jesus attracted a following. On the one hand, he insisted that he adhered to and maintained the tradition, and that the most important thing was not simply to acknowledge these laws, but to fulfil them and put them into practice. On the other hand, he called his teaching a new one, both in content and in form: 'new wine [in] new wineskins' (Mark 2:21–22). This new teaching in new form called for the radical reform of the old tradition. As such it was naturally resented and then persecuted by the upper classes of the Jews and by the authority of the Roman state. When Jesus was arrested, his disciples were scattered, and at least one of them denied all knowledge of him. The soldiers who were responsible for his imprisonment and persecution, the bystanders who passed by, and even the 'robbers' who were crucified along with Jesus, mocked him and hurled insults at him. These facts, according to Christian doctrine, were signs of human sin. However, from a historical viewpoint, they were evidence that, at that time, the real disciples of Jesus were few, his teaching was radical, and under pressure his followers were vulnerable.

The conclusion of Jesus' life was his crucifixion. He was condemned by the high priest and sentenced and executed by the Roman governor. However, his death marked the transformation of a radical Jewish sect into a new religious movement. It was believed that, three days after being executed, Jesus had been raised from

the dead and that he was subsequently taken up to heaven. Before
he ascended, it was claimed that Jesus gave his final instructions
to his disciples:

> All authority in heaven and on earth has been given to me. Therefore,
> go and make disciples of all nations, baptising them in the name of
> the Father and of the Son and of the Holy Spirit, and teaching them
> to obey everything I have commanded you. And surely I am with
> you always, to the very end of the age. (Matthew 28:18–20)

Encouraged by Jesus' resurrection and obeying his instruction, his
disciples carried out this great mission and proclaimed the kingdom
of God. They took Jesus' promise as a fulfilment of the long-held
hope, and his resurrection as a symbol of the new kingdom of
God. Although what they intended was not the establishment
of a new religion to confront the Judaism in which they had
grown up or to replace the state cult of the Roman Empire, their
practice was still regarded as dangerous and revolutionary by both
Jews and Romans. Besides troubles from without, Christians in
the first century were divided by different understandings and
practices among themselves. Disputes led to disorder, and conflict
greatly reduced the strength of the church, especially when it faced
opposition and persecution. Christian leaders realized that the only
way to recover from confusion and to proceed from weakness to
strength was to unite Christian believers into a single organization
and to establish a single identity which would be recognized by
everyone. Gradually, and with great effort, Christian groups were
organized into a single, universal church with commonly accepted
creeds, holy writings and liturgy, which were clearly distinguished
from those of the Jewish synagogues. Christianity came into being,
not only as a new faith but also as a new institution, soon to become
the most powerful religious organization humanity had ever seen.

During its nearly two thousand years of history, in the course
of which Christianity has evolved from a limited movement to
a universal religion, it has interacted with, as well as benefited
from, many distinct sources. Among these sources, the Jewish
tradition provided most of the original theological assumptions
and religious practices of Jesus and the first Christians; the Greek
tradition strongly influenced the philosophical expression of Christian faith and its mystical rituals; the Latin influence contributed
directly to the organization and institution of the new religion;
the monastic movement, through its style of living in monasteries,

promoted the ideals of Christian communities; the Renaissance, by combining sacred pursuit and secular civilization, created a glorious tradition of Christian art and humanism; the Reformation, in the name of reforming the old rituals, emphasized a return to the tradition and 'simple faith' of the Bible; the Enlightenment developed, though indirectly, the use of the critical spirit and rational principles in Christian theology; and last, but by no means the least, the missionary movement, from the Mediterranean area in the first century to the whole of the world in the twentieth century, not only extended the sway of Christianity, but also absorbed a rich nutrition from other cultures. With so many sources and influences, there is a need for us to discuss selectively the most important ones, to present a recognizable picture of Christian faith.

Christian doctrine was a new expression of religious faith. However, like that of Confucians, it came out of a living tradition, the Israelite tradition. From this tradition, Christian theology received not only a mythology of God, but also a human history. The strong influence of the Israelite tradition on Christianity is to be seen in its concept of God, its expectation of a Messiah, and its understanding of the relationship between human beings and God. For this reason, Christianity included the classics of the Israelite religion as part of its Holy Bible, and took the Jewish concept of the Creator as active in human history and its warrant in antiquity as the ground of their own Christian beliefs. However, Christians did not model their theology completely on the Jewish one. They also created their own sacred scriptures, that is, the New Testament. They viewed Jesus as the Messiah, Jesus' ministry as the beginning of God's kingdom, Jesus as a new Moses giving the people a new Covenant, and the Church as the new Israel. In this way, they moved away from their Israelite origins for a new destiny.

Scholars, from Judaism and from Christianity, may differ concerning who Jesus was and what he taught, but they agree that Jesus, at first, was a prophet, and that Jesus' teaching brought new life to an old expectation and started a new sect on the basis of an old tradition. The novelty of his message was not that he created a new theology and religion, but that he emphasized and developed certain aspects of the old tradition. Although this message was firstly about the coming kingdom, it was not totally irrelevant to the social life and political structure of his time. The kingdom of heaven had to be built on earth, and would begin with the purification of the human heart. Thus, Jesus' teaching about the generosity of God and his coming kingdom had strong practical applications. He consorted with the socially outcast, preached non-violence and love of enemies, challenged the established religious authorities, led an itinerant life and condemned those whose primary values were family, wealth, honour and religion.

This message might not have been convincing but for Jesus' death and resurrection. The early gospel writers described how the tomb was found empty and, except for the earliest manuscripts of Mark, how Jesus appeared in different ways to his disciples. Whatever different meanings have been added to this mythical faith, nobody would deny this: 'Belief in the Resurrection was historically decisive in the origins of Christianity, and at the centre of almost all forms of Christian worship.'[36] Christians believe that Jesus' sacrifice and resurrection inaugurated the new covenant between God and his people, that is, not only those of Jewish descent but all who believed and trusted in God's promises.

The Christian gospel was primarily about what God had done for his people in the life, death and resurrection of Jesus Christ, and thus, at least partly, was in keeping with the old Israelite faith. As in the Israelite religion, faith in God as Creator and supreme Lord was a central point in Jesus' teaching. Jesus, by his words and actions, confirmed that there was one and only one Supreme God. When Jesus was asked what was the most important of all the commandments, his answer started with the claim that 'the most important one is this: Hear, O Israel, the Lord our God, the Lord is One . . . ' (Mark 12:29). However, as a concentration upon certain traditional themes in an intensely focused manner, Jesus preached 'a new teaching' with authority (Mark 1:27), emphasizing on the nearness of God. Therefore, 'the kingdom of God is near' became the basis of the good news. The God who draws near offers to forgive sin and promises a new life. God cares, not only for the righteous and the good, but also for the lost and the outcast. God also calls for obedience and discipleship. Only those who obey God and his will can be forgiven. 'All the sins and blasphemies of men will be forgiven them. But whoever blasphemes against the Holy Spirit, will never be forgiven; he is guilty of an eternal sin' (Mark 3:28–29). This line drawn between ordinary sin and eternal sin was a reinterpretation of the traditional separation between those chosen and those not chosen. This reinterpretation in terms of a present reality of the Spirit of God did not detract from the traditional authority of the transcendent God, but rather served to transfer attention from the external to the internal, from bare commandment to living experience, marking a religious shift between religions.

Christianity was first known only as a radical Jewish sect. However, in due time, a break took place. The first sign of this break was that Jesus was recognized as the Son of God, not only in the sense of a human being whose mission was to restore the kingdom of Israel, but in the sense of Lord and Saviour – God the Son, who with the Father and the Holy Spirit was the One God in Trinity. Jesus was not only honoured as a teacher, or master, but also as the Lord of all. Christians ascribed to him the honour and functions traditionally reserved for God. The central point of the Christian gospel was that 'God is near'. But how could the people see the nearness of God? Through Jesus. In the life, death and resurrection of Jesus Christ, and through sending the Holy Spirit promised for the 'last days', God had done what he had determined to do. If we say that God, as the creator and law-maker, is above human beings, then according to Christian logic, it becomes obvious that, in Jesus, God is among human beings. We find again the transformation from one religion to another.

The Israelites had a tradition of belief in a Messiah, who 'will not judge by what he sees with his eyes, or decide by what he hears with his ears, but with righteousness he will judge the needy; with justice he will give decisions for the poor of the earth' (*Isaiah* 11:3–4). Christians affirmed that in Jesus the Messiah had now come. For the Israelites, a Messiah was an individual human being anointed by God, and a messenger of God, but no more. Christians believed in such a Messiah, but they further affirmed that the Messiah, or Christ, interpreted in terms of the 'Suffering Servant of the Lord' mentioned in *Isaiah*, was none other than Jesus. They further believed that Jesus, though rejected by his Jewish contemporaries, was anointed by God to proclaim and initiate his kingdom of righteousness and peace for all the nations of the world. Furthermore, they were not satisfied with the idea of Jesus only as a messenger; they worshipped him as Saviour and Lord, or, as it is said, 'the Son of God' with full divinity. This development of the tradition also led to another concept, that is, of the two natures of Jesus as God and as human. As divine, Jesus presents the mystery and transcendence of God, while as human he reveals God's immanence and presence. The duality of Jesus' humanity and divinity enables him to be a mediator through whom human beings can be restored to their true relationship with God. It is because of this dual nature, which is a central point in Christian doctrine, that Christianity appears to be not only a theistic religion but also a religion with a strong humanistic colour: the relationship between God and human beings has to be understood not only from the point of view of God but also from that of human beings themselves. God, invisible and unapproachable for the common people according to the traditional concept, has been revealed in the person of Jesus and therefore has become accessible to everyone. In Jesus, God is revealed as he really is – holy and righteous indeed, but also the perfection of kindness, compassion, love, grace and benevolence. Jesus' sacrifice of himself is taken to be further evidence of God's grace, as well as a source of hope for all humans: for Jesus is 'the Lamb of God, who takes away the sin of the world' (John 1:29). The universal claims of God, his self-giving love (*agape*), and the divine–human nature of Jesus as the Christ, were three of the most important factors in Christian belief that contributed to its eventual triumph.

This break was accelerated by Christian emphasis on the grace of God rather than on God's Law. In Jewish tradition, supreme emphasis was placed on God's law. Therefore, the relation between God and human beings was expressed primarily in terms of law. God was indeed gracious, and brought the people of Israel out of Egypt; but since the observance of his law was seen as the primary means of maintaining relations between human beings and God, God could become first and foremost King and Judge, a supernatural sanction for carrying out his own law. Obeying this law, an individual or a nation would be protected, loved and saved; breaking this law, he or they would be punished and destroyed, as recorded in many instances in the Old Testament.[37] However, when grace rather than law was emphasized, God was seen not only as a supernatural sanction, Creator, all-powerful and all-present Being, but also as the source of wisdom and loving-kindness. Some of the features ascribed to God in the Israelite tradition either disappeared or were presented much less strongly. In their place, prominence was given to God as a loving Father full of compassion for human beings. God did not come to punish those who had sinned, but to call them back to him and to save them. This new emphasis brought out a new character in the concept of worship. In the tradition of Israel, 'there was a ban on graven images, which helped to separate Israel from many of the fertility and other cults of the area'.[38] In their actual worship, however, the Israelites were not clearly distinguished from those of other cults in terms of their rituals. 'Many of the sacrifices were expiatory in character, where a person gave up something of worth, for instance, a goat or a sheep, in a concrete manifestation of his feeling of sin or guilt at something he had done.'[39] Although in the Old Testament we read that the true sacrifices to God should be a broken spirit and a humble heart, the radical consequences of this understanding of worship were not fully realized. God was understood to enjoy animal sacrifices and burnt offerings, and to accept sacrifices on his altar (*Isaiah* 56:7). While Christians inherited the ritual of worshipping a single Supreme God, and forbade sacrifice to other spirits, they developed this ritual in the light of their special understanding of the relationship between human beings and God. They saw the traditional sacrifices fulfilled in and superseded by the sacrifice, or self-offering, once and for all, of Jesus himself. Thus the Eucharist, or Mass, or Holy Communion, was interpreted as a recalling of Jesus' sacrifice, and a sacrifice of praise and thanksgiving. This enabled Christianity to put more emphasis on the direct communion with God in the Spirit which the sacrifice of Jesus had made possible.

The separation of Christianity from Judaism was completed when Gentiles were admitted to full membership of the Christian church. Traditionally, the Israelites stressed that they were the people chosen by God to carry out his mission, while other nations were condemned, either because they broke God's creation laws, or because they persecuted his chosen people. Therefore, there was a huge, sometimes impassable, chasm between the chosen and the condemned. Jesus defied this tradition and made his claims universally applicable. His followers continued his practice and came to believe that exclusion of non-Jews from the worship of God was contrary to God's will, because God was Father and Saviour of all human beings, not only of Jews. God's mission could not be carried out by a single nation, but by all people who would follow Jesus Christ. Paul, known as 'apostle to the Gentiles', resisted demands that Gentile converts must abide by Jewish ritual regulations. Mainly through the early Christian missionaries, Christianity spread quickly to the whole of the Greek world and diverged sufficiently from the tradition of Israel to become a new religion.

Christians of the first century believed that God's kingdom would come soon, and that all, both the dead and the living, would be judged at Jesus' return. Supported by this faith, they concentrated on preaching the gospel to others and paid little attention to the practical aspects of theological doctrine and community order. However, year after year, the kingdom did not come as predicted, while organizational problems and theoretical difficulties accumulated to such a point that they would have destroyed the whole structure of Christian communities had they not been resolved immediately. To establish a complex system of doctrine, theology and discipline for all the Christian communities, to compete with other faiths, and to resist persecution from the authorities, a model of an institutional structure and a deeper philosophical system was needed. The Roman Empire provided the former, while Greek philosophy provided the latter.

Although a two-way influence between Christian teaching and Greek thinking had taken place from a very early time, the first to accept the challenge coming from educated unbelievers were those Christian Fathers who had received a thorough education in Greco-Roman philosophy.[40] Their efforts were resisted by others on the ground that there should not be any mixture between Christian faith and so-called Greek and Roman 'paganism'.[41] However, 'ultimately it was the synthesizers who won out'.[42] The Christian theologian Augustine (354–430) was also a synthesizer of Christianity with the Greek, especially the Platonic tradition. He transformed the neo-platonic division between soul and matter into a duality between love of self, the driving force of the earthly city, and love of God, the driving force of the city of God. When we come to the medieval ages, we see the complex works of the Dominican Thomas Aquinas (1224–74), such as his *Summa Theologiae* and *Summa Contra Gentiles*, in which Aristotelian concepts, the ideas of St Augustine, the theology of the Eastern Church, and the writings of St Paul were synthesized into a coherent doctrine, based on a correlation between faith and reason, and between divine and natural virtues. This left a lasting stamp on Christian thought. These epic efforts resulted in a blend, not only of various ways of life, but also of diverse traditions and cultures. Through such works, Christian faith was founded firmly on the combination of the Jewish tradition and the values of the Hellenistic world and the Roman Empire, and the Christian church was supported positively by a profound philosophy and a deeply devout theology. After three centuries of uncertainty, struggle and persecution, Christianity, with Greco-Roman philosophy providing its theoretical structure, was accepted by the edict of Milan (313). Under Theodosius I it became the official religion of the empire. After that, however, the disputes predominated within the Church as Christianity carried out its internal mission within the state and at the same time confronted other faiths from outside. These differences and disputes were accentuated when East and West developed their own distinctive understandings of Christian theology and their own forms of liturgy. For example, in theology, the Western Church was more concerned with the problems of sin and salvation, while the Eastern Church focused its attention on Christ's cosmic role and the divinisation of human life through Christ; and in institutional structure, the Christian Church in the West was organized on the basis of the papacy, while the Christian patriarchs of the East rejected the Pope's claim to supremacy. These differences and disputes were further encouraged by political division and secular rule. In 1054, the traditional date of the first schism, the final separation within Christianity occurred: Eastern Orthodoxy was separated from Western Catholicism.

A few centuries later, the second great schism occurred, when the movement for religious reform, beginning in Germany and then spreading over the whole of Europe, shattered the unity of Christendom in the West. The Reformation was not, in origin, a remaking of Christian doctrine, but a protest over the church's institution. However, it protested against several points of medieval Catholic teaching and implied a break with the current understanding of the relationship between the believer and God. Martin Luther rejected the concept of salvation by merit and reliance on the penitential system and insisted that God's love and salvation could come only by grace through faith. He also rejected the mediation of priests and believed that the Word of God could be discovered in the hearts of believers through the Holy Spirit. For him, all believers were equal in the sight of God, and the monastic way of life had no advantage over ordinary life in respect of access to God and God's grace. The Protestant reformation not only renewed its own understanding of God and grace, but also led to reformation within Catholicism. Within both groups, and between both groups, there appeared room for a variety of understandings, radical and conservative. Since then variety of expression of Christian faith has become significant throughout the Christian world.

CONFUCIUS AND JESUS

The substantial encounter between Confucianism and Christianity was primarily initiated by Christian missionaries, who came to

China and found a comrade as well as a rival in the Confucian tradition. The initial sympathy between Christianity and Confucianism was grounded in the fact that Christianity as a theistic religion has many humanistic characteristics, while Confucianism as a humanistic religion has some theistic characteristics. These common characteristics enabled them to agree on some forms of religious belief, practices and even rites. They also provided a basis for them to co-exist and to co-operate in the struggle against other religious faiths, such as Buddhism. However, the common characteristics shared by both sides did not reduce their fundamental differences. The attempt to conceal these differences went badly wrong, and the consequent misunderstanding of each other made the situation even worse. To illustrate their differences and similarities as well as to prepare our comparative study between their principles, *jen* and *agape*, a comparison between their masters, Confucius and Jesus, is needed to complement our presentation of the two traditions.

It has been claimed that the position Jesus enjoys in Christianity is similar to that which Confucius enjoys in Confucianism. Both were, are and will be followed, acknowledged and worshipped in their own circles. For their firm followers and believers, they are not only the founders of great traditions, but also the hope of transcendence. A sacred light is focused on them and an interpretive narrative concerning them has been developed in the respective traditions and handed down from generation to generation. What was publicly observed to have happened to them in history has been interwoven with what was believed to have been the deeper significance of what happened or what was imagined to have happened. This raises problems concerning our knowledge about their life and their teaching. However, since the early eighteenth century, there has been a thoroughgoing attempt, with greater or less success, to distinguish between the Jesus of history and the Christ of faith. Under the influence of the spirit of scientific research, Chinese scholars as well as Western sinologists have also re-examined the tradition about the Confucian master, and the picture of Confucius has become much clearer.

For a comparative study in religion, the difference between the historical data and the facts as religiously interpreted is not as crucial as it might be for a purely historical inquiry. On the other hand, these two presentations of the facts, as found in the gospels of the New Testament and in the sayings and stories contained in the *Analects* of Confucius,[43] must be considered together so that the real significance of their teaching for their followers can be identified.

The key for comparing and contrasting Jesus and Confucius in theological terms is the fact that, in the language of classical Christology, Jesus has two natures (very God and very man) in one person, while Confucius has only one nature in one person. As a result, in terms of humanity, there are more similarities than differences between Confucius and Jesus, while in terms of alleged divinity, Jesus differs significantly from Confucius.

From a first glance at the source books it is not difficult to conclude that both Jesus and Confucius are truly human. Throughout the gospels we can see the full humanity of Jesus. As human, Jesus was born and his mother was a woman called Mary. Like all other human beings, Jesus felt hungry when in need of food (Mark 11:12; Luke 4:2); felt sorrow when depressed (Mt. 26:37); grew up (Luke 2:40); slept at night (Luke 8:23); felt outcast (Luke 9:58); needed clothing (John 4:6); and was angry when the fig-tree turned out to have no fruit (Mark 11:13–14). An emphasis on Jesus' humanity served to distinguish mainstream Christianity from various 'heresies'. Some modern theologians, especially Barth, Pannenberg and Rahner, attach great importance to the humanity of Christ. For Karl Barth, the character of God and the character of man as new humanity are closely associated in the person of Jesus. Without the humanity of Jesus, there would be a gap in Christian teaching. John Robinson in his *The Human Face of God* explores the significance of the psychological aspects of Jesus for Christian doctrine. The new humanity that Jesus is believed to bring with him is not only in his inner feelings and emotions, but also in his love for other men and women. Jesus' human origin and character, although they might seem to detract from his position in the spiritual world, has broadened his appeal for ordinary people. Emphasis on the humanity of Jesus inevitably suggests an equality between him and other humans. If Jesus can communicate with God and be loved by him, so logically can everybody else: 'Whoever lives by the truth comes into the light, so that it may be seen plainly that what he has done has been through God' (John 3:21). The humanity of Jesus also tends to give to Christianity the character of a humanistic religion, though it never becomes dominant and is frequently overshadowed by its theistic correlate.

The same can be said concerning the humanity of Confucius. When young, Confucius was humble. In order to carry out his mission, he and his disciples had to travel from one state to another, enduring hardship from starvation and from being threatened and mocked by followers of other schools. Although he devoted himself to studying the ancient Way, he frequently felt that his talent might be of no use, because there was no sage-king. In private life, Confucius enjoyed reading poems, composing music, travelling and observing ritual dance. In one instance, it is recorded that he was so ardent a lover of music that he even forgot the taste of meat for three months after hearing a particular piece (*Analects*, VII, 14). The experience of Jesus that 'only in his home town, among his relatives, and in his own house is a prophet without honour' (Mark 6:4) was one that Confucius shared, so that he behaved carefully and spoke unassumingly in his native village (*Analects*, X, 1).

Both Jesus and Confucius were teachers of their times. Jesus was often called 'teacher', or 'rabbi', not only by his disciples, but also by others when they addressed him (Mark 12:14; 13:1). This was also true of Confucius, who was called '*fu tzu*', meaning teacher or master. However, their views of teaching were very different. For Confucius, the role of a teacher was to teach arts, politics and ethics, so that his students could one day use them to serve the government and bring peace to the chaotic world. The disciples of Jesus, on the other hand, were instructed to carry out his mission and preach the good news of the coming Kingdom, and so there was no need for them to study the human sciences, ethics and philosophy. While Confucius and his students advised rulers that the aim of politics was first to correct the ruler himself, so that all the people in the world would follow him, Jesus taught that, in order to be reconciled to God, humans had to repent of their sin, put their trust in God and prepare for the coming of the Kingdom. Because Jesus subjected humanity to the rule of God, the humanism of Jesus was not a simple one. Indeed, neither Jesus nor his disciples had any intention to develop such humanism into a full-blooded doctrine. At best, it was regarded as a step on the way to knowledge of God. By contrast, Confucius and his followers fully developed their understanding of humanity in which transcendence can be attained, so that a humanistic tradition was established.[44]

Although it is not clear whether Jesus thought of himself as the Anointed One (Messiah) or not, he believed that he was sent by God to preach the gospel. The good news is taken by later Christian theologians as that in Jesus Christ, in his preaching and sacrifice, God recreated 'a new people' in a new relationship to God himself.

Similarly, Confucius claimed to be carrying the mission of *Tian* to bring Heavenly *Tao* to the world. Confucius showed a strong faith in *Tian*, and he believed that it was *Tian* who begot *te* (virtue or power) in him (*Analects*, VII, 23). He had a firm belief that his mission was endowed by *Tian*, and that it could not be disrupted by anybody else other than *Tian*. When all his disciples were afraid of danger from the enemy, Confucius was not anxious but put his faith in *Tian*. Believing that *Tian* did not intend to destroy the ancient culture which had come down to him from King Wen, what had he to fear from human beings? (IX, 5). When his favourite disciple Yan Yuan died, he felt so sad that he asked if *Tian* intended to bereave him (XI, 9).

It seems, therefore, that Jesus and Confucius have a similar relation towards the Transcendent. However, we cannot find in the *Analects* passages similar to those in the New Testament, in which a father–son relation is expressed. Neither Confucius nor any other Confucian claimed a son–father relation between himself and *Tian*. Nor, in later history, was Confucius worshipped as the Son of *Tian*. The attempt by popular faith to make Confucius equal to a god is not the mainstream of Confucian tradition, and Confucius remains for the greater part of history a perfect human or teacher rather than a deity related to God. At this point, the Christian Jesus differs from the Confucian Confucius. In Christianity, Jesus the Christ is God incarnate, and so he becomes the focus of Christian faith. God cannot be understood solely by inference from his creation, but can by God's revelation of himself in Jesus Christ. To be in or with Jesus is the only way to be in God. Therefore, Jesus is both the Transcendent and the way to transcendence. In Confucianism, Confucius is held to be the way to transcendence, but not the Transcendent. Confucius functions as the sage who, by his own effort, has reached the supreme goal of the human world and has become a humanistic 'divine' sage: 'the culmination of humanity' (*The Book of Mencius*, 4A:2). Since human beings are essentially the same, and are equal in terms of their moral potential, other people can, at least in theory, achieve what Confucius has achieved. That this is possible is shown not only by the fact that Confucius himself expressed his admiration for many other sages who were fore-runners of Confucianism, but also because it is in conformity with Confucian teachings. Transcendence from a divine perspective must necessarily involve religious focus and religious perceptions dif-ferent from a human conception of transcendence. Consequently,

Christianity and Confucianism offer different ideals of life: a life lived in accordance with the image of God in which human beings were made, and a life that fulfils its human potential. Jesus offers an example of the former, while Confucius provides a model of the latter.

Both Jesus and Confucius affirmed that they were under the command of the Transcendent. However, their concepts of the Transcendent differ. For Jesus, God was Father in Heaven, Creator of the world, and Lord of human beings. Jesus showed neither hesitation nor ambiguity in paying homage to Him, and fully accepted the faith in YHWH of the Israelite tradition, although he seems to have spoken more about the kingdom of God than about God himself. When we turn to Confucius' conception of the Transcendent, we detect an ambiguity. The Confucian transcendent Being is 'Tian', which, as an independent term, appears a total of eighteen times in the *Analects.* Among these eighteen times, there are twelve that are uttered by Confucius himself. Three kinds of *Tian* can be detected in these twelve uses. The first is the natural heaven, or the natural cosmos (*Analects*, VII, 19; VIII, 19); the second is the moral *Tian*, or the universal righteousness (III, 13); and the rest refer to a Personal *Tian*, the Lord of Destiny, or the Sovereign of Heaven (VI, 28; VII, 23; IX, 5; IX, 12; and XIV, 35). This ambiguity of reference reveals that in Confucius' mind, although attention should be paid to the Transcendent, *Tian* is not the focus of human transcendence. *Tian* should not be distanced from human beings. *Tian* and human beings are interdependent, whether in the past or in the present. *Tao*, the Way, which guards and guarantees the human cause is from *Tian*, while it is humans who can carry out and glorify the Way. The degeneration of human beings from their original golden age to their current disorder is not a counterpart of the Christian myth that human beings sinned and fell from God's paradise. For Confucius, *Tian* and human beings are essentially the same, and the principle of Heaven is also the principle of humanity. *Tian* provides a motive for human action, not an alternative to action. To be fully human is the best way to be near *Tian* or to be in accord with *Tian*. Confucius admits that there is a destiny for everyone and that this is endowed by *Tian*. However, truly to fulfil this destiny is fully to commit oneself to one's human duties.

Both Jesus and Confucius concentrated on the human pursuit of transcendence. Their unremitting efforts in preaching their message (*tao*), their readiness to sacrifice themselves to serve the people, and their staunch faith in their mission were major factors which led and encouraged people to pursue eternity. However, because of their diverging conceptions of the Transcendent, the ways they prescribed to attain transcendence also diverged.

To enhance his appeal, Jesus declared that he was sent by God to tell the people God's message. The writers of the gospels used a paragraph from Isaiah (42:1–4) to convince the reader that Jesus was the long expected Messiah of Israel, who came to proclaim justice to the nations (Matthew 12:18). Jesus was accepted as the Way through whom human beings could be reconciled to God, and as the Word by whom humans could be forgiven and saved. The seeker after truth was promised the reward of truth and the seeker after righteousness the reward of righteousness. Thus, there was no need to be concerned about clothes, food or a house. The only thing one should be concerned about was the kingdom of God and his righteousness (Matthew 6:28–34). This emphasis on God and his kingdom derived, it is believed, from Jesus' special relation with God, and in later Christian reflection the message and the person of Jesus were seen as one: 'For God so loved the world that he gave his only begotten son, that whoever believes in him shall not perish but have eternal life' (John 3:16).

Compared with Jesus, Confucius' way to transcendence was humanity-oriented. He himself believed and earnestly instructed his pupils that a good student should always think about the Way of *Tian*, never worrying about material conditions like clothes or food. By learning and practising this Way, one could easily be satisfied with regard to all these things. However, in his teaching, Confucius manifested a different spirituality from that of Jesus. *Tian* is mainly understood impersonally as the Way, rather than personally as a Being; this Way is accessible to everybody, not necessarily through Confucius himself; and to transcend the limitation of life, one is required to engage in cultivation of humanity and bring peace to the world.

Because of the special relationship between Jesus and God the Father, and because Jesus' coming signalled the end of the old age and the beginning of the new, to transcend is to follow Jesus who is the Son of God. The 'Sonship' of Jesus is taken as the symbol of the nearness of God and functions as the bridge between the believer and the saviour. To stress this sonship with God, the writers of the Gospels retold many stories, either of Jesus' own experience or of their witnesses. According to Mark, when Jesus came out of the water after being baptised by John, he saw the heaven being torn open and the Spirit descending on him like a dove, and heard a voice from heaven: 'You are my Son, whom I love; with you I am well pleased' (Mark 1:10–11). Jesus' status as the Son of God was confirmed not only by the voice of God, but also by Jesus' hearers, who admitted that Jesus taught them as one who had authority, not as the teachers of the law (Mark 1:22); by the centurion who had heard Jesus's cry and saw how he died: 'Surely this man was the Son of God!' (Mark 15:39); and by the evil spirits, who had been driven out by Jesus: 'I know who you are – the Holy One of God!';'You are the Son of God'; 'Son of the Most High God' (Mark 1:24; 3:11; 5:7). Only the Son of God could teach with the authority that Jesus had, or exercise the power to drive out unclean spirits, heal various illnesses, order the storm to be quiet, and feed several thousand people with a few loaves of bread. And only in terms of his special relationship with God can it be understood that Jesus' extension of family claims to the universal 'family' of those who did God's will (Mark 3:32–35) is primarily theological.

For Confucians, Confucius had a similar role in leading them to their transcendence. Confucius was venerated as the ancient teacher to have enlightened the people who would otherwise have been ignorant and uncultivated, and as the perfect Sage to bring the way of humans into accord with the Way of Heaven. The real significance of 'the ancient teacher' and 'the perfect sage' for Confucians is much more than that conferred by its English translation. To understand this, we have to keep in mind the Confucian ideal of the ancient golden age, their reverence for teacher–master–sage, and the significance of ancestral worship. Thus the perfect sage can be understood only in the light of the 'Divine Sage', the 'Highest Sage', the 'Triad with Heaven and Earth', and the ancient teacher in the light of the 'forefather', the 'model for ten thousand generations', the 'enlightened' and even the 'Saviour', which is vividly revealed in the well-known saying that 'The whole history [of human beings] would have been in darkness, had *Tian* not sent Confucius to the world'.

It is of great interest to note that, while Jesus is worshipped as the Son of God and Confucius as the perfect sage, neither of them ever stressed or elaborated this. Jesus admitted his distance from God: 'No one knows about that day or hour, nor even the angels in heaven, nor the Son, but only the Father' (Mark 13:32), and admonished the people never to call him good, because 'no one is good but God alone' (Mark 10:18). Similarly, Confucius himself never presented himself as a sage and never claimed to be perfect. According to his own description, he was only a person who devoted himself to learning of the ancient classics and tried his best to restore the great Way of the ancients. The differences between the image of Jesus and Confucius as they were and their image as they are believed to be are of great theoretical merit and practical value. The secular experiences and humble self-descriptions distanced the masters from the Transcendent but neared them to the people, while the sacred nature and saviourship strengthened their appeal and bound all their followers together. In both traditions, the holy image of Jesus and Confucius shone out through their humanity, or as Tu points out when he discusses the image of Confucius, 'He [Confucius] was a sage to his followers but not to himself, and for that reason he became the exemplar of sagehood itself.'[45]

Calling human beings to enter the new kingdom, Jesus believed that the secular institutions were only secondary to the transcendental goal. For him, norms, rules and institutions were matters of this world. In the coming kingdom, all of them would lose their value and appeal. For example, marriage was important only in the human world, not in the kingdom of God or in the post-resurrection life of those who had died. 'When the dead rise, they will neither marry not be given in marriage; they will be like the angels in heaven' (Mark 12:25). However, for Confucius it was essential to learn not only the transcendental knowledge about *tao*, but also all the human arts and sciences, which were believed to be necessary for one's emancipation. The way to be free was, for Confucius, the way of morality and performance of one's duties in this world. Therefore rules, institutions and moral codes were needed, not only in social life but also in the pursuit of transcendence.

Both Confucius and Jesus taught the people to be faithful to their teachings and to be reverent to the Transcendent. However, when dealing with human affairs and the divine calling, their attitudes exposed their divergence. Although Jesus did not deny the necessity of performing human duties, he made it clear that trust in God and faith in his kingdom were distinguishable from human duties, and one should always choose the first whenever these two conflicted. When he said that 'no one can serve two masters' (Matthew 6:24), he implied more than a mere distinction between serving God and serving money: having faith in God is the only way to human transcendence. In telling a questioner to 'give to Caesar what is Caesar's and to God what is God's' (Mark 12:17), Jesus not only avoided possible political persecution, but also affirmed that there was a distinction between relative human authority and the absolute authority of God. In this way, Jesus made religious faith the basis of social duties, and placed the former above the latter and subjected the latter to the former. However, for Confucius, there was no such distinction. Religious faith was composed of, or consisted in, faith in humanity, and therefore one should first perform one's human duties if one wanted to attain to transcendence. 'If a person cannot yet serve humans, how can he serve the spirits?' (*Analects*, XI, 12). It was through the first service, through performing human duties, that one could learn the proper relationship between the human and the Transcendent, between this life and the life to come, and so make it possible to transcend the limitation of life and find the ultimate meaning of life.

For a theistic religion, faith is considered to be the gift of God and belief is a response to that gift. A humanistic religion, on the other hand, focuses on human duties, and so faith grows from human nature and can be cultivated in one's true self and nourished by sincerity. In a theistic view, the world is supernatural, full of the unexpected, and calls for a large measure of idealism, while in a humanistic view, it is natural and knowable, in which realism offers the best way to achieve one's goal. This is why Jesus and Confucius adopted different attitudes towards miracles. As a religious master, Jesus used miracles to show God-like power and to let the people know that the Kingdom was at hand. But he insisted that miracles had to be understood as the gift of God, and that any misuse was against God's will. Consequently, Jesus sometimes warned against miracles and refused to perform them, as he did to the demon and the crowds who asked for a 'sign'. For Jesus, miracles were nothing but God's power. Faith or trust in God was primary and miracles only secondary. 'Without faith any miracles could not be done' (Mark 6:51), while with faith the unexpected would become the expected, the impossible the possible, and the supernatural the natural: 'Anyone who says to this mountain, "Go, throw yourself into the sea", and does not doubt in his heart but believes that what he says will happen, it will be done for him.'[46] When we come to Confucius' attitude towards faith and miracles, we see a humanistic spirit. While Jesus tended to use miracles as a support to faith, Confucius seldom talked about them.[47] Confucius said that, even if he was not understood by his fellow people, he would not complain to *Tian*, but would keep his faith that *Tian* had understood him (*Analects*, XIV, 35). Since *Tian* and humans had been identified, to trust in *Tian* was to trust in humans. Therefore, it needed no miracles nor any other supernatural power to support human faith in *Tian*, but only the confidence of human beings in themselves. In this system of humanistic religion, there was no room for the performance of miracles.

Ethical teachings are an important part both of the New Testament and of the *Analects*. The moral ideal, the designations of morality for human relations and for social life, are cherished extensively and remain basic norms for today's world. However, the distinction between the teachings of Jesus and Confucius is not indiscernible. One of the prominent characteristics of Jesus' ethical teaching, corresponding to his understanding of the Transcendent and his way to transcendence, is that he subordinates ethics to religion and subsumes morality under spirituality. For him, moral teaching was based on the human response to God's coming kingdom. Although there are no demands of the kind we find in the Old Testament, which were grounded in God's direct commands, and although Jesus appeared more humane and accessible to the common people, he nevertheless emphasized faith – awareness of the absolute claim of God rather than the relative claims of human morality. To repent of one's sin was not primarily for the relief of conscience or for social benefit, but in readiness for the coming kingdom. In this sense, the value of moral teaching was secondary, and should not be allowed to distract from the primary religious concern. For example, on the one hand, Jesus told the people to obey Moses' command to love their parents. On the other hand, when he felt it necessary to weigh the claims of God against the claims of human beings, he immediately grounded morality in religion by saying that 'anyone who loves his father or mother more than me is not worthy of me, and anyone who loves his son or daughter more than me is not worthy of me' (Matthew 10:37). In contrast to Jesus' religious ethic, Confucius established an ethical religion in which ethics was pre-eminent over, or identical with, religion. Morality was central to the Confucian way to transcendence, and it was valued, not because it was a means to serve human needs, but because it made it possible for humans to find the eternal in the temporal. In the mind of Confucius, to seek the eternal was to be moral. Thus he required his followers to 'behave well to their parents at home and to their elders abroad, to be cautious in giving promises and punctual in keeping them, to love the common people and to be near the virtuous' (*Analects*, I, 6). Thus, one's own self-cultivation becomes the focus of the Confucian way to transcendence. When he was asked how to reach the ideal, Confucius replied with three requirements, of which the first was to cultivate in one's self the capacity to be diligent in one's tasks; the second was to cultivate one's self in order to ease the hardship and misfortune of others; and the third was to cultivate one's self in order to give peace and security to all people (XIV, 42). Self-cultivation was elaborated in later Confucianism in three aspects of self-improvement: (1) meditation on one's own good nature to realize one's self as a part of the whole universe, so that one can identify oneself with the cosmos; (2) learning of human sciences, especially moral rules and propriety of behaviour; (3) practising virtues in human relationships, especially in the family and in communities according to these rules and propriety. In this sense, self-cultivation presents the characteristic of Confucian spirituality which is in contrast to the 'self-denial' presented in Christian spirituality (Mark 8:34).

On a number of ethical issues, Jesus and Confucius began their teaching on the same basis, but were then led to different conclusions by their different emphases. Both of them, for example, set 'perfection' as the human goal. For Jesus, a human should be perfect, because to be perfect was the requirement of the heavenly Father: 'Be perfect, as your heavenly Father is perfect' (Matthew 5:48). For Confucius, perfection was a goal required by human nature, and to be perfect was regarded as the highest aim of true learning. Again, both of them speak of 'love' as the basic ethical principle. However, in the mind of Jesus, the first and most important meaning of love was to devote oneself to God, and loving others follows from love for God. By contrast, Confucius described *jen* as loving others and as bringing benefit or dignity to people. He said that to love people was to put the Five Virtues into practice everywhere in the world: respectfulness, liberality, faithfulness, diligence and generosity (*Analects*, XVII, 6). Again, both of them spoke of trusting others. However, Jesus, having in mind the conflict between God's kingdom and the human world, taught his disciples to 'be on your guard against men' (Matthew 10:17), since it was humans who would persecute them. The contrast between this age and the age to come was such that those who belonged to this age were always a danger for people seeking God's kingdom. For this reason, Jesus seldom talked about trust and friendship in the social context, which paled into insignificance in the friendship with God and in God's love for human beings. Confucius, on the other hand, had a full confidence in humanity, although he warned against being intimate with those who had a bad character. The trust and respect between people were thus of significance not only for one's success in one's career, but also for one's seeking transcendence.

Both Jesus and Confucius experienced hardship in proclaiming their message, and showed an admirable character and a strong will. Jesus lamented that, while even animals and birds had their holes and nests, he himself (the Son of Man) had no place to rest (Matthew 8:20). Nevertheless he continued preaching, because of his divine commission. Confucius ate only coarse food, drank plain water and used a bent arm for a pillow, but still felt happy to persist with his *tao* (*Analects*, VII, 16). He was so intent upon enlightening those eager to learn that he forgot his hunger, and he was so happy in doing so, that he forgot the bitterness of his lot and did not realise that old age was already near (VII, 19). Even when he was not understood, he still took as his motto: 'Do not grieve that other people have not recognized your virtue but worry that you could not recognize theirs' (I, 16).

In their attitudes towards tradition, both Jesus and Confucius were reformers as well as sustainers of old traditions. They claimed that they were successors rather than creators. Jesus proclaimed:

> Do not think that I have come to abolish the Law or the Prophets; I have not come to abolish them but to fulfil them. I tell you the truth, until heaven and earth disappear, not the smallest letter, not the least stroke of a pen, will by any means disappear from the Law until everything is accomplished. Anyone who breaks one of the least of these commandments and teaches others to do the same will be called least in the kingdom of heaven, but whoever practises and teaches these commands will be called great in the kingdom of heaven. (Matthew 5:17–19)

However, his understanding of the tradition was radical and he claimed that these prohibitions, laws and moral requirements were made for men, not men for these laws (Mark 2:27). When the Pharisees and some of the teachers of Law asked Jesus why his disciples did not live according to the traditions of the elders – the disciples were eating their food with 'unclean hands' – Jesus rebuked their hypocrisy. He contrasted the rules taught by men with the commandments of God, and insisted, as he always did, that the former must be allowed to give way to the latter. Man-made rules focused on external behaviour, while the commandments of God penetrated to the heart: 'Nothing outside a man can make him "unclean" by going into him. Rather, it is what comes out of a man that makes him "unclean" (Mark 7:5–9, 15–16). In this way, Jesus radicalized the Jewish understanding of sin: an evil intention was as great a sin as an evil deed. 'You have heard that it was said to the people long ago, "Do not murder, and anyone who murders will be subject to judgement". But I tell you that anyone who is angry with his brother will be subject to judgement'. 'You have heard that it was said, "Do not commit adultery." But I tell you that anyone who looks at a woman lustfully has already committed adultery with her in his heart.'[48]

For Confucius, the ancient *tao* was sacred. He spent the whole of his life propagating and preserving the ancient tradition and took the way of life in ancient times as his ideal. All he did was to *restore* this *tao*. However, Confucius actually did *change* and *reform* the tradition. He believed that *tao* must adapt to new circumstances: it was humanity who could make the *tao* great, not the *tao* that could make humanity great (*Analects*, XV, 29). He insisted that a full and correct understanding of the ancient *tao*, lay not only in abiding by the rules but also in cultivating inner sageliness. Since the ancient *tao* existed in the world as well as in human beings, to cultivate human morality and enhance human well-being were the best ways to carry on the ancient tradition.

Through a comparison of Confucius and Jesus we have found that Confucianism and Christianity are two different traditions with certain important similarities. Central to their difference is the distinction between humanism and theism. While Jesus is a human, his power and spirit come from God and he is identified with God. Humanism is present in Christianity and is one of the characteristics of Christianity. However, it is overshadowed by theism and is subordinate to theism. While Confucius is regarded as a 'god-like' sage, he is essentially a human or a perfect human. His knowledge and virtues come mainly from his own cultivation and learning. A theism that calls for devotion to the Transcendent exists in Confucian teaching and sometimes is even taken as the basis of the whole of Confucian doctrine. However, it is not the central theme running through the system of Confucian teaching. Rather, it is to serve a humanistic purpose: humanity attains to transcendence by itself.

3

Jen in Confucianism and *Agape* in Christianity

Any kind of religion, whether theistic or humanistic, must provide people with a universally practicable principle that is related closely to its transcendental foundation as well as to its religious pursuit and ethical application. Such a principle comes from its profound faith and sets the ultimate goal for the whole of doctrine. Therefore, it is the heart and soul of this religion and characteristic of its nature as a religious tradition. *Agape* and *jen* are respectively the heart and soul of Christianity and Confucianism.

As heart and soul, the principle possesses both a universal character as the essence of *a* religion and special features as the guiding line of *this* religion. The duality of the character of a religious principle is a reflection of the dual nature of the human expression of a religious view. On the one hand, a principle has its special origins and is expressed in its particular form, function and application. Any study of a religion would be superficial if it neglected these particularities. On the other hand, the principle of one religion shares many aspects with the principles of other religions, whether or not they belong to the same category of religious typology, and a study of it will require a careful examination of its universal elements. Only by appreciating this characteristic duality of a religious principle can we give a faithful presentation of the universal and particular aspects of a religious principle.

It is true that Confucianism and Christianity are different religions and have different principles with different implications. Thus, some have correctly argued that there exists a significant difference between *agape* as the Christian principle and *jen* as the Confucian principle, since *agape* is essentially or originally a divine energy while *jen* is basically or practically a supreme human quality.

However, we may go on to argue that this difference between a theistic religion and a humanistic religion is only one side of the picture. There is another side. Confucian *jen* and Christian *agape* can be contrasted in their particular aspects, but share a great deal in their universal aspects. If we take into account only the difference presented by their particular factors, we shall be blind to their universal elements. We must see both sides of the picture and study them in their relationships. Generally speaking, Christian *agape* and Confucian *jen* diverge in regard to their focus, the one centring on theological transcendence, the other on humanistic progress. Nevertheless, they converge in regard to most of their functions and implications. In an examination of their convergence and divergence we shall come to a deeper understanding of the two profound traditions in which these two principles play their roles. To reveal the functions and implications of Confucian *jen* and Christian *agape* hidden in their scriptures and doctrines, we shall in this chapter undertake a general examination of the historical origins and main interpretations of each in its own tradition; and then in the following three chapters we shall move to a specifically comparative study of their particular implications.

JEN IN CONFUCIAN TRADITION

Jen has been widely used in Chinese literature both by Confucians and by Taoists and Buddhists. In *Tao Te Ching*, which is generally regarded as the first classical expression of Taoist philosophy, we read that 'It was when the greatest *tao* declined, then *jen* and *yi* (morality) arose'; 'After *tao* (the Way) was lost, then came *te* (Power or Virtue); after *te* was lost, then came *jen*'.[1] In contrast to Lao Tzu, the alleged author of *Tao Te Ching*, who would not mention *jen* unless he felt it necessary to do so in order to mock Confucian or conventional moral views, another Taoist master, Chuang Tzu (369–296? BCE), gave much more attention to the concept of *jen*, so that it could be absorbed into Taoist terminology. For Chuang Tzu, *jen* refers not only to a moral quality which is connected with Confucianism, but also to a presentation of the essence of the cosmos, thus having gained an ontological significance. Chuang Tzu contrasted these two kinds of *jen* and termed the latter 'great *jen*', 'true *jen*', or 'perfect *jen*', and the former 'small *jen*', 'normal *jen*' or 'defective *jen*'. Chuang Tzu repeatedly claimed that 'Great *jen* is not *jen*'; 'Perfect *jen* is a lofty thing – words like filial piety would never do to describe it'; '*Te* is harmony, *tao* is order; when *te* embraces all things, we have *jen*'; 'Perfect *jen* knows no affection'.[2] The prejudice of earlier Taoist philosophers concerning *jen* was modified in later Taoist works, where *jen* was understood in its moral sense and thus was considered necessary for human attaining to immortality. For example, in the *Book of Huai Nan Tzu* of the second century BCE, it is said that 'a person of *jen* never hurts his life by satisfying his desires'. Ko Hung of the fourth century CE connected *jen* closely with Taoist immortality and took *jen* as a path necessary for a long life or for becoming immortal. He said, 'those who seek immortality must set their minds on the accumulation of merits and the accomplishment of good work. Their hearts must be kind to all things. They must treat others as they treat themselves, and extend their humaneness [*jen*] even to insects . . . '.[3] *Jen* was thus integrated into Taoist philosophy and the Taoist understanding of the world. Following Taoism, many other schools of thought or religious movements, which flourished in the period of the Chin dynasty (221–206 BCE) and the Han dynasties (206 BCE–220 CE), took *jen* as one of their main themes. Even Buddhism, which was not an original religion in China and proclaimed an escape from this world, embraced the term *jen* as soon as it entered Chinese culture. Not only is the term *jen* used as an honorific title for the Buddha (*jen wang*, King of *jen*, the person who has practised *jen* to its utmost), but it is also used for worthy Buddhists (*jen che*). *Jen* is also frequently used in titles of some sutras (*jen wang Ching*, the Book of the Buddha), in referring to temples (*jen tsu*, temples of *jen*), and in naming pagodas (*jen ta*).[4]

However, a more comprehensive study of these usages in different philosophies and religions tells us that, although *jen* is used in various ways and by various schools, its fundamental connotation is to be found in Confucian cosmology, philosophy, ethics and religion. Whether it is rejected or embraced, *jen* is treated as the religious and moral principle or substance of the universe, which has a specific relation to the Confucian political ideal, its philosophical exploration and religious pursuit. *Jen* is nothing other than the symbol of Confucianism.

The origin of *jen* can be traced back to the earlier parts of Confucian classics. *Jen* first appeared in the *Book of History*, where in some instances it is written as the character for JEN (Humans) with the same pronunciation. In the *Book of Poetry*, *jen* is used in some poems and prefaces which are commonly regarded as later productions.[5] *Jen* appeared to be an important moral and religious concept at the beginning of the period of Spring and Autumn (770–476 BCE); and by the time that *The Spring and Autumn Annals* was annotated, *jen* must have become commonplace. In these contexts, the implications of *jen* range from a specific moral quality to a number of virtues, especially relating to loving people, doing good to others and practising filial piety to parents. The development of *jen* as a key term during the period of Spring and Autumn prepared for its Confucian understanding.

The first person to attach pre-eminent importance to *jen* and finally to establish it as the basis, or keystone, of Confucianism was Confucius himself. Confucius inherited and developed previous usages of *jen* in the ancient classics, but reinterpreted it in the light of his humanistic spirit and promoted it as the highest ideal. The essence of the ancient tradition and the fundamental spirit of the unities between *Tian* and humans, between ancestors and descendants, and between the sage and the common people, were all integrated into the single concept of *jen*, so that *jen* became an inclusive concept that signified not only human excellence but also transcendental principle.

Confucius taught on many matters and commented on many events. At the same time he believed that all his ideas were based on a single principle. He once said to one of his disciples that all his teachings had one thread that ran right through them (*Analects*, IV, 15). On the other occasion he told another student that, although he had tried to learn and teach as many things as possible, there was a central point around which all his ideas were developed (XV, 3). Again on another occasion, he confirmed that there was a single word that could be put into practice for the whole of life (XV, 24). From these paragraphs we can infer that there is a central theme in all Confucius' teachings and a key concept in all his doctrine. What remains for further study is what this central theme, or key concept, is.

There are two ways of identifying the central theme in Confucius' teaching: first by summarizing his conversations to see what is revealed, and secondly by examining the implicit intention of the relevant conversations. Following the first method we find that the central concept of Confucian teaching is indeed *jen*, not only because *jen* is one of the most frequently used concepts, but also because it encapsulates the characteristic content of Confucian doctrine. However, at this point there seems to be an insoluble contradiction for all commentators of the *Analects*. On the one hand, *jen* is indeed a central topic in Confucius' conversations: it appears 105 times, and 58 out of nearly 500 chapters in the *Analects* are directly concerned with its meaning, function, or practice.[6] On the other hand, it is said that 'The Master seldom talked about profit, fate and *jen*' (IX, 1).[7] However, this contradiction disappears if we appreciate that Confucius did not talk much about *jen* because he was cautious in discussing such a fundamental issue, but that most of his conversations concerning *jen*, just because of their importance, were recorded and compiled into the book of the *Analects*. Consequently the very matter about which Confucius spoke comparatively little – in the context of all his conversations throughout his life-time one hundred occasions were by no means many – appears more frequently than others. Since such unusual treatment could be given only to a fundamental and vitally important concept, there can be no doubt that *jen* is taken to be such a key concept in the Confucian system.

This matter seems even more complex when we try to draw a conclusion from Confucius' tacit intentions in some of his conversations. It is true that neither Confucius himself nor his disciples referred to *jen* immediately after their discussions of the 'thread'. Rather, there was a time when *shu* – do not do to others what you yourself do not desire – was said to be the word which should guide one's whole life. Based on this fact, a syllogism is invented by some commentators:

> *Jen* is the central concept of Confucius' teaching;
> *Shu* is said to be the key word guiding one's whole life;
> Therefore, *jen* is *shu* and *shu* is the thread running through
> Confucianism.

The conclusion of this syllogism has found wide approval, because *shu* is indeed a very important aspect of *jen*. It is *shu* that makes it possible for *jen* to be expressed and manifested. *Shu* is the primary procedure through which *jen* is practised. However, this important aspect and primary procedure of *jen* cannot justify the view that *shu* is *jen*.[8] In Confucian teaching, *jen* is to be understood on two levels: what *jen* is itself, and what embodies *jen*.

On the first level, *jen* is understood as the underlying principle and substance, the primary motive of all action and behaviour, and the essence of human nature and Heaven, and therefore, it is

undefinable, although not unknowable. Confucius seems to understand this difficulty, and does not spend much time in exploring *jen*
at this level. What he wants to say about *jen* is mostly on the second
level, on which *jen* is manifested as ways and procedures of realizing
this principle and actualising this substance. *Shu* is one of the most
successful approaches in this task. Many have seen the importance
of *shu* for *jen*, but they have failed to see the difference between *shu*
as the procedure of *jen* and *jen* itself. Robert Allinson, for example,
argues that the central thread running through Confucius' teaching
is none other than *shu*, the negatively formulated Golden Rule.
Unfortunately, he goes too far and equates *shu* with *jen*. He believes
that in the *Analects* (XII, 2), *shu* is used 'virtually interchangeably
with *jen* as a complete definition of *jen*'.[9] However, a reading of
this paragraph points in a different direction: there are many ways
of carrying out *jen* and *shu* is only one of them. When Confucius is
asked what *jen* is or how to practise *jen*, he mentions three ways
of practising *jen*, or three conditions for realizing *jen*. The first is
to have absolute sincerity in dealing with others. In Confucius'
words, when one goes abroad, one should behave to everybody
as if one were receiving a great guest, and deal with people as if
one were assisting at a great sacrifice. The second is what is meant
by *shu*: do not do to others what you yourself do not like. The
third is to cultivate one's virtues so that one never complains of
others, either in affairs of state or at home.[10] These three conditions
are equally important for *jen*,[11] but with different emphases. The
last is concerned with cultivating one's character, so that *jen* can
be manifested in one's behaviour and attitudes; the second with
restraining oneself from bringing harm to others, by reflecting on
one's own experience; and the first with treating others sincerely,
trying one's best to do good to others and carrying out one's
duties faithfully, whatever one does and wherever one is. By way
of comparison, the first two are used more frequently to portray
the procedures of *jen* as love, while the last is taken as the basis of
one's practice of *jen*. Not to bring harm upon others is elsewhere
called *shu* (*Analects*, XV, 24), and to do good to others and to deal
with one's business honestly is elsewhere named *chung* (*Analects*,
IV, 15). '*Chung*' is usually translated as 'loyalty'. However, it does
not merely mean a faithful attitude to one's prince, or superior, as
later Confucians believed it to mean. Confucius thought of *chung*
as a generalization of altruism based on sincerity: cultivating one's
character earnestly, and therefore performing one's duty faithfully

and treating others sincerely. In his own words, 'One who wishes to establish himself must first establish others; one who wishes to be prominent himself must first help others to be prominent' (*Analects*, VI, 28). Compared with *shu*, *chung* connotes a positive intention and action.[12] To be *jen* to others, it is not enough not to impose upon them what one does not like oneself. One must try one's best to help others achieve what they want. On the other hand, *chung* and *shu* share the same principle of practising *jen*, moving by analogy from what is close to what is not so close. The closest to anyone is one's own self. Thus one should be able to know from oneself what others like or dislike. Guided by this analogy and motivated by sincerity, one can establish an affirmative relation with others.

Shu and *chung* are closely related and are equally important procedures of *jen*. There is no ground for believing that *shu* is more fundamental and is actually the unifying thread in Confucius' teachings, while *chung* is only another expression for *shu*.[13] Since they are two ways of practising the same principle, or two procedures of the same ideal, *shu* and *chung* must be taken together to illustrate how to practise *jen*. Both are involved in the relationship between oneself and others, and will be realised in the movement from oneself to others. Although *chung* places more emphasis on one's sincerity and *shu* more on reflecting on others, it is not correct to say that *chung* means only the full development of one's own mind while *shu* means only the extension of this mind to others. Some scholars read how Chu Hsi interpreted *chung* as developing one's own sincerity and *shu* as extending one's sincerity to others, and therefore render *chung* as 'conscientiousness' and *shu* as 'altruism': 'it is the Confucian golden rule, or *jen* (humanity), with *chung* referring to the self and *shu* referring to others'.[14] However, what is intended by 'developing one's own mind' and 'extending to others' in the context of Chu Hsi is to illustrate the different emphases of *chung* and *shu* in realising *jen*, not to cut *jen* into two halves with *shu* and *chung* each occupying a half. *Jen* is essentially the relationship between oneself and others. As two procedures of *jen*, *chung* or *shu* must each involve the whole of this relationship, both the self and the others. *Shu* and *chung* differ only in their ways of carrying out *jen* in the full relationship between oneself and others, doing good to others or refraining from harming others. In this sense, each of them is both 'developing fully one's own sincerity' and 'extending one's own sincerity to others'.

However important *shu* and *chung* are for understanding the central theme of Confucian doctrine, they are not equivalent to the theme itself. Confucius told Tseng Shen, one of his favourite disciples, that there was one thread running through his teachings. Logically, Tseng Shen might have been expected to explain what this thread was. When asked, however, what was meant by the Master, instead of stating that the *thread* was *chung* and *shu*, Tseng Shen explained the words of his master by saying that all the teachings of Confucius were *about chung* and *shu (Analects,* IV, 15). One implication of the fact that Tseng Shen replied in this way is that, since the thread runs through all Confucius' teaching, penetrating all virtues and practices, it can be seen only in its manifestations. *Chung* and *shu* are its manifestations, or applications, and can be used to summarize what Confucius taught. Since *chung* and *shu* are both 'cultivating one's own mind' and 'extending it to others', they are the ways of realizing the highest ideal, that is, *jen*. As manifestations, or applications, or practices of *jen, chung* and *shu* are essential for the central thread running through the whole doctrine, but they are not the thread itself.

From the age before Confucius to that of Confucius, and from Confucius to the neo-Confucians, the discourses on *jen* were continuingly enriched and extended. Each generation of Confucians inherited the earlier explanation of *jen* and added its own understanding to it. From a linear point of view, the evolution or development of *jen* within Confucianism is properly summarized by Wing-tsit Chan as follows:

> From the original idea of *jen*, which was used in the *Book of History*, as '(1) kindness from above, it was broadened to mean (2) benevolence, still a particular virtue but no longer restricted to rulers, and further extended to connote (3) perfect virtue, which includes all particular virtues and applies to all men. In its application it was understood as (4) love, and, more specifically, (5) affection and, more emphatically, (6) universal love. On the psychological level, it is (7) man or (8) man's mind. Under the influence of Buddhism, it became (9) impartiality, which was in danger of becoming merely a state of mind, as was *jen* in terms of (10) consciousness, and so it was quickly modified as (11) impartiality embodied in the action of man. Finally, it was expanded to the limit to become (12) one body with the universe and the generative force of all things, namely, (13) process of production.'[15]

Complex and divergent as these interpretations are, they can be integrated into a single principle, underlying all other concepts in

Confucianism. This single principle, in turn, may be presented in three dimensions: human-cosmic unity, moral-metaphysical goodness and practical-universal love. These dimensions are explored in such an intensive manner in the Four Books that they signal the completion of a philosophical and religious enhancement of *jen* from an experiential quality to a universal principle, from a psychological state to a cosmic substance, and from love as a human affection to love as an ethical commitment and religious mission. It was through this innovation that the Confucian understanding of *jen* obtained its fulfilment in Chinese tradition: *jen* is defined as the essence of human beings and of the universe, as the guiding line for human life and as the creative force of the cosmos. Thus, *jen* is clearly presented in three aspects of Confucian humanism: (1) *jen* as humanity; (2) *jen* as virtue; and (3) *jen* as love.[16] Each of these three aspects is inseparable from the whole of *jen*, which specially emphasises (1) that all three are essentially one, distinguishable but not separable, and each of them enriches the *jen* as the Confucian principle rather than detracts from it. *Jen* as the heart and soul of Confucianism and as the unique basis for Confucian doctrine is embodied in these three dimensions; (2) that in the last analysis, *jen* as love is more fundamental than *jen* as humanity or virtue, and therefore *jen* as love is the heart of the heart and soul of the soul; and (3) that the purpose of exploration of *jen* is constantly on the practical side rather than on the theoretical side. To understand the world one must study extensively, be steadfast of purpose, inquire earnestly, and reflect on what is at hand. However, the aim of this learning and practising is to become a person of *jen* (*Analects*, XIX, 6) which can be realized only by fulfilling humanity extensively, cultivating virtue sincerely and practising love universally. Through these practices one learns what are the natural laws and the moral rules, and how to abide by them. When one has done this, one is able to be a person of *jen*. When one becomes a person of *jen*, one can be said, though with qualifications, to have transcended the temporal and limited realm, having fulfilled one's value as a human and integrated oneself with other humans and with the whole cosmos. When this integration is completed, a person of *jen* will become a sage who can help the transformation of Heaven and Earth and who therefore possesses the nature of eternity. This is the ultimate goal of the Confucian doctrine of *jen*.

The discourses on *jen* in the Four Books were carried on in later Confucian development, in which *jen* is taken as the centre of Confucian cosmology, metaphysics, philosophy, politics, education, ethics, aesthetics and religion. Hundreds of books, articles and commentaries have been produced to expound the meaning and function of *jen*. Although many of them are valuable for a discussion of the Confucian doctrine of *jen*, from the methodological view the Confucian understanding of *jen* is especially distinctive in the writings of three great Confucians, Tung Chung-shu of the Han Dynasty, Chu Hsi of the Sung Dynasty and Wang Yang-ming of the Ming Dynasty, where the doctrine of *jen* was systematized and characterized in association with their specific understanding of the Confucian world-view.

As a result of political suppression in the Chin dynasty and the subsequent chaotic situation, Confucians in the former Han dynasty were faced with a society penetrated by the ideas and practices of Legalism, the school of yin–yang and the Five Elements and Taoism. Confucianism had to adapt to this new situation, and the mystical tendency in Confucianism was encouraged and developed against this background. The distinctive feature of Confucianism in this period is its mystically exaggerated view of the unity between human beings and the universe, integrating Confucian ethics, concepts of yin–yang and the Five Elements, and the conception of change, into a systematic doctrine. Its representative is the greatest Confucian of the Han dynasty, Tung Chung-shu (179?–104? BCE). Tung Chung-shu on the one hand developed the mystical and religious aspects of Classical Confucianism, and on the other hand expressed them in the terminology of yin–yang and the Five Elements, thus moulding religion, politics, history, ethics and philosophy into a single system in a way unprecedented at that time. In its cosmology, the unity of heaven, earth and humans is the base, the interaction between yin and yang is the motive force, and the right orders among the Five Elements are the laws of movement. He further developed a religious philosophy. This philosophy starts with the correlation of human beings and *Tian* (Heaven), which he saw as a divine order or personal Lord, and whose Mandate or Decree, if not followed, would be withdrawn, so that the withdrawal would sooner or later lead the dynasty to break down. By this close correlation, Tung Chung-shu provided a justification for the view that human qualities, not only physical features but also moral sense, were endowed and animated by heavenly spirit: 'Heaven, when it constituted man's nature, commanded him to practise love [*jen*] and righteousness, to be ashamed of what is shameful, not to be concerned, like birds and beasts, solely with existence and profits'.[17] He propagated Confucian ethics and required that humans should model themselves on the virtues of heaven; that is, on virtues like *jen*, righteousness, propriety and wisdom, which originally came from the will and evolution of *Tian*. Few modern scholars have given special attention to Tung Chung-shu's treatment of *jen*. It is believed that Tung's theory of *jen* is at best an unsystematized comment on the earlier theories of Confucian *jen*. However, Tung did contribute a great deal to the Confucian doctrine of *jen*. This contribution was made in two ways. The first was that he associated *jen* with *Tian* the creator of the world in his exploration of the correspondence of humans and *Tian*; and the second was that he confirmed and explained that *jen* was 'to love others or to love all'.

Tung agreed with Mencius that *jen* should be understood not only in the light of human action, but also in the light of the unity between *Tian* (Heaven) and humans. For him, there is only one origin or source from which all beings and humans come, which is *Tian*. Since humans have their beginning and end in this origin, their nature, behaviour and virtues are predetermined by it. 'What produces (man) cannot (itself) be man, for the creator of man is Heaven [*Tian*]. The fact that men are men derives from Heaven. Heaven, indeed, is man's supreme ancestor.'[18] *Tian* (Heaven), as the creator of humans, not only produced the human body but also created the human spirit as well as the rules of community life, and thus *jen* comes directly from the will or operation of *Tian*. *Tian* in Tung is presented in two forms: the creator, commander and governor of the universe who is identified with *jen* and takes care of human business; and the spiritual force underlying the production and reproduction of humanity and myriads of things, in which the benevolence and beneficence of *jen* is fully manifested. As the creator and commander, *Tian* is *jen*, manifesting the love of *jen* in his producing and nurturing of all things in the universe and in his constant concern over humanity; and *Tian* commanded *jen* in humanity: 'Heaven, when it constituted man's nature, commanded him to practise love [*jen*] and righteousness [*yi*] . . . '[19] As the cosmic force, *Tian* is the source of *jen*. The unity and correspondence between humans and the cosmos is obvious. There are *yang* and *yin* [two cosmic forces]: thus humans have their nature and feelings. The outward manifestation of human nature is to be found in the virtue of *jen*, and that of human feeling in the quality of covetousness that derives from *yin*. In this sense, *jen* is directly associated with the *yang* force of the universe, or is its embodiment in human nature. Coming from the origin of the cosmos and being rooted in human nature, *jen* is given a universal status and profound role in unifying the human realm and the cosmic world.

By the transforming influence of *Tian's* will and operation, human vigour is directed to become *jen*. However, humans may not participate in this influence because of their imperfect intelligence and morality. Only the sage can relate things and human affairs to the One and the origin. In order to teach humans how to regulate their relationships as well as to reconcile humans with their origin, the sage or sage-king formulates the virtues of *jen* and *yi*, and makes them into practicable rules for self-cultivation and social life. In carrying out activities in community and in cultivating their character, humans internalize the universal principle as particular virtues. As both principle and virtue, *jen* consists in loving others, not in loving oneself: 'if one loves oneself very much but does not apply one's love to others, one cannot be considered humane [*jen*].' Wing-Tsit Chan comments on this paragraph that 'This understanding of humanity [*jen*] as love is found in ancient philosophers . . . but for them it was one of several possible meanings, but in Tung Chung-shu it is *the* meaning. This interpretation is characteristic of practically all Han Confucianists, and Tung was the first.'[20] From Confucius, who defines *jen* as loving humans (*Analects*, XII, 22), to Mencius, who insists that no one is not loved by a person of *jen* (*Book of Mencius*, 7A:46), and to Tung Chung-shu, who explicitly explains *jen* as loving others but not loving oneself, the function and implication of *jen* is further defined in respect of human relationship.

Chu Hsi (1130–1200) was a great neo-Confucian in bringing the rationalistic school to full maturity. He was also the greatest thinker in Confucian history since the time of Confucius–Mencius in the sense that he created a syncretistic version of Confucianism that dominated the Confucian world until the twentieth century. While he built up a system of syncretistic Confucianism, based on his exploration of the Great Ultimate (*tai chi*), Principle (*li*), and material force (*chi*), he also made a great effort to systematize the Confucian understanding of *jen*, and to him, 'the concept of *jen* was clearly far more important than those of the Great Ultimate and other philosophical categories'.[21]

Chu Hsi opposed the theories of *jen* popular at his time, that *jen* means forming one body with all things or that *jen* is a state of consciousness. He stressed the productive force and the integrating power of *jen*. For Chu Hsi, *jen* is received by humans from the mind [*hsin*] of Heaven and Earth, which produces all things. The moral qualities of this mind are four: the power of origination, flourishing, advantage and firmness, while the power of origination unites and controls all their operations. These four qualities become Four Virtues in the human mind: *jen*, *yi* [righteousness], *li* [propriety] and *ch'i* [wisdom]. Correspondingly, *jen*, like the power of origination in the mind of Heaven and Earth, embraces all the functions of these virtues. It is in *jen* that we can find the virtue of the human mind as well as that of the mind of Heaven and Earth. The chief virtue of *jen* is to produce or to give life. All virtues are like seeds, while *jen* alone makes it possible for the seeds to grow. Just because *jen* is the mind of growth, it is taken as the root and source of all other virtues and good deeds. Like Confucius and Mencius, Chu Hsi laid the responsibility of preserving the mind of *jen* on the conscious activities: respectfulness in private life, seriousness in handling affairs, and loyalty in dealing with others. To express the mind is to practise the virtues: be filial in serving parents, respectful in serving an elder brother and altruistic in dealing with others. Further, Chu Hsi argued that *jen* was not only the virtue of mind but also the principle of love.[22] As the virtue of mind, *jen* penetrates virtuous actions, activities and conscious states. As the principle of love, *jen* enables Heaven and Earth to produce ten thousand things as well as human beings and to make them grow; and it enables humans to love all. In his commentaries on the *Analects* and *The Book of Mencius*, he repeatedly argues that the mind of *jen* is the mind of love: the substance of *jen* is seen in love and its application is made through love. However, *jen* as the principle of love is not only ordinary love. It is like the root of a plant and the spring of water. It is the source of all forms of love and expresses itself in all forms of love. Therefore, *jen* is the nature of love and love is the feeling of *jen*, or *jen* is the substance of love and love is the function of *jen*.[23]

Although Chu Hsi defines *jen* both as the virtue of mind and as the principle of love, his emphasis is on the side of the principle, the objectivity of which is in obvious contradiction to those who believe that *jen* is fundamentally in the subjectivity of mind. For the latter, *jen* is nowhere but in the mind. The mind is not only one's own mind, but the mind of all humans and of the universe. Therefore, defining *jen* as mind it naturally results in the saying that *jen* is to integrate oneself with the universe. Cheng Hao (1032–1077) argued that the person of *jen* forms one body with the universe and the myriad of things. Cheng I (1033–1107) asserted that the person of *jen* regarded the universe and all things as one body.[24] However, it was in Wang Yang-ming (1472–1529) of the Ming Dynasty that this theory of *jen* received the finest defence and strongest argument. For Wang, the mind of one is also the mind of others; the human mind is also the mind of the universe. This mind is none other than *jen*. Because human beings and all things participate in the same mind and same *jen*, they form a unity. Wang's argument for *jen* as one body with the universe starts with the psychological experience used by Mencius. When one saw a child about to fall into a well, he argued, one could not help feeling alarm and compassion. This fact showed that one's *jen* formed one body with the child. Further, when one observed the pitiful cries and frightened appearance of birds and animals about to be slaughtered, one could not help feeling an 'inability to bear' their suffering. This fact, he again argued, showed that his *jen* led him to unity with the birds and animals. Even when one saw plants broken and destroyed, one could not help a feeling of pity. This fact showed that his *jen* led him to unity with the plants too. Even when one saw tiles and stones shattered and crushed, one could not help feeling regret. This fact showed that one's *jen* formed one body with tiles and stones.[25] The unity of all things lies in the mind of *jen* that is our Heaven-endowed nature. The mind–heart in itself has bright and manifest virtues which are present in all men, either great or small, so long as it is not obscured by selfish desires. Evil, such as greed for gain, destroying and killing, is aroused by the selfish desires which are contrary to the original heart–mind of *jen*. However, the bright virtue of *jen* and the innate good nature can manifest again if people cultivate their character by reducing these desires, in which case one is reunified with Heaven, Earth and all things and all beings.

Like most Confucians at that time, Wang takes *jen* as the source of all virtues, which is the expression of the principle of production and reproduction of living beings. Other virtues are like branches or shoots, while *jen* is like the root. The root is the life of a tree. It enables the tree to grow up, first the shoots and then the trunk and then the branches. This justifies the view that *jen* is to form a unity with all beings and things, that is, to love all one's fellow creatures. It also justifies the view that to love all, one first has to love one's parents, brothers and relatives, which are the ways in which *jen* grows.[26]

From these three representative theories of Confucian *jen*, we see clearly that Confucians discuss it at three levels. At the metaphysical level, *jen* is taken as the principle of the universe, which is responsible for the growth and evolution both of human beings and of all things. The principle of the universe may be in a spiritual form, or it may not. In whatever form, the emphasis of the doctrine of *jen* is not on the relationship between the giver and the receiver, but on their unity and harmony, of which *jen* is the foundation and source. At the psychological level, *jen* is taken as the essential stuff of human consciousness. The world shares the same consciousness embodied as the universal principle. The principle is expressed in the human mind where it actualizes itself as human nature. Since every human being born shares the universal principle as well as human nature, he is equal to everyone else. At the ethical level, *jen* is taken as the root and source of the virtuous life. The root and source should be understood not only in the sense of a provider, but also in the sense of the activator and motivator. From the point of view of *jen*, human beings are able to live a moral life because of the nature of *jen*. *Jen* is the power and the ability of human morality. From the point of view of humans, *jen* must be carried out in human life and activity. To live a virtuous life, one first has to preserve and cultivate the root, and to create the proper circumstances for *jen* to grow, of which learning and practice are taken as the necessary ways.

AGAPE IN CHRISTIAN TRADITION

While *jen* is the soul and central theme of Confucian doctrine, *agape* or its popular translation, love, is the soul of Christian teaching. It is common Christian belief that God is the God of love, Jesus Christ is an embodiment of love, and consequently Christianity is a religion of love. Christian theology and philosophy are established around the concept of love and countless writings have been concerned with the exploration of love and its significance. As John Macquarrie puts it in his *In Search of Humanity*, 'within Christianity love has been explored and interpreted in a depth that goes beyond anything we find in other religions or in secular philosophies'.[27]

Love, indeed as it is used in our daily language, is an umbrella word covering many aspects and activities of life, from positive attitudes to other people to affirmative action towards other things. Religious love and secular love have been spoken of without differentiation, and intellectual love and emotional love have been interwoven without care. Behind every usage of love, it is argued, we can find a rich history, and in every usage of love we can come, through different ways, to an appreciation of Christian faith. However, among all these usages, only one is of fundamental significance for Christian doctrine since it is the foundation of its conception of love: love as a special relation between God and humans and a special relation between human beings themselves, the second relation having its source in, and being the enrichment of, the first. These relations of love have in Christian doctrine been crystallised into one word: *agape*, the love of self-giving, either from God to humans or from humans to God and to their fellowmen, the love with all one's heart and soul.[28] There are many Greek terms corresponding to the English word love, each with a different connotation and origin. For example, *phileo* is the most common word for love or affectionate regard, but it is often used to denote love between friends or love for learning; *stergo* means to love, feel affection, especially the mutual love of parents and children, but it is also used for love of a ruler, love of a tutelary god, and even the love of dogs for their master; *eros* denotes originally the love between man and woman of longing, craving and desiring, but later it also embraces the mystical searching and striving for perfection, goodness and immortality; while *agape* has a wider application in its meaning, essentially it is not a longing for possessions or worth, but a generous move by one person for the sake of the other.[29] From this interpretation of *agape*, the biblical writers and translators developed a concept of love that refers to God's self-giving love for his creatures. Although *agape* is still used in other senses on occasions – for example, it refers to the love of man for woman in the Song of Songs and it is almost interchangeable with *philia* in John 21:16–18, it is overwhelmingly adopted for the relationships of humans with God and with their fellow men; indeed, later theological discourse gives it even narrower and more specific meaning so that it refers exclusively to the love of self-giving. Since God is believed to be wanting nothing, he is the source of *agape*, and his love is pure self-giving. Under the influence of this understanding of God's love, human *agape* is also associated with self-giving rather than self-seeking (I Corinthians 13). Since Christian love is *agape*, it would be correct for us to use the term *agape* as the principle of Christian doctrine, and thereby to distinguish it from ordinary forms of love, either the love of private life or the love of social relationship.

There have been countless writings in which Christian love has been described, discussed and commended. However, the focus of this chapter will be on the original teaching of Christian teachers, especially that contained in the biblical sources, and on representative theories in later development of Christian doctrine. We make this selection not only because it offers a means of grasping the value of Christianity without overstretching our attention, but also because it is a path leading us directly to the centre of Christian doctrine and avoiding the possible prejudice created by others' presentations and arguments. In the original teaching of Christianity, as we have seen, Christian love has three dimensions, which are surprisingly in agreement with the triangular religious structure we presented in the first chapter: a transcendental compassion from God towards human beings, a religious devotion from human beings to God, and an ethical care from one human being to another. However, while it is convenient to say that Christian love has three dimensions, we must remember, as we emphasized in dealing with the three dimensions of Confucian *jen*, that these three dimensions are in the mainstream of Christian doctrine actually one, as against any suggestion that God's *agape* to his creatures is separable from human devotion to God and completely different from human love for their neighbours. Each of them is essential for understanding Christian love, but none of them on its own constitutes the whole. To reveal the rich content of Christian love, we must pay attention to each of these three dimensions. In order to come to a true conception of Christian love both as a single principle and as a unity of three dimensions, we will follow the way in which we discussed Confucian *jen* – first, in this chapter, examining the historical development and religious function of *agape*; and then, in the following three chapters, discussing its three aspects which are respectively: (1) *agape* as grace; here we will mainly discuss the theocentricism of Christian love in which *agape* is understood first of all as the relation of God to human beings; (2) *agape* as the human response to God's grace; here we will concentrate on the human internalisation of God's calling and on the unity and tension between human motivation and divine command; and (3) *agape* as neighbour-love; here we will explore the ethical application of *agape* through one's attitude and action towards others, whether friends, strangers or even enemies.

Within European culture, the promotion of love as the heart of faith did not begin with the coming of Christianity. Long before the Christian era, the concept of love had been explored both by the Israelites and by the Greeks, who had created a rich source of terms to express their understanding of love, divine love as well as human love, and the role of love in their religions. Scholarly study of the Hebrew Scriptures reveals a variety of Hebrew terminology denoting what is meant by love. When this tradition overlapped with that of the Greeks, the meanings which originated in Greek culture made their own contribution to Israelite understanding, so that there emerged a common conception which provided a background for the Christian understanding of love.[30] It is suggested that the root of these terms may be located in one of the most original and basic human relations: that between man and woman. Although there is not yet sufficient etymological evidence to support this suggestion, and sexual relations play a limited role in the O.T. literature, we can at least presume that in the pre-Christian tradition, love had already been more concerned with personal relationship than with the relationship between humans and things, and it is from this basic usage that the wide range of application of these terms arose.

The application of these terms has been classified by O.T. scholars into two broad categories, secular love and religious love. In its secular sense, love varies from sexual desire to personal attachment. According to Quell, love of this kind is found in three basic meanings in the O.T.: the vital urge of the sexes towards each other; family relationship, friendship and legal association; and the norm of social relationship and therefore an aspect of the legal code. In its religious sense, love essentially belongs to the theological relation between God and his chosen people. This classification is open to question. The secular and the religious are seldom distinguishable in most religious traditions, and even less so in the tradition contained in the O.T. literature. It is inappropriate, therefore, to exclude the feelings and behaviour displayed in sexual and family relationships from those proper to religion. Behind and within every so-called secular love there is ultimately a religious significance and explanation. From this point of view, the applications of love in the O.T. may well be classified into three categories, as we have done in our general approach to religious studies: theological, religious and ethical. Since theological, religious and ethical are different aspects of the same religious structure, all usages of love both in the O.T. and in the N.T. are essentially of a religious nature.

The essence of love in the O.T. is that its theocentric application predominates over its other applications, and love of God is always superior to, or is constantly taken as the basis of, human love, whatever form it may presume. As a vertical relation between humans and God, love moves in two directions: God loves humans and humans love God. However, the downwards movement takes precedence over the upwards movement. In terms of the Covenant as well as the belief in creation, the emphasis is constantly put on the former movement, and the latter is believed to be only its extension or derivation (Deuteronomy 10:14–16). The characteristic of the downwards movement from God in the O.T. is that his love is addressed in the first place to the people generally (especially to the Israelites) rather than to individual persons. An exception occurs when God's love is directed to kings, such as Solomon (II Samuel 12:24 and Nehemiah 13:26). However, the king in question should be seen as the representative of the people rather than as an individual person. Any attempt to develop the idea of God's love outside of his relationship with the chosen people would, in the context of the O.T., be fruitless.[31] God's love is constantly related to the covenant, although there is a determined attempt in Hosea to 'pull down the theory of Covenant, in order to expose God's love as its foundation, and then builds it up again with righteousness, judgement, loving-kindness and faithfulness'.[32]

When we turn to human love, we find that love is displayed in two kinds of movement: upwards, so that love is directed to the almighty and creator God; and horizontally, from one person to another.[33] The reason why humans must love God is not properly explored in the O.T. God's love for humans, which is developed in the theory of creation and Covenant, is simply taken as the fundamental reason for human love. In other words, the reason for human love for God cannot be found anywhere except in God's love for humans. Love for God is simply a direct response to God's love: one should love God *because* God loved one's ancestors: God 'set his affection on your forefathers and loved them, and he chose you, their descendants, above all the nations, as it is today' (Deuteronomy 10:15). In terms of the collective religion of Israel, this is a sufficient reason for the response from humans. As a response to God's love, human love is 'a fundamental motive in all communion with God. To love God means to enjoy him and seek him instinctively. Fundamentally, those who love God are the truly pious, whose life of faith bears the stamp of originality and genuineness: they seek God for his own sake.'[34] God created the human world in the overflow of his love, and also laid his commandment of love on humans. Therefore, human love for God is primarily a commandment of God: 'Love the Lord your God with all your heart and with all your soul and with all your strength' (Deuteronomy 6:5). Since love is said to be a commandment, there is a possibility that humans may or may not obey it; they may love God with all their heart or only half-heartedly. This is crucial for human relationship with God, and God is said to be the only judge to know how this relationship stands.

Contrary to Quell, who takes the human love for the neighbour displayed in the O.T. literature as a purely secular love, not only is this love ethical, it also has a fundamental theological and religious significance. First, human love for the neighbour is not merely personal affection, but a moral relationship between humans based on the relationship between humans and God. All human beings are God's creatures and their relationship should be modelled on God's relation with his creation. Secondly, this love is not based on pure sexual desire, nor on personal favour, but on a universal awareness that love is the very stuff of one's life, as vital as one's own soul. Thirdly, when this love is summarized in terms of neighbour-love in Leviticus (19:18), it is not a secular feeling, nor even a legal relation, but the devotional care to others, which is commanded by God. As a secular feeling, love may be denied to one's enemies. As a legal requirement, love may or may not be given to a stranger. However, as a divine commandment, love is to be extended to help strangers, aliens, even one's enemies.[35] Although love for strangers, aliens and enemies is not yet clearly expounded and promoted in the O.T. literature, it nevertheless lays a good foundation for later Christian development, in which universal love becomes the core of Christian ethics.

The Christian concept of love originates and evolves out of this background. Although there were other words available, the writers of the Gospels adopt *agape* in nearly every case to refer to God's relationship with humans, Jesus' love for humans and human love for God and Christ. By God's *agape*, which has created the new realities among humans, humans are provided the motive and power to love one another. It is clear that neither the command to love God nor the command to love one's neighbour nor the Golden Rule was invented by Jesus.[36] While Jesus persisted in the ancient tradition that the theological love of God was the precondition of all other forms of love, he appears to have developed God's love in a distinctive way, in which compassion and forgiveness are central. Compared with the O.T., God's love in the N.T. is bestowed less collectively and more individually, less predetermined by one's ancestry and more by one's own life and faith.[37] God's love is understood as God's compassion for human suffering and forgiveness of human sins. Although humans constantly violate God's will, God is believed to love them and forgive them as soon as they show their love and faith in God. When Jesus says that a woman's 'many sins have been forgiven – for she loved much' (Luke 7:47), he reveals the absoluteness and superiority of this love: love itself is the only condition for salvation. Anybody who loves will be saved because he or she has faith.

Jesus explored at a deeper level and in more varied aspects the meaning and value of human love for God and for neighbour. Jesus is said to be the first to have combined (Mark 12:28) the two commandments of loving God (Deuteronomy 6:5) and loving neighbour (Leviticus 19:18); as a consequence the three-fold relationship between God and man, man and God, and man and man, becomes one relationship, that of love. Jesus is also believed to have been the first to present love as the principal commandment, so that the other commandments find their true meaning only when they are incorporated into that of love. He is also believed to have been the first to make love the final criterion of righteousness, so that righteousness, which had a central role in the Jewish structure of religion and politics, is surpassed by love and must be understood in the light of love.

In human love for God, love is explained as a service to God or attending to him like a slave (Luke 17:7), faithfully obeying his orders, submitting to his lordship and seeking the extension of that lordship before every other aim in life (Matthew 6:33). Because of the sinful nature of the world, the unity between love for God and love for others has been broken, and therefore Jesus puts first the love for God, even at the expense of human relations. In this sense Jesus even spoke of love for one's Heavenly Father as involving hating one's natural father and mother (Luke 14:26). Love for God means abandoning everything one has or everything one desires. A person who loves property or money cannot love God, nor can a person who desires prestige love God with all his heart. Jesus also turns the focus of love towards himself because of his special relationship with God. No love is greater than that of a father for his son, and God's love is bestowed on Jesus as on an only beloved son. Loving or not loving the Son of Man, the inaugurator of the new age, becomes the only criterion for judging whether or not a person has faith in God and in the kingdom-to-come. Because he himself represents the new age, Jesus calls for unconditional devotion to himself: 'Anyone who loves his father or mother more than me is not worthy of me; anyone who loves his son or daughter more than me is not worthy of me; and anyone who does not take his cross and follow me is not worthy of me' (Matthew 10:37, 38).

Jesus extended love for God to include love for others. The term 'others' refers here not only to members of the elected people of the Old Israel, but also much more generally, possibly to the whole of humankind, although Jesus did not explicitly say so. The aim of love is especially to succour the poor, the sick and the sinners, who were outcast in Jewish society. The universality of Jesus' love is more clearly seen in his call to love one's enemies. 'When Jesus demands *love of enemies*, he sets himself consciously in opposition to Jewish tradition.'[38] In the O.T., there are occasions when help to enemies is required. However, help is not the same as love, and help and love do not fully coincide. One can help one's enemy without loving him or her, but one must help one's enemy if one loves him or her. This break with tradition is justified by Jesus' special mission, to prepare for the coming of the new kingdom of God. With the coming kingdom, the reward for loving one's enemies becomes real, and the motive for loving one's enemies derives from God's gracious will for all to be saved through Jesus Christ.

If we say that Jesus initiated the identification of love with the heart of Christian faith and even with the Spirit of God, we have also to say that it was Paul and John who developed and deepened this process. The Christian doctrine of love matured in their theology. This maturity is signalled first and foremost by the theological unity established between God's love, Jesus' love and love of the elect. The grace of God is fully shown in his love, especially in sending his son, Jesus Christ, to the sinful world, and it reaches its peak on the Cross on which Jesus gave up his life. For Paul, this love is for all people who are willing to follow Jesus Christ, and it is so powerful that it creates new men, who are fully free and therefore able to respond to God's love. In the relationship of love between God and humans, God is always the source and the initiator. All forms of love stem from him and all forms of human love are responses to him. Faith in God comes directly from his love, and God's love is said to have been in Christ Jesus, the Lord of the world (Romans 8:39). The traditional concept of law is firmly based on that of love: love is the fulfilling of the law. God's spirit is one of love, and the Holy Spirit is none other than love that is the life-giving power of the new age (II Corinthians 3:6). Love stands at the centre of the Christian triad: faith, love and hope, and is treated as the soul of the triad.[39] Of faith, love and hope, the greatest is love, and love is indeed above faith and above hope. In other words, faith, love and hope are actually one. Faith and hope are only different expressions of love. Faith is meaningful only in the light of love and faith in God must express itself or work through love. Hope can lay hold of the future only because of love. Love is said to be the greatest gift of the Spirit, and therefore Paul puts the Spirit (*pneuma*) and love (*agape*) side by side (Galatians 5:22), taking love as the driving force for Christian communities. Human love for God has to express itself in love for one's neighbours. Like Jesus, Paul emphasizes the tradition of neighbourly love, but grounds this love on the new basis of faith in Jesus Christ. Since Paul expects the new age to come swiftly, he identifies neighbourly love with the brotherly love of the Christian community: serving fellow-members of the new community of Christ enables him to identify the 'beloved' and the 'brother'.[40] This identification may be interpreted as broadening the range of neighbour-love, in so far as 'brother' applies to everyone. However, it may also be understood as narrowing the range of neighbour-love, in so far as 'brother' excludes those who have not heard, or have not been converted to, Christianity.

Compared with Paul, John gives more emphasis to the religious function of love and uses love as his motif for evoking a response from his readers. *Agape* is used more frequently in its absolute form, as a noun without an article and as a verb without an object. Love becomes the underlying basis for Christian doctrine: God is love, Jesus Christ is love, and faith in them is also love. John stresses the salvational meaning of Jesus' death, in which all God's love is concentrated, and through which God's love shines into everyone's heart. In John, love primarily and essentially is a downward movement: from God the Father to the Son Jesus Christ, and from the Son to the world. As receivers of this love, humans should model themselves on the love of God and show brotherly love: 'let us love one another, for love comes from God. Everyone who loves has been born of God and knows God. Whoever does not love does not know God because God is love' (I John 4:7–8). In brotherly love, God's love is fully completed and finally fulfilled. Since John gives emphasis to the downwardness of love, he more than others stresses love as a commandment. The commandment of love is one which encompasses all other commandments. To love is to obey God's command, and through love one will gain eternity and never die: 'we know that we have passed from death to life, because we love our brothers' (I John 3:14).

Since New Testament times, among the various schools of Christian thought, many attempts have been made to explore the role and value of Christian love. In these explorations some have stressed this aspect of love and others have emphasized that aspect, highlighting different characteristics in their theories of Christian love. The interpretation of Christian love has, according to Daniel Day Williams, taken three major forms: the Augustinian type, the Franciscan type and the Reformation type, and each of them has been echoed by a number of modern theologians.

'St Augustine formulated the conception of love at the critical point in the development of early Christianity, and his vision in some way informs all subsequent Christian thought in the West'.[41] One of the contributions to Christian love made by St Augustine is that he combines the Christian doctrine with the philosophy of neo-Platonism, in which he establishes an eternal trinity of love: the Father is love; the Son is love, and the Father and the Son are unified in the Spirit of love. Humans can find love and rest in God's love and in their love for God. Everything and every being are essentially what they are in the mind of God, who is the ultimate good, self-sufficient, changeless and absolute, in contrast to everything else, which is lesser, non-sufficient, mutable and dependent. The meaning and motive of human love for others can be found only in love for God, because we must love them not for their sake but for God's sake. Human love is a reflection of God's love and seeks its perfection in God's love. However, humans are innately weak: they have the power to know the eternal but are unable to hold it fast. Human love for God is thus constantly diverted through restlessness, curiosity and anxiety, and is directed to lesser things which can give momentary satisfaction. Love for the divine is replaced by love for the secular. In seeking temporary satisfaction, humans often forget to seek eternal happiness. From his own experience, Augustine believed that it was necessary to distinguish between love of God and love of the world, to seek the former and resist the latter. In making this distinction, Augustine is 'close to a saying that to love God is to turn away from love for whatever is changeable. Thus a kind of asceticism of the temporal is introduced into Christian theology, which has affected the whole course of the conception of love.'[42]

Another characteristic view of love in Augustinian doctrine is that there is a hierarchy among the forms of human love, love for God being at the top, with other loves such as sex coming much lower and having much less value. Therefore, in order to refine one's love, one must turn all other forms of human love into love for God. Augustine did not disagree with the view that the Greek virtues of temperance, fortitude, justice and prudence are very important for human life. However, he did insist that these virtues must be understood in relation to love and that all the virtues are in fact forms of love: 'Temperance is love giving itself entirely to that which is love; fortitude is love readily bearing all things for the sake of the loved object; justice is love serving only the loved object, and therefore ruling rightly; prudence is love distinguishing with sagacity what hinders it and helps it'.[43] These forms of love are virtues because they are all directed to God alone. However, because of the wretchedness of human nature, human loves are not always directed, nor are all people ready to bring their loves, to God. Instead, they tend to love themselves and to love things which will bring immediate benefit to themselves. For those who give priority to themselves, love is praised and appreciated because of its nature as self-love. The duality of human nature produces two kinds of people: one living in the city of God and loving nothing but God; the other living in the city of earth and loving nothing but themselves. Fortunately, the movement from the earthly kingdom to the heavenly kingdom is willed by God and will be forwarded by God, through such means as religious institutions, social conventions, asceticism and morality. This gives hope to human beings, because human salvation cannot come from humans themselves.

The second type of Christian love, according to Williams, is that of St Francis of Assisi. The characteristic of his doctrine of love derives from his insistence that salvation should not be understood as an instantaneous occurrence. A true response to God's love cannot be a matter of empty words or mere emotion. In return for God's

love to them, humans have to devote their humble service to
him, by establishing a personal union with the spirit of Jesus.
Such love is endowed with the spirit of radical freedom, breaking
through established institutions, the ethical order and personal
relationships.[44] Therefore, to love is to give up everything one
has, including one's social obligation, and to live a life of monastic
order, or as Francis put it, 'To buy love I have entirely renounced
the world and myself'.[45] In order to demonstrate one's will to live
such a life of unreserved equality and love, the first thing one must
do is to sell all one has and give it to the poor. Possession of anything
except the most basic necessities of food and tools is taken as 'evil'
and as a departure from the spirit of love. In return for giving up
one's possessions, one acquires the qualities of love: goodness,
kindness, forgiveness and repentance. Since love is first of all a
gift from God, it has nothing to do with ordinary knowledge. Love
cannot be acquired merely from learning. Rather, the accumulation
of knowledge often leads to pride, which is the worst of sins and
blocks one's access to the love of Christ, the source of all love.[46]

The third type of Christian love is expounded by the theologians
of the Reformation, especially Luther and Calvin, who 'understand
the love of God as grace, as forgiveness to man, rather than as a
spirit which can be directly and immediately realized in man'.[47]
This doctrine explains love in the light of faith and is based on the
belief that humans can do nothing on their own to counteract their
sins. The love that comes from God is the only hope and salvation
for human beings. Only by faith in God's mercy can humans have
hope to be saved. With faith in God and in Christ, humans are
filled with love and experience the reality of being loved and of
loving. Without faith, humans know nothing of Christian love,
only of self-love, which contrasts the self-giving love of Christ.
The meaning of human love can be seen only in the light of the
love of God and God's love is given to each individual. Between
individuals and the love of God nothing, neither church nor priests,
can stand. Whether one can receive grace is decided not by these
intermediaries but by one's direct communion with Jesus Christ.
From the love of God one can receive everything needed for loving
God, loving Jesus Christ and loving one's neighbour. This love is
realised in one's service to God and to others and also in one's
daily work. The Reformation in Christian tradition was more or less
equivalent to neo-Confucianism in Confucian tradition, in the sense
that both were attempts to transform and transmit the tradition of

a thousand years, and both made a new contribution to their own tradition by re-emphasizing an original doctrine. For example, when the theologians of the Reformation stressed that in theology one must rely on Scripture alone, this stance was similar to that of the Rationalist School of neo-Confucianism, which insisted that learning (the Confucian classics) was the only means by which the Way of the sage could be known. When the reformers denounced the Catholic approach to salvation and insisted that human salvation depended solely on faith rather than on works, their approach to salvation was similar to that of the Idealist School of neo-Confucianism, which held that *Tian* bestowed the same mind upon sages and ordinary people alike, and that inner reflection, rather than external exploration (whether of the Classics or of general knowledge), was the only way to the ideal. However, in making such comparisons, we must always remember that there is a great difference between neo-Confucianism and the Reformation in their underlying views of the theistic–humanistic relationship. Although both spoke of faith and the approach to the ideal, their understanding of faith and ideal were far from in agreement, the one being theistic faith, the other being humanistic pursuit.

Christian love continues to be explored in the modern world, and different views are put forward by different scholars, whether in its theological, religious or ethical dimension. However, old and new explanations of Christian love share certain basic features which serve to distinguish Christian love from other forms of love as understood in other religions and traditions: in the relationship between God and humans God's love is prevenient and decisive, while human love is a response to God's love; in the relationship between humans, fundamental is the love commanded by God and evidenced by Jesus Christ. These essentials determine the theistic orientation of Christian *agape* and permeate every part of Christian doctrine.

A PARALLEL BETWEEN TWO TRADITIONS

There is not the slightest doubt, from what we have discussed, that *jen* plays a commanding role in Confucianism parallel to that of *agape* in Christianity. Each is the central theme which runs through a complicated system of various theories and practices. Each is the fundamental principle that guides or underlines every aspect of its metaphysical doctrine and ethical applications. Each is the bond of virtue that gives meaning to human goodness and harmonises virtues as ideal. Each aims at reconciling humans with the Transcendent and thus paving the path to human own transcendence, although in different ways. For these reasons, Confucianism is often called the doctrine of *jen*, with *jen* being its heart, and Christianity is often referred to as the religion of *agape*, with *agape* being its soul.

Neither *jen* nor *agape* is a simple concept. In its history, *jen* is given as many as thirteen meanings according to Wing-tsit Chan, from *jen* as human beings to *jen* as universal love, from the macrocosmic principle in the universe to the microcosmic entity in the human heart. However, among all these meanings there is an inner harmony. The question frequently raised by Confucians is not whether such harmony exists, but how to define it. For us this harmony exists in the inclusive nature of *jen* and in the unity of the Confucian principle with its three dimensions: humanity, virtue and love. These three dimensions are often functioning together and it is difficult to separate one from the others. Compared with *jen* in Confucianism, *agape* is dealt with more consistently in Christianity, with 'love' being its unchangeable central meaning. Christian doctrine and practice, faith and ritual, are all based on its understanding of love; they become manifest in love and aim at bringing out love. However, the unified meaning of Christian *agape* does not imply that *agape* in Christianity has only one face. In fact, the different aspects of *agape* are emphasized by different writers in different ages with as much variety as those of *jen* in Confucianism. Some emphasize the divinity of *agape*, others stress its humanity, taking it more as human love than as divine love. Human love is consistently an important aspect of *agape*. However, differences also arise from different treatments of human love. It may be a spontaneous reaction in one instance, and a deliberate response in another. There are various theories concerning the nature, function and usage of *agape*, either human or divine, which describe from different angles the Christian understanding of the presence of the Transcendent, the relationship between human love and divine love and the role of love in human transcendence.

As far as human beings are concerned, both *jen* and *agape* are closely related to human goodness. In the Christian claim that *agape* is the source of human virtues and provides the basis for particular forms of the moral good, we have found a doctrine parallel to the Confucian teaching that *jen* underlies morality and virtue, although the humanistic implication of this underlying function is stressed as strongly as possible in Confucianism, while its theocentric value is promoted to a supreme level in Christianity. Confucius argues that *jen* is superior to all other forms of human virtue and is the quality that human beings cannot be without. The Confucian ideal is the perfect human. To be a human is to possess *jen*. If one only follows social norms and abides by moral rules but forgets that the most important thing is to have *jen* in heart, one is in no way a Confucian human. Neither the abundant knowledge of propriety nor a good grasp of music enables such a person to be called '*jen*'. According to the mainstream of Confucian tradition, although the reason that a person is perfectible is inherent in what he or she is, he or she existentially is not what he or she ought to be, that is, a person of *jen*, a transcendental person living and acting in human contexts. To proceed from what one is to what one ought to be, or from the surface of one's being to the origin of one's being, or from the temporal existence to transcendental existence, one has to progress through self-cultivation. However, self-cultivation is not to seek the ideal beyond human existence, nor is it purely psychological contemplation. On the one hand, it is like a work of digging and drilling a well. The deeper one digs, the nearer one is to one's true self. The fullest realization of the original *jen* cannot be achieved until one has penetrated to the deepest ground of one's nature. On the other hand, it is a practice fulfilling humanity in social contexts, performing one's duties as a member of family, community and humankind.

Following the same logic, Christianity argues that *agape* precedes every good attitude and all good behaviour, and is the only way by which one will live in eternity, or as Paul once claimed:

> If I speak in the tongues of men and of angels, but have not love, I am only a resounding gong or a clanging cymbal. If I have the gift of prophecy and can fathom all mysteries and all knowledge, and if I have a faith that can move mountains, but have not love, I am nothing. If I give all I possess to the poor and surrender my body to the flames, but have not love, I gain nothing. (I Corinthians 13:1–7)

In this paragraph, we can identify three characteristics of *agape*, which are constantly stressed in Christian writings, either explicitly or implicitly. The first is that *agape* is not only a negative response, but a spirit that God planted in the human heart and Jesus Christ replanted through his life and death. Without this spirit, humans cannot respond to God's command properly. The second is that the essential quality of humans is *agape* rather than faith. Faith can grow and function only because it is rooted in love and supported by love. The third is that love is not equal to external altruism – giving up one's property to help others, nor to ascetic practices – giving up one's physical desires or even one's physical body. Love is more than that, and it is in the heart rather than merely in behaviour. On the one hand, these characteristics clearly place the Christian doctrine of love in the same category as the Confucian doctrine of *jen*: it is first benevolence and then beneficence. On the other hand, they serve to distinguish Christian *agape* from Confucian *jen*: *agape* comes from the divine source rather than origins in human nature. For a Confucian, because of the fundamental unity between *jen* and humanity, whatever one is doing or one does, and indeed any of one's practices, though not yet enabling one to the ideal, contributes to one's final enlightenment. For a Christian, however, there can be no enlightenment nor is there an ideal to be realized, until one is already in God's *agape*, because of human detachment from God's *agape* in sin, although it may be argued that the Holy Spirit that is love can be present and active in human nature, which is made in the image of God and not completely corrupted by sin, so that humanity may pursue the ideal out of his own nature.

Both *jen* and *agape* are creative, actively creating and penetrating. The creativeness of *agape* is rooted in God's creation and grace. To talk about love is, in Christianity, to talk about God. Without God and God's creation, there would be no love at all. However, God not only created, God is also creating, continuingly creating human goodness through Jesus' sacrifice. Human fulfilment should be realized only in community and the common good. It is possible for *agape* to be manifested in human relationships, because all these relationships are prescribed by the law of God as the way of life and the discipline of grace. However, the law of God is not mere rules binding people from doing wrong. It is understood to be more encouraging than punishing. It is expression of God's love, in which human flourishing is desired. The creativeness of *jen* is based on humanity and on the unity between humanity and the universe. To talk about *jen* is, in Confucianism, to talk about humanity. Without humanity and human unity with the universe, there would be no *jen* at all. Humanity is not a static state but a dynamic creation, and human unity with the universe is not in the existing balance but in the continuingly creative efforts made by human beings, in the proper relationships between humans themselves, between humans and communities, and between humans and things. All these relationships are properly regulated, and actively engaged in, by *jen*, while the potential goodness in human nature is realized and fulfilled in cultivating *jen*, both in the heart and in community life. In order to manifest the original virtues, Confucianism calls for unswerving efforts in learning, which, according to the *Great Learning*, consists of eight steps: to investigate things in the world and affairs in society, to extend one's knowledge of physical and metaphysical principles, to make one's will sincere, to rectify one's heart, to cultivate one's personality or character, to regulate one's family, to govern the state rightly, and to bring peace to the world.

Both *jen* and *agape* are underlying concepts. In Confucianism, humanity and virtue are promoted and refined as a fundamental principle of universal love, by which Confucians search for transcendence. Love is at the centre of all the meanings of Confucian *jen*, which embraces all beings and things, and is recognized as the integrating force of the Confucian world. In Christianity, *agape* is primarily revealed by the light of God's grace, and God's love is the model and source of all other forms of love. The source and meaning of human love are said to be found only in God's love, which is the foundation of all Christian teaching and of all Christian churches.

As far as human love is concerned, there are many terms that are used to express the conception of love in these two traditions. However, in their selection of terms, we find that they follow a similar way. Confucians use the term *jen*, and Christians use the term *agape*, to mean a special relationship between one person and another (whether humans or spiritual beings), of respect and care, in which the utilitarian consideration has been reduced to its minimum; *ai* in Confucian books, and *philia* in Christian classics, are used to refer to a general feeling of love towards others, emphasizing the aspect of fondness and reciprocity; Confucian *chin* and Christian *storge* are both used in the sense of 'affection, especially of parents to offspring, and also of offspring to parents'; and *hse* in Confucianism, and *eros* in Christianity, are usually used to denote the sexual aspect of love. Carefulness in adopting the correct terms for what is meant by love is obvious in their source books. Since respect and kindness are defined only by one's self-giving love rather than by the beloved, *jen* and *agape* can easily be made universally applicable; since affection and liking exist in family and between friends, *ai* and *philia*, *chin* and *storge* are applied in the framework of family and society to the members of these communities; while sexual love, referred to by *hse* and *eros*, is in most cases excluded from love proper.[48] It is also similar that in Confucianism *jen* does not reject *chin* and *ai* but includes them as the constituting elements of human relationship and takes them as efficient ways to its realization, neither does Christian *agape* deny the elements both of *philia* and of *storge*. It would not be in harmony with either of two traditions if we insisted that *jen* and *agape* must be studied only in their pure forms, excluding the elements of friendly and family love.

Different from these elements, sexual love has little place in Confucian *jen* and even less in Christian *agape*. Confucius contrasts *jen* as virtue and love as sexuality. He deplores with regret that there are few people who pursue the virtue with the same eagerness as they pursue the pleasures of sex. A person of virtue, therefore, should always be on guard against the seduction of sexual love. In Christianity, *agape* excludes any element of sexual love. Similarly to the Confucian way, it is taught that one must resist any tendency to sexualize *agape*. Either to realize *agape* as an ideal or to carry out *agape* as the principle of action, one has to be unmoved by the temptations of sex. This contrast and conflict between *agape* and sexual love is obvious in most Christian writings. However, the case becomes more complicated in the Christian tradition, because *eros* is used not only in the sense of sexual love but also in the sense of the mystical longing for perfection, especially by those influenced by the Platonic writings. The interaction between divine love and human longing gives rise to 'a series of arguments in which the exclusion of *eros* from, or its inclusion in, *agape* has been maintained. From this point of view, we may say that *eros* plays a much more significant role in the Christian conception of *agape* than *hse* plays in the Confucian idea of *jen*.

The relationship between *eros* and *agape* has enjoyed the attention of modern theologians. The celebrated thesis put forward by Anders Nygren has dominated the discussion of Christian *agape* for several decades in the western world, and attracted a great deal of support as well as objection.[49] Nygren, basing his argument on the contrast between *eros* and *agape*, asserts that there are two traditions and two types of religion, *eros*-religion and *agape*-religion. His descriptions of these two religions bear upon our own comparison between Confucian *jen* and Christian *agape*, although he would certainly disapprove of any attempt to compare them. Hence a consideration of his argument will be helpful in our own examination of the differences between Confucian *jen* and Christian *agape*.

Nygren's argument starts with the difference between the mono-theistic world and the pagan world. He believes that this difference produces different ideals of love, *agape* in the former and *eros* in the latter. In their origins and early development these two conceptions

> had nothing at all to do with each other, and are by nature completely antithetic, and yet in the course of subsequent history have become so thoroughly interwoven that it is now difficult for us to think of the one without thinking of the other.[50]

It is therefore Nygren's task to look for the reason why they were interwoven, and then to separate them properly so that people may appreciate 'them as two fundamental religious ideas, as two opposite attitudes to life, as two answers to the fundamental questions which Mankind is compelled to ask concerning the meaning of life'.[51]

For Nygren, it is obvious that *eros* is the rival of *agape*. The essential meaning of *eros* is 'the Platonic love . . . the desire of the soul of man to attain salvation by detachment from earthly objects of desire, and by seeking after heavenly things'.[52] *Agape*, on the other hand, is God's love and the divine desire of charity to save humans from their sins. These are two different principles of religion and two different ideals of human life, from which two 'utterly different religious and ethical types',[53] egocentric and theocentric, are produced. The essential difference between these two types of religion is found in their understanding of the relationship between humans and God. What is meant by 'ego-centric *eros*-religion' is, in the language of this thesis, a religion that focuses on human beings and human efforts to achieve eternity. The relation between the divine and the human is such that there is a gulf between them but it is not impassable. Humans share the divine nature. The difficulty in doing so comes only from the fact that humans do not sincerely pursue the divine and are frequently distracted by the temptations of the world. As soon as humans realize this, they can turn to the divine and enter the realm of the eternal. What is meant by theocentric *agape*-religion is a religion in which God is the centre.

Between God and humans there is an impassable barrier, which humans from their side can never cross, or as Nygren claims:

> Every effort of man to exalt himself to the Divine is regarded as an act of presumption like that of the Titans; so far from bringing man into a right relation to God, it is the extreme of godlessness. The gulf between God and man can only be bridged by God himself. Man can never by *eros* attain to God.[54]

In the light of human relationship with the divine, what has been said by Nygren about the difference between *eros*-religion and *agape*-religion is, by and large, applicable to our contrast between Confucian *jen* as the principle of humanistic religion and Christian *agape* as the ideal of theistic religion. In the conception of *jen*, humanity stands at the centre and is credited with the ability to cross the gulf between the temporal and the eternal; while in the conception of *agape*, God stands at the centre and is the only hope for human salvation. Although few Christian theologians deny all human responsibility for their destiny, nevertheless, most of them agree the ultimate responsibility in this matter rests with God.

However, we do not intend to continue this application of Nygren's typology to the point where he further contrasts *eros* and *agape* and gives eleven specific instances of their differences.[55] Here we need not determine whether or not these differences are true to the theoretical and historical contrasts between *eros* and *agape*, although we might argue that in his detailed discussion Nygren violates the logic of his argument. He gives us the impression that he is discussing the differences between **two types of religion**, when the majority of his contrasts are between **two concepts**. What we must do now is examine to what extent his contrasts are significant for those between Confucian *jen* and Christian *agape*.

The essence of the differences between *jen* and *agape* is that one is humanistic and centred on human progress and self-transcendence, while the other is theistic and centred on divine salvation. Humanity is the source of all forms of Confucian *jen*, while God's charity is the source of all forms of Christian *agape*. Confucian *jen* can be realized in the context of human life, while Christian *agape* looks beyond the human community for its fulfilment. On the one hand, we must always keep these contrasts in mind whenever we come across these two concepts. On the other hand, we must also guard against the temptation to contrast human *jen* and divine *agape* in the way that Nygren contrasts *eros* and *agape*, without being aware of two different understandings of the Transcendent and two different ways to human transcendence.

Within the range of humanity, neither *jen* nor *agape* is selfish, in so far as they are universally applicable principles and seek the ideal by reuniting humans with that which transcends them. The equation between the anthropocentric and the selfish, which is an essential feature of Nygren's contrast of *eros* with *agape*, cannot be justified in the case of Confucian *jen*. *Jen* is certainly an anthropocentric principle, because the responsible self is the start of Confucian *jen*, and the doctrine of *jen* is developed along the line of self-cultivation and human growth. However, it rejects individualistic self-centredness. *Jen* pursues universality and eternity in the virtue of individuals. It is indeed the case that *agape* is theocentric, not only as regards its source but also as regards its function. However, it does not totally cast away human flourishing. Rather, it is regarded as the means to human fulfilment, through reconciliation with God. The absolute self-giving of *agape* may be possible in God's love, but not in human love. For some Christian theologians, there seems to be something deficient in a personal love, whether divine or human, that does not care whether it arouses any positive response or not. They argue that such a love is surely benevolence, but it would be difficult to say it is the whole of Christian love. For them a proper understanding of Christian love is that God's love is self-giving and his creation is an act of sheer overflowing self-giving; however, love that wants nothing creates a love that wants a response, the love of his creature. Therefore, human *agape* is always associated with the divine *agape*. In this sense, human *agape* differs from *jen* only in the sense that *jen* is **directly** anthropocentric, while *agape* is **indirectly** anthropocentric.

As universal principle, neither Confucian *jen* nor Christian *agape* is determined by its objects. *Jen*, whether as humanity or virtue or love, is itself self-sufficient and complete. The realization or actualization of *jen* depends solely on the agent – 'Is *jen* far away? It comes as soon as I desire it' (*Analects*, VII, 30) – who alone can decide how to act and in what way to act. *Agape* as human love also depends on the agent. There is a spontaneity in human *agape*. It is given not simply because God commands it, but also because God freely elicits it. God loves evil-doers as well as the good, and humans love their enemies as well as their friends. However, neither *jen* nor *agape* is purely spontaneous. In Christianity, humans love as a response to the command of God, while in Confucianism *jen* is activated by one's own self-cultivation. To respond to God, one has to have firm faith in God; to cultivate one's self, one has to have a responsible self. In fact, in both *jen* and *agape* it is impossible to separate what is spontaneous and what is caused.

As behaviour, neither *jen* nor *agape* is a passive process. They actively create and participate in their objects so that the lover and the loved are constantly interflowing. In love, *agape* creates a new people in a transformed world, and in self-cultivation and extension of one's virtue, *jen* creates the harmony between humans, and between humans and the universe. *Jen* is not simply a reflection on its objects as Nygren believes is true of *eros*. It is also a fundamental force for advancing both humanity and the world towards their ideal. Therefore, like *agape*, not only can it *see* value in its objects, it can also *create* value in its objects. This work of creation establishes humanity, promotes virtue and practises universal love, and thereby a new generation and a new world is brought forth, or more precisely, the Golden Age of the ancient time is brought back.

4

Jen as Humanity and *Agape* as Divinity

The source of a humanistic principle is humanity; in other words, a humanistic principle is like a tree, which has its root in, and gets its nutrition from, humanity. The centre of a theistic principle, on the contrary, is God, and its root is in divinity. This difference illustrated in Confucian *jen* and Christian *agape* reflects a fundamental divergence between the Confucian understanding of transcendence and the Christian idea of transcendence. Since *jen* has its primary meaning in, or is identified primarily with, human beings, the majority of Confucians believe that to transcend is to develop one's humanity, which is one's own responsibility. Since *agape* has its primary meaning in, or has identified itself essentially with, God, most Christians insist that to transcend is to live in God's grace, for which only God is accountable. This is the first contrast between *jen* and *agape*: *jen* is rooted in humanity in the mainstream of Confucianism and Confucian transcendence is taken primarily as perfection of humanity, while *agape* is rooted in divinity and Christian transcendence is essentially to participate in the life of Christ. However, *jen* and *agape* are not completely in contrast, even where their conception of transcendence is concerned. They share many characteristics. *Jen* as human nature is believed by most Confucians to have been endowed by *Tian*. In this sense, *jen* may also be said to have been initiated divinely, if we recall that *Tian* is taken as the transcendental foundation of Confucianism, especially in the earlier part of the Confucian classics. On the other hand, *agape* as God's grace is not totally opposite to human nature. When God creates humanity, the nature of *agape*, which is the essence of God, has also given orientation to human nature. Although this good nature was corrupted by original sin, most modern theologians, especially those of the Catholic tradition, tend to believe that it has not been absolutely excluded from human nature, or in other words, human nature was only distorted, not totally corrupted, by their sin. In this sense, human beings are not totally self-centred and self-concerned; they may be orientated by self-giving love, especially when this love is initiated by the Holy Spirit. Therefore, at least for some traditions within Christianity, to transcend is not only to give up one's life, nor only to wait passively for 'salvation', but it is also involved with human effort, and it is to live one's life in the Spirit of Christ and to participate actively in the life of God.

JEN AS HUMANITY

The character *jen* (仁) originated in the character JEN (人 human beings).[1] From the fact that we have not yet found the character of *jen* in the 'oracle bones' inscriptions, nor in the bronze inscriptions, which are the earliest known writing systems in China, and the further fact that the character *jen* is represented by the character JEN in the earlier part of Confucian classics, we can infer that *jen* as a philosophical and religious concept came much later than the concept of JEN as humans, and that it was from JEN as human beings that the character *jen* as a human quality or relationship evolved. The primary root of *jen* lies in human beings. But what is the distinctive characteristic of human beings? It is not life, nor desire, because even plants have life and animals have desires. No part of the characters of *jen* and JEN points in that direction. The rise of Chinese humanism led to the idea that the essence of human beings is their sociality, arising out of their social relationships. With this understanding, the character *jen* was created by combining two parts, JEN (人 human) and er (二 two).[2] Human beings were related by kinship as well as by social interaction, and thus they were distinctive both in their existence and in their activity. However, in earlier days, the distinction between human beings was mainly one of flesh and blood, from which came the contrast between freemen and slaves. Only after a long journey of exploration into the reality of their humanity did the Chinese realize that there was something more important than the mere fact of existence. This 'something' did not come from physical features, such as beauty and strength, nor from status, such as wealth and rank, but from personal and social qualities, such as moral character and virtue. In physical terms, human beings must be treated with 'equality', so that they could be collectively distinguished from animals. In moral terms, however, human beings were to be considered as unequal, differentiated into distinct categories.

The need for distinction might have been the social motive for the emergence of the character *jen*. There were two ways of differentiating human beings. The first was a sociological distinction, classifying human beings into aristocrats (JEN) and the mass (MIN). This distinction reached its peak in the Shang dynasty and in the first half of the Chou dynasty. Alongside a deeper consciousness of human destiny came the second distinction, classifying human beings into the good and the base. This second distinction, which was essentially an ethical distinction, provided the social background as well as the intellectual reason for the popularity of the concept of *jen* in the period of Spring and Autumn. Of course, these two distinctions were not at that time completely exclusive. Even in the time and writings of Confucius and Mencius, as seen in their writings, these two distinctions were not always clear-cut. Rather, they frequently overlapped each other in this or that way. Although Confucius did not completely exclude the old idea that what made a being a 'JEN' was his/her nobility of existence, in the majority of the conversations of Confucius the sociological distinction was deliberately not identified with the ethical distinction, which was later developed by Mencius into a celebrated doctrine of agreement and disagreement between human nature and human fulfilment. The distinction between the good and the base is not in physical terms, and therefore cannot be conveyed by the factual concept of JEN itself. Only the evaluative concept of *jen* can do this. Thus by the concept of *jen* they established that human nobility could not be inferred from status, but only from a qualitative excellence in performing one's duties. *Jen* is not merely a state of existence, but a degree of ethical achievement. By *jen* human beings acquire their human dignity, and without *jen* a being can no longer be a proper human, because he has not yet gained, or because he has already lost, his value as a human, although in physical terms he is no different from others. A person can become a person of nobility only when he determines to fulfil his *jen*, which has been allotted and revealed to him by *Tian*.

In distinguishing the good from the base, Confucius dramatically changed the implications of the old ideal personality (*chun-tzu*),

infusing it with a full realization of *jen* and promoting it as the new
ideal for his followers. *Chun-tzu*, translated variously as 'superior
man', 'princely man', 'ideal man' or 'gentleman', etymologically
referred to a 'son of a ruler', and was extended to refer to the
descendants of the ruling house, and then to the members of the
upper classes, indicating their aristocratic birth and noble descent.[3]
Although this old usage was still followed here and there and a
chun-tzu could be taken to mean a superior in contrast to an
inferior, the term was used distinctively by Confucius to signify
the totality of superior human qualities, which are obtainable by
action rather than mere existence. On the lower level, a *chun-tzu*
is someone whose action is free from violence, whose bearing is
completely sincere and whose speech lacks all vulgarity. On the
higher level, however, a *chun-tzu* is someone who can be entrusted
with the destiny of the whole state, who willingly bears such a heavy
burden as serving the state and the people and who perseveres in
fulfilling his *jen* in the world (*Analects*, VIII, 4, 6, 7). *Tao*, the Way
or the Truth, is the only thing a *chun-tzu* is seeking after, even if
his doing so brings him into poverty. 'A *chun-tzu* seeks the *tao*
and not mere living . . . and a *chun-tzu* worries about *tao* and not
about poverty' (XV, 31). In *tao*, the ideal previously connected with
physical existence and social status is now linked closely with
achievement and determination in fulfilling one's mission, and
thus becomes the goal that both upper and lower classes can strive
for. One cannot choose one's parentage, but one may choose to be
a noble or base person. Among Confucius' disciples, many came
from poor families with lower social status. However, because of
their sincere attitude towards learning and their unremitting effort
in carrying out *tao*, they were praised by Confucius as noble, moral,
or wise, the qualities equivalent to those of a *chun-tzu*. At a later
stage of Chinese history they were even worshipped as Confucian
saints.

Since a *chun-tzu* is considered a person of superior dignity and
strong moral conscience, this ideal is primarily associated with *jen*,
or with one's pursuit of *jen*. To pursue *jen*, one has to be consistent
in learning *tao* and in cultivating one's character. Poor and low as
one may be, a *chun-tzu* enjoys *jen*, or his achievement in cultivating
jen. However, modern scholars disagree as to whether or not we
should identify a *chun-tzu* and a person of *jen*. For example, Tu
Wei-ming insists that 'it is not too difficult to become a *chun-tzu*
(gentleman) but hardly anyone is qualified to be called a *jen*-JEN

(a man who embodies *jen*)'.[4] However, there are interchangeable usages between these two terms in the *Analects*, and we can find little or no evidence that *chun-tzu* is separated from *jen*. It is said that as soon as a *chun-tzu* is separable from *jen*, he is no longer a *chun-tzu*. 'A *chun-tzu* who ever parts company with *jen* does not fulfil that name. Never for a moment does a *chun-tzu* quit *jen*.'[5] If there are differences between these two terms as used in Confucius' conversation, then these differences are: (1) a *chun-tzu* is the realization of *jen*, while *jen* is the essence of *chun-tzu*. A person who has embodied *jen* is a *chun-tzu*, while a person who has ignored *jen* is a degraded, or base, person; (2) a *chun-tzu* is a stage which a person can reach by cultivating his *jen*, while *jen* is a continuing process of moral effort, which is everlasting and constant for the whole life; (3) a *chun-tzu* is a function of *jen*, while *jen* is the substance of *chun-tzu*. Through a *chun-tzu*, *jen* can be presented in tangible form, and by *jen* a *chun-tzu* is supported with a boundless source for his excellence. With these subtle distinctions between a *chun-tzu* and *jen* in mind, we may well say that it would not be proper to translate *chun-tzu* sweepingly as 'princely persons' or 'aristocratic persons' in Confucian contexts. Rather, a '*chun-tzu*' refers to a 'person of virtue', or a person who has manifested the virtue of *jen*.[6] A person who is fully in *jen*, or embodies human nobility, is a true human. In this sense, a 'person of *jen*' and a '*chun-tzu*' are interchangeable in describing one's achievement in cultivating *jen*.

One further question is whether a person can be a person of *jen* by himself or whether one can reach this goal only by other means. This question is made more complicated by the fact that the traditional usage of *chun-tzu* as the title for the superior was adopted in some paragraphs in the *Analects of Confucius*. Generally speaking, Confucius and his followers laid the responsibility on one's own self: *jen* came from moral activity rather than from social status, a person becomes a person of *jen* because of his own efforts rather than because of anything else. For them, the Way of the ancient kings did not die along with their death. It continues to exist in human beings. Those who have realized the major part of the Way are the wise or worthy, while those who understand only a small part are the unwise or unworthy. So there is no one who lacks access to it (XIX, 22). The same holds for *jen*. *Jen* does not exist outside humans; it is in the human heart. *Jen* is not far from one's reach. It depends upon oneself to practise *jen* rather than upon others (XII,

1). The significance of 'depending on oneself rather than on others' is that it reveals the power of humanity and provides the profound source for human virtues: humans can freely choose to be good and destiny does not prevent them from doing so. The requisite is only that one shall have a determined will to pursue or to nurture it. If a person resolutely desires to practise *jen*, he will become a person of *jen*. Confucius said that he had never come across a situation where a person who failed to pursue *jen* was because he had not sufficient strength to do so (IV, 6).

Although *jen* is within everybody's reach, Confucius denied that any person could naturally or automatically become a person of *jen*. *Jen* comes only from practice and learning, and one's worth depends on one's will and action, regardless of ancestry and family. From this, David L. Hall and Roger T. Ames interpret *jen* as a person-making process.[7] As a person-making process, *jen* is not only a necessary quality of human beings, but also a dynamic force in creating and renewing humans. Humans exist at three levels: in the middle, a human is an individual person, who exists naturally; above, he is an 'authoritative person' (or 'Great Man') who becomes a fulfilled human in the productive activities of *jen*; below, he is a 'retarded person' (small or base person) in whom *jen* is unproductive. The purpose of learning and practice is to initiate the creative activities of *jen* that has been bestowed when a person is born. *Jen* is an essential part of humans proper, or as the *Doctrine of the Mean* puts it: 'The fulfilled transformation of oneself is called *jen*' (chapter 25). *Jen* is the transformation from the natural existence of an individual person to the fulfilled existence of a human, in which *jen* is both the result (the fulfilled human) and the moving power (the integrating and transforming force).

At the higher level of human development, Confucius described several models of the human ideal, and regarded the sage as the highest of them. A sage is certainly more lofty than a *chun-tzu*, and sublimer than a person of *jen*. However, just because a sage is so lofty, it seems that for Confucius the sage has left behind the human realm and entered the divine realm. A sage is not only a model for human beings, but also one who has been raised from the human world to the spiritual world, unifying the secular and the sacred, and a spiritual power nourishing reverence for Heaven and Earth. Given the loftiness of the sage, Confucius recognized how difficult, if not totally impossible, it was to be a sage. Therefore, as a realist, Confucius spoke more of the human effort to become a person of

jen, or a *chun tzu,* than to become a sage. 'A Sage I cannot hope
ever to meet; the most I can hope for is to meet a *chun-tzu.'*[8] The
difference between a person of *jen* and a sage is obvious. Some
modern scholars have seen that there is an identity between a person
of *jen* and a *chun-tzu,* but have mistakenly taken the further step of
identifying all these three titles used in the *Analects* – person of *jen,*
chun-tzu and sage.[9] While both the person of *jen* and the sage can
exist by reason of their moral quality, for Confucius the former is an
embodiment of human existence and activity at their highest, while
the latter is the transcendental embodiment of humanity by which
one's own humanity has been extended widely to all people. When
one of his disciples asked whether a person who not only conferred
wide benefits upon the people but also was able to succour the
multitude could be called a person of *jen,* Confucius replied that it
would no longer be a matter of a person of *jen: such a person* would
no doubt be a sage. Even Yao and Shun [the ancient sage-kings]
would have found this difficult to achieve![10]

To be *jen* is not a final achievement, but a continuing effort. To
make efforts in obtaining *jen* is not that one expects to be enlightened
suddenly as envisaged by Chan (Zen) Buddhism, nor to be as in
some forms of Taoism like the immortals, who can enjoy eternity
once they have reached a certain stage in meditation. Rather, a
person of *jen* is in an endless process of moral cultivation. One
has to be diligent in such cultivation throughout the whole of
life, without a moment of relaxation. Although, compared with
the sage, a person of *jen* can much more easily achieve his goal,
it is still very difficult for a person to adhere to *jen* for the whole
of his life. For this reason, Confucius was reluctant to give the
title of *jen* or good to other people, and even more reluctant to
claim it for himself. When he talked about himself, Confucius
was even humbler: 'How dare I claim to be a sage or a person
of *jen*? What I can be described is that I learn unwearyingly and
teach others without impatience.'[11] From this paragraph we can
see that Confucius believed that there were three stages which one
could possibly reach in one's life: a person who devotes oneself
to learning; a *chun-tzu,* or a person of *jen,* or a good person,
who has grasped *tao* by learning and practice; and a sage who
has completed what is bestowed from Heaven by manifesting
one's virtues and thus bringing peace and harmony to the world.
Throughout all these three stages, one must practise *jen* so that it
can become integrated completely with one's existence: whatever

one does and whatever one desires, it is always in agreement with the requirements of *jen*.

After Confucius, the most important thinker to place great emphasis on *jen* was Mencius. The identification between *jen* and humanity was strengthened by Mencius in his proposition that '*jen* is humanity',[12] and his belief that *tao* would not prevail unless *jen* and human beings were integrated. However, when Mencius said that '*jen* is humanity', he had also modified the connotation of the original identification of *jen* with human beings. In Confucius, the integration of *jen* with human beings was a process of human effort rather than an inborn nature, an ideal rather than a reality, and an activity rather than a state of existence. In this sense, Confucius rejected, not only the traditional idea that *jen* was mainly associated with one's family origin, but also the common-sense notion of his time that *jen* was a reward for superior status in social life. For Confucius, *jen* was bound up with the moral struggle to perfect oneself and society, and nobody could be born with *jen*. Even for a *chun-tzu*, it was still necessary to guard against alienating himself from *jen*, because it was always possible for a *chun-tzu* to abandon *jen* on this or that occasion. Mencius agreed with Confucius that *jen* was the characteristic quality of human beings and that human effort was needed in manifesting this quality. With this quality, a human life was full of value; without this quality, it could be regarded only like that of an animal or a bird. However, in contrast to Confucius who believed that *jen* existed solely in human activity, Mencius stressed that *jen* existed innately in everybody. *Jen* was human nature and provided the basis and possibility for a person to become a *chun-tzu*. Moral effort was useful, because it could help to protect and develop one's original good nature, the nature of *jen*. Psychologically speaking, the identification between *jen* and human nature rendered *jen* not only an ideal but also a reality, not only an activity but also a predisposition. In human nature, the passive and the active, consciousness and behaviour, the ultimate and the ways to the ultimate, are integrated into one: the innate good mind or heart.

In associating the two concepts *jen* and *yi*, Mencius also differed from Confucius, who took *jen* as the single concept on which his humanism was based. Mencius wrote that '*jen* is the human mind and *yi* (morality) is the human path'; and '*jen* is the peaceful abode of human beings, while *yi* is their righteous path'.[13] From these paragraphs, many scholars suggest that Mencius contrasted *jen* and *yi* and took them as two distinct qualities. This is a misleading interpretation. The relation between *jen* and *yi* in Mencius' discussion is presented at two different levels. At the ethical level, Mencius argued that *jen* and *yi* were two aspects of one nature, or two embodiments of one quality. Since they were different reflections of human nature, they appeared in different forms. For example, Mencius described the connection between *jen* and the inborn feeling of sympathy, and between *yi* and the inborn feeling of shame and dislike. However, at the ontological level, *jen* is spoken of in the sense of the one and the universal, which underlies all human existence and qualities, and represents that by which a human is a human being; while *yi* represents the particular and the many, which result from the application of *jen* in different situations and on different occasions. That is why Mencius attacked those who took *jen* as internal and *yi* as external, and argued that the internal and the external could apply only to the operations or functions of *jen*, and not to *jen*, that is, the substance or essence of all human virtues. Although human beings had many inborn feelings, all of them were based on a single mind–heart (*hsin*), which could not bear to see the sufferings of others. This is the beginning of *jen* (*The Book of Mencius*, 2A:6; 7B:31). Cultivating this mind, a human being can be full of *jen*; destroying this mind, a human is degraded to an animal.

The identification of *jen* with human beings was extended further to the macrocosmic level. The cosmos and human beings are essentially unified by *jen*. *Jen*, being the essence of human beings as well as of the cosmos, functions as a governing principle and supportive substance, motivates the unity and variety of the universe, underlies all forms of action and expresses itself in the nature of all beings. In the metaphysical sense, a human is a human because he or she is part of the universe and partakes of the *jen*. However, human beings are not merely an ordinary part, they are the most advanced part of the world. Human beings can consciously carry out *jen* to its utmost, and *jen* has to depend upon human effort to be manifested and enlarged. By human efforts, *jen* is transformed from a cosmic principle to particular embodiments, from essence to operation, and in human beings the operation and embodiment of *jen* are fulfilled and completed. Although there is *jen* in everything and everywhere, and *jen* can be observed from any operation and movement of the cosmos, the full nature of *jen* is revealed in human beings and in their conscious activities. *Jen*, as the essence of the cosmos, has

to be recognized in the creative action of human beings. *Jen* is
never an abstract entity, but constantly full of humanity which
not only motivates the action of human beings, but also motivates
the movement of the universe. What makes a person a human is
also what enables all the beings in the cosmos to be integrated.
Since human nature is the same as the nature of the cosmos and
the nature of all things, a person of *jen* is expected to extend his
own *jen* to all things and to the whole cosmos. Since all share the
same root and the same nature, it is both possible and justifiable
for a person of *jen* to do so: a person of *jen* regards that which fills
the universe as his own body, and considers that which directs the
universe as his own nature.[14]

It was Mencius who first systematically explored the theory that
jen was the active force which drives human beings to strive for the
unity between themselves and the universe. According to Mencius,
a great human was not limited, because he lived in the spacious
dwelling of the world, stood in the correct seat of the cosmos and
walked in the great path of the universe (*The Book of Mencius*,
3B:2). The unity between human beings and the universe could
be achieved by human efforts, that is, by cultivating one's own
'great *chi* [spiritual or moral power]': 'nourish it with integrity or
sincerity [*cheng*] and place no obstacle in its path so that it [great
chi] will fill the space between Heaven and Earth'.[15] In the end, a
person who has attained *jen* would include the whole cosmos in
his own self: 'All the ten thousand things are there in me' (7A:4).
With this process of identification, one reaches the highest possible
point of self-cultivation, which is also the turning point from his
being a human to becoming a transcendental being, from knowing
the mandate of *Tian* to carrying out the will of *Tian* and serving
Tian.

In the *Doctrine of the Mean*, the approach to the unity between
human beings and the universe is further explained thus: a person
who cultivates the beginning of *jen* possesses sincerity [*cheng*]; by
possessing sincerity, one transforms both oneself and others; by this
transformation one is integrated with the universe; and by being
integrated with the universe one assists in the transformation of the
universe.[16] An integrated universe is a universe full of *jen*; therefore,
it is a universe with perfect humanity.

This idea was accepted and developed by neo-Confucians in the
Sung and Ming dynasties. *Jen*, the mind–heart, the principle [*li*], and
sincerity [*cheng*], are all the same in their function of integrating

human beings and the universe. Chang Tsai (1020–77) combined *jen* with a central idea in the *Book of the Change*, and established that not only human beings but also all creatures are related in *jen*. 'By extending one's mind [of *jen*] one is able to embody the things of the whole world . . . As he views the world, there is in it no one thing that is not his own self'. Therefore, 'Ch'ien [Heaven] is called the father and K'un [Earth] the mother . . . (All) people are my blood brothers and (all) creatures are my companions.'[17] Another neo-Confucian, Cheng Hao (1032–85), made it clear that '*jen* is something that makes for oneness with Heaven and Earth'. For him, a student who wants to learn and practise *jen* has first to understand that *jen* is the unity of the cosmos and human beings, and therefore that, by extending one's *jen*, 'the person of *jen* takes Heaven, Earth and all things as one with himself'. 'The person of *jen* is inextricably one with all things'. For a person of *jen*, the universe and all things are nothing but parts of his self. Because *jen* of human beings and *jen* of the universe are originally one and the same, human beings, by activating *jen* in themselves, at the same time obtain integrity with the universe. 'The universe is one great stream of life and one great *jen*; therefore it is the man imbued with *jen* who is capable of achieving oneness with the universe.'[18] Since human beings share the same principle with heaven and earth, they share the same mind and *jen*. Therefore, *jen* is not only a human quality, but a creative force of the cosmos. As Chu Hsi put it, 'In Heaven and Earth, it is that mind to produce things which fills the universe. In man it is that gentle mind which loves men and is kind to other creatures.'[19] For him, *jen* is the total substance and universal function of the whole universe by which each being is shaped and supported. Both human nature and the laws of nature operate on the same principle of *jen*. Wang Yang-ming (1472–1529), an idealist of neo-Confucianism, developed this theory to its metaphysical limits in his assertion that Heaven and Earth and the myriad things were one body, the world was one family and the country was one person, because all of them partake *jen*.

All these neo-Confucian writers tried to defend the belief that *jen* is the nature of human beings as well as that of the cosmos, and that *jen* unifies human operation and the cosmic movement. For them, a person who has realized that his essence is also the essence of the universe can reach eternity in cultivating his humanity. When a person cultivates his *jen* to its utmost, he can identify himself with the universe; and when he can identify himself with the universe, he has realised his *jen*. By this metaphysical argument neo-Confucianism came to the conclusion that *jen* is not only *an* essence of a being, but *the* essence of all beings and of the whole universe, which is the unifying power or force between the Confucian Transcendent and the Confucian ways to transcendence.

AGAPE AS DIVINITY

In contrast to a humanistic religion, where the fundamental principle is rooted in the existence and quality of human beings, the principle of a theistic religion is rooted in the presence and power of the divine. Christianity is essentially a monotheistic religion, and the Christian principle, *agape*, is thus based on its theology of God and its understanding of God's relationship to human beings.

Christianity arose out of the Israelite tradition, and the Jewish conception of God was consequently taken as the basis of the Christian conception of *agape*. Accordingly, *agape* is essentially and fundamentally understood in terms of the being and character of God. Without the succour of God's sovereignty and grace, the great tree of Christian love cannot grow. Divine *agape* is thus the reality and value of the Christian principle, divine grace the basis of all forms of Christian love, and divinity the source of all Christian virtue and goodness.

Agape as divinity is presented in three forms in the Bible as well as in the Judeo-Christian tradition: in God's creation; in God's making a Covenant with his people; and in the person of God himself and his Son Jesus Christ. As creator, God initiates human evolution; as covenant-maker, God actively participates in human history; and as lover, God enters into human relationships. However, these three manifestations of God are but three aspects of Christian divinity and are three manifestations of the divine grace, which later become three pillars supporting the same arch of Christian love.

1. *Agape* as God's Creation. The divine love is first seen in the Judeo-Christian myth of God's creation. The O.T. begins with the description of the process of God's creation and with God as the creator of the universe. In the beginning, there was nothing but God. God created the world of his free will; consequently, this very first act of creation is an expression and realisation of the divine *agape*. According to the O.T., God did not act without care, nor did he create arbitrarily, but he was personally involved in the

whole of his creation, compassing it with an all-embracing love. Through this love, order and law were imposed on the chaos, and there were heaven and earth; through this love, light was brought to the darkness, and there were day and night; through this love, blessing was given to all living and moving creatures, and the creatures were able to multiply rapidly. The last, as well as the most valuable expression of the divine grace of God, was in his creation of humans in his own image, and so humans were granted the right of ruling the earth on behalf of God. In all these processes of creation, God saw that his creation was good (Genesis 1:1–31; Isaiah 42:5). Goodness, love and creation are unified in God's grace: the creatures are created out of love, they are good because they are created, and they are loved because they are good. The involvement of love with goodness became a characteristic mark of divine grace in later Christian theology.

According to the Judeo-Christian tradition, God creates out of love, and his creation brings him great pleasure. This love is said to apply universally to all forms of his creation, and so it combines universalism and particularism. From this unity comes another characteristic of the Christian concept of divine love. On the one hand, God creates the world personally, bestowing his love fully upon all his creatures, so that each being or thing has its own position and function in the harmonious cosmos. On the other hand, God's grace, which is embodied in his creation, is independent, self-affirming and self-giving. God is above his creatures as well as in his creatures. Since humans were the last to be created and the most cherished of his creatures, God took special care of them, made them in his own image, and endowed them with his own nature of love. In his love towards human beings, God's grace also combined universalism and particularism. All human beings are the offspring of God's creation, and are taken care of and blessed and embraced in his love. However, humans betrayed God's love and committed sin. In order to restore the primary harmony between himself and his creatures, God chose one people from all the peoples of the world and revealed himself to them alone as their God.

Agape as divine creation is a completely self-giving and self-affirming love. However, since the process of creation is hidden, the realization of his love can be seen only in the universal order of creation, in human history and in human love. This leads to the conclusion that God's love is involved with, and is realized by, the love of his creatures, especially by human beings created in the image of God himself. Therefore, on the one hand, it must be admitted that *agape* as divine grace is unique, and that the holiness of God's love emphasizes its difference from human love, as Anders Nygren has correctly demonstrated; on the other hand, it must also be affirmed that there exists an unbreakable connection in the Christian tradition between divine love and human love, so that there cannot be an absolute gulf between the divine and the human.[20] To divorce human love from God's creative love will either cut off the divine source of human love or isolate God's act of creation from his creatures. If the harmony of God's hiddenness in creation and personal involvement with his creatures is properly appreciated, there would be no difficulty in making a change of emphasis from theistic grace to humanistic love, and this would have a significant effect on the Christian principle.

Christian theologians further explain the traditional concept of *agape* as God's creation in the light of their doctrine of the Trinity: God's creation is through Jesus Christ, and God's love is also the spirit of Jesus Christ. 'There is but one God, the Father, from whom all things came and for whom we live; and there is but one Lord, Jesus Christ, through whom all things came and through whom we live' (I Corinthians 8:6). The unity of God and Jesus Christ is not only a unity of will and revelation, but also a unity of creative action. Jesus was endowed by God, not only with the mission to save the world, but also with the task to recreate the world. 'In the past God spoke to our forefathers through the prophets at many times and in various ways. But in these last days he has spoken to us by his Son, whom he appointed heir of all things, and through whom he made the universe' (Hebrews 1:1–2). This identification of God with Jesus Christ in creation is essential for the understanding of Christian love, and serves to distinguish Christianity from Judaism. In Jesus Christ, some Christian theologians see the incarnation, death and resurrection of God; others see the great process of continuing creation by God. The world was made out of love and it is remade out of love when God sends his Son to redeem humankind. Through this revelation of love, the hiddenness of God's creation is replaced by the appearance of Jesus Christ, and the unidentifiability of God's love becomes, through his presence in Jesus Christ, the identification of God with all humans. The reason why the world exists, why life is meaningful, and why this meaning is eternal, is that Jesus Christ has come and has gone, in which process he overcomes the old and sinful world and creates a new people in the new world of God's Kingdom. Thus, Christ's creative activity belongs not only to the past but also to the present and the future. The divine grace of creation is not, in the main, directed towards the bodily life of humans, but towards their spiritual life. Without this grace, the spirit fails; and without the divine love, the heart is barren. A barren heart results in a meaningless life and a failing spirit leads to eternal ruin. The ignorant and blind think of nothing but how to preserve their own bodily life. However, to gain the eternity of the spiritual life of love, one must be prepared to give up one's bodily life and follow Jesus, as Jesus himself said, 'Whoever wants to save his life will lose it, but whoever loses his life for me and for the gospels will save it' (Mark 8:35). By the creative love of Jesus Christ, which was demonstrated on the Cross, human sins are forgiven, human life secured, the human future promised and human love sustained. With the sacrifice of Christ, life in the flesh has given way to the life in Christ (Galatians 2:19–20). The love of Christ not only motivates the new life but also sustains it (II Corinthians 5:14). One who follows Jesus is described as coming out of the darkness into light, out of death into life (John 3:16–21, 5:24, 8:31). Such is believed to be the real significance of Jesus Christ as the embodiment of God's love and the true identification of God with his creation.

Augustine maintained that God created not only bodily life but also spiritual life, and argued that the latter should be appreciated more than the former. He asked how, if flesh, sense, soul, mind and understanding were all given by God, it could be said that goodness and righteousness were not? Compared with the creation of one's being, the creation of one's goodness is more excellent. 'If Thou hast given me being and another has given me goodness, the giver to me of goodness is better than the giver to me of being'.[21] Without the mercy of God, humans are helpless and have nothing to be proud of. Against Pelagianism, which claims that since humans have received their nature from God they are capable of choosing between good and evil and can by their own efforts avoid sin and pursue the good, Augustine argues that a distinction must be made between knowledge and action. What humans know to be good they cannot do and what they know to be evil they cannot avoid, because human beings simply lack the power and ability to do what is good. Furthermore, Augustine believes that humans cannot truly know what is good and what is evil, because they do not really love the good and hate the evil, and because they cannot themselves find

delight in righteousness and enjoyment in love. Only in Christ are
humans taught to do the works of righteousness and love, since the
knowledge and will to do so come, not from themselves, but from
the Holy Spirit given to them.

2. *Agape* as God's Covenant with Humans. *Agape* as divine grace
appears in the doctrine of the Covenant, which is characteristic
of the Judeo-Christian tradition. There is no doubt that for the
Israelites the covenant is the sign and focus of God's love for
human beings, represented by his covenant people, or God's love
for humanity manifests in such a covenant. The whole of the Old
Testament, it may be said, develops around the notion of a covenant
between God and Israel.[22] In the New Testament this covenant is
renewed. By his sacrifice on the Cross Jesus establishes a new
Covenant between God and all who are willing to follow him.
What is conveyed by the covenant is not so much a binding
treaty to be observed, but a sure love to be sustained. The close
association of the Covenant and love in the Bible enables Quell
to conclude that 'There can be no doubt that the Covenant is
an expression in juridical language of the experience of God's
love: the whole Covenant theory is based on the idea of love.'[23]

The first and fundamental mark of this covenant is that it was
made by God with his chosen people, so that he might fully display
his love for them. There have been various attempts to trace the
earliest covenant as such. Some believe they have found it in the
covenant made between God and Adam, or between God and Noah,
and that these represent a universal treaty between God and human
beings.[24] However, the original covenant forming the basis of the
religion of Israel did not occur until the time of Moses when God
made a covenant with Israel on Mount Sinai, after Moses, under
the protection and guidance of God, had led the Israelites out of
Egypt: 'You yourselves have seen what I did to Egypt, and how I
carried you on eagles' wings and brought you to myself. Now if
you obey me fully and keep my covenant, then out of all nations
you will be my treasured possession. Although the whole earth is
mine, you will be for me a kingdom of priests and a holy nation'
(Exodus 19:4–6). The core of this covenant is expressed by Jeremiah
'I will be your God and you will be my people' (Jeremiah 7:23).

God showed his love for Israel by making with them his covenant.
This 'Covenant-love' is a translation of *chesed*, which means 'mercy,
loving-kindness and grace', although it can also be used for human
love, when it means 'faithfulness, loyalty or piety'. However, in

a way that distinguishes it from other terms for 'love', *chesed* is conditional upon the existence of a covenant, and represents 'that attitude to a covenant without which that covenant could not continue to exist'. When it is used solely for the Covenant between God and Israel, its primary meaning is the 'sure love' of God which maintains the covenant. However, it also carries with itself a universal meaning similar to *agape*, because *agape* 'applies to the Old Testament *chesed* of God, His covenant-love for Israel. It applies also to the New Testament development in *charis* and in the Grace of Protestant theology'.[25]

It is maintained that God could and can exist without his creatures. However, he chose to create humans. He also chose Israel rather than any other people as his own people and made his covenant with Israel. In all that he does, God remains unaccountable to human judgement. This is an axiom of theistic religion. Humans can presume only that God acts because he is God and because he wills to act. If God should will to abandon his chosen people, there is nothing to prevent him from breaking the covenant. However, God does not and cannot will this because of his love for Israel, and his love becomes even more gracious when Israel's insistent waywardness is considered. The faithfulness of God thus becomes the basis of his covenant-love.

The O.T. prophets came to realize in their own experiences the might and faithfulness of God's covenant-love for his people. For example, Hosea discovered in his relationship with his wife the nature of God's love for Israel: a strong and unswerving determination to be true to his part in the Covenant obligation; and Jeremiah realized through his childlessness how deep was God's fatherly love to his people. 'This is a love which nothing can destroy, not all her [Israel's] waywardness, not her apostasy.'[26] Because of this love, the covenant between God and Israel could never finally be broken even though the Israelites continuingly transgressed it. However, the prophets had also seen the danger inherent in the unfaithfulness of Israel, namely, that it would call forth the punishment of God, in which nobody could escape.[27] The constant theme of the writings of the prophets, therefore, is that of recalling unfaithful Israel to repentance and faithfulness. Their belief is that God is a forgiving God and will restore the relationship of the Covenant. Jeremiah goes even further; he prophesies that, such is God's unswerving love for his people that he will make a covenant with his people and write it on their hearts (Jeremiah 31:31–34). We may suppose that it was this prophecy that Jesus had in mind when, at the last supper, he inaugurated his new covenant.

This new covenant is symbolized by the cup of wine, which represents Jesus' blood (Luke 22:20, 29), sealed by his sacrifice on the cross and completed by the resurrection and gift of the Spirit. The heart of the New Covenant is forgiveness rather than punishment, whereby *agape* as divine grace finds its new function: taking away the sins of the world, so that human beings will be able to return to God. From Pauline teaching recorded in II Corinthians (3:7–18), we can see how the difference between the old covenant and the new has resulted in the following aspects. First, while the old covenant was made known through Moses by letters engraved on stone, the new covenant is made through the Spirit of Christ by the sacrifice on the cross. Secondly, while Moses veiled himself so that the Israelites should not see the splendour of the covenant fading, this veil has been taken away in Christ so that anyone who turns to the Lord can immediately behold his glory. Thirdly, while the effect of the old covenant was to condemn men, the effect of the new is to establish them in righteousness. Thus, the glory of the old covenant has faded away, and the glory of the new increases and lasts for ever. In summary, the old covenant emphasized God's law, with its demand for obedience, while the new emphasizes God's mercy and love, which restores freedom to everybody. Of course, Paul also believes that there is an essential convergence of purpose between the old and the new. God is and remains gracious. The new covenant does not abolish the former covenant, it fulfils it. Although there are two covenants, there is only one will of God, the will of love.

3. *Agape as God's Love. Agape* as divine grace finds expression in God's creation, in God's Covenant and, more immediately, in God himself. God's creation and covenant cannot be separated from God's love. The absoluteness, unchangeability and eternity of God are revealed not only in his being the creator of the universe and maker of the Covenant, but also in his being the lover of the world. In one tradition to be found in the O.T. literature, God is described as unconditional, divine and sovereign love. God loved and chose Israel, not because Israel was better than any other people, nor because of what Israel had done or had been, but simply because God chose and loved her. In the face of God's love, Israel was neither good nor great. On the contrary, Israel was frequently condemned for her wickedness. Why God continued to love such a wicked

people was a question that often troubled the prophets, and the answer given was that, since God loved their forefathers, so he must also love their descendants: God would keep his promise to the forefathers whom he loved. This was hardly a satisfactory answer to the question of why God's love was so faithful and constant. The real value of such an answer, however, lies in its implicit concept of God: God loves for his own sake, or for his name's sake (II Kings 19:34). Or to be more precise, God loves because love is God's essential nature. As to why God bestowed his love upon Israel, this can be explained only by God, because God is who he is. Of course, the writers of the O.T. did not state explicitly that God was love. For them, the divine love was fundamentally a love of choice or election, which, in focusing on one, excluded all others. Such exclusiveness troubled many of the prophets: they acknowledged it, but could not respond to it. Therefore, a vicious circle was formed: God chose Israel because he loved her; God loved Israel because he had chosen her. This circle was broken only by the teaching of Jesus and, more particularly, by those early Christian theologians who boldly replaced the chosen people with the chosen Son, Jesus Christ. The division between those who were chosen and those who were excluded was brought to an end by the death of Jesus. God's love was now freely available to whoever loved Jesus, no matter what his class or race was: 'If anyone loves me, he will obey my teaching. My Father will love him, and we will come to him and make our home with him' (John 14:23); and 'Grace to all who love our Lord Jesus Christ with an undying love' (Ephesians 6:24). From this there naturally arose the universal conception that: God is love and Jesus Christ is the Lord of love. This marked the mature doctrine of Christian love, and also signalled its divergence from the restrictiveness implicit in Judaism.

Since God is love and God's love is in Jesus, then salvation is the salvation of love. God is universal love; his salvation must extend beyond the chosen people to all people who follow Jesus. Generally speaking, there is in the O.T. a harmony between the holiness and the nearness of God's grace, and God is seen as redeemer and saviour. 'This insistence upon the redeeming activity of God and the consequent alteration in the fortunes of Israel can be seen by the way in which, whenever the prophet [second-Isaiah] mentions the sins of the past, he immediately speaks of forgiveness and redemption'.[28] However, the notion of God as redeemer and saviour was in most cases restricted to the relation between God and his chosen people.

Redemption was used in its original sense of a master buying back a slave as the property of the original owner (Isaiah 41:14). Universal salvation was not taken as the essential element of divine love: 'God is going to establish His will and vindicate the right. He is going to do this with particular reference to the righteous poor, a phrase which in time comes to mean the godly humble remnant of Israel who, through all the perils of their way and in spite of every disability and oppression, have conformed to the norm (*tsedeq*) which God has established.'[29]

The theme of the universalism of God's love, which appeared here and there in the writings of the prophets, was central to the teaching of Jesus and was further developed by his followers. According to Luke, Jesus claimed that the scripture from Isaiah 61:1 was now being fulfilled in the hearing of his audience: 'The Spirit of the Lord is on me, because he has anointed me to preach good news to the poor. He has sent me to proclaim freedom for the prisoners and recovery of sight for the blind, to release the oppressed, to proclaim the year of the Lord's favour' (Luke 4:18–21). Christian teachers developed this teaching to the full, and love was realized in the freedom of the slave, in the forgiveness of sinners, and in the hopes of those who suffered. All these acts of salvation are possible because God is none other than love. Thus love is said to be, not one of the many attributes that God possesses, but the essential nature of God. God cannot be known and understood except in his love and by his love.

The contrast between the old and the new is central to the identification of God and love in the N.T. and in later Christian writings. Although God created and cared for his human creatures, commanding them to be faithful and good, they chose to disobey and go their own way. Thus a sinful world developed which was in opposition to God's will. To save sinners, God sent his Son, Jesus Christ, to earth, summoning them to believe in him, forgiving their wrongdoing, and redeeming them from their sins.[30] Thus, this love is fully revealed in God's identification with his Son Jesus Christ and in the life and death of Christ: 'God so loved the world that he gave his one and only son, that whoever believes in him shall not perish but have eternal life' (John 3:16); 'God demonstrates his own love for us in this: while we were still sinners, Christ died for us' (Romans 5:8). In this way Christian faith merges with Christian love: love as divine *agape* is alone the saviour of the world and the hope of humankind, and Christian hope manifests in divine *agape*: without the raising power of the Holy Spirit, humans remain sinners, and transcendence is impossible.

TRANSCENDENCE IN HUMANISM AND THEISM

The similarities between Confucian *jen* and Christian *agape* in respect of their roots and their relationship with the Transcendent are, at first glance, very few. Humanistic *jen* is rooted in humanity and grows from secularity and temporality to sacredness and eternity. Humanity is the life and spirit of the Confucian principle, whether as a religion or as a philosophy. When humanity is taken as the root of *jen*, it is associated with its transcendental understanding of the world. The transcendence in Confucianism is understood essentially as a process of self-transcending, and it is in human life that humanity pursues their ultimate. Since the ultimate for human beings is also the ultimate for the universe, to strive for perfection in one's own nature and to bring forth human flourishing in the world are the way to transcendence. To be perfect is to fulfil one's *jen*; to fulfil one's *jen* is to extend one's self to its widest degree; to extend one's self is to commit oneself to human common good and to be in harmony with the universe; and to be in harmony with the universe is to transcend the limitations of one's own life and to find the ultimate meaning of life in *jen*. Therefore, transcendence and the ways to transcendence in Confucianism constitutes a circular movement with both its starting point and the end being in the self and self-cultivation. Throughout the whole process *jen* is always a motivating power.

By contrast, theistic *agape* is rooted in divinity and flows downwards from the divine to the human, thus raising temporal existence to eternity. Unlike Confucian *jen*, according to which the ascent from the temporal to the eternal is a developmental process motivated by *jen* and effected by self-cultivation, the ascent from the temporal to the eternal in Christian *agape* involves a conversion motivated by God's self-giving love and effected by divine grace. Thus divinity is the life and source of the Christian principle, whether through theological reflection or through religious experience. The possibility of human *agape* depends on its source in divine grace, which has revealed itself in creation, in the special covenant and in the suffering of Jesus Christ. Human beings, although created in the image of God and with an inclination towards self-giving love, have distorted this image and spoiled this inclination by their sin. Therefore they have no source of *agape* within themselves and cannot restore the nature of *agape* by themselves. Human transcendence is God's work of restoring and renewing the spirit of *agape*. Understood as such, Christian transcendence and its approach to transcendence also constitutes a circular movement. However, neither its starting-point nor its end is within humanity. This process is initiated by divine *agape*, draws its power from divine *agape* and its final goal is to participate in divine *agape*.

Thus, Christianity and Confucianism provide us with two different understandings of transcendence and two different approaches to the Transcendent. First, transcendence is understood in Confucianism essentially as a human affair, for which humanity alone is responsible; while transcendence in Christianity is taken primarily as a divine mission, for which only God is accountable. Secondly, for most Confucians, to transcend is to develop one's good nature to its utmost; while for most Christians to transcend is to put hope on Christ. Thirdly, as a human affair, Confucian transcendence is involved with all aspects of human life, and everything – such as morality, institutions and rituals – that is conducive to human fulfilment is taken as a way to attain transcendence; while as a divine mission, Christian transcendence cannot be helped by anything that belongs to humanity, only God's mercy alone can bring it about.

A full appreciation of Confucian *jen* and Christian *agape* in respect of their transcendence, however, must take note not only of their differences, but also of their similarities. These similarities are more easily overlooked than those in other areas because of the fundamental divergence in the two concepts of transcendence. Some people hold that there is no common ground at all between Christian theism and Confucian humanism in their understanding of transcendence and approaches to it, or else that the contradiction between them is so sharp that it excludes any common concern. Others admit that there is this or that piece of common ground between *jen* and *agape* in so far as transcendence is concerned, but go on to argue that this ground is too small to provide a solid base on which the two conceptions of transcendence can communicate with each other. A careful examination of them, however, will show that neither of these views is fair, and that the differences and similarities between *jen* and *agape* are interwoven.

In one sense, an understanding of transcendence comes from reflection on the experience of the ultimate, and to transcend is to be one with the ultimate. For Confucianism, the ultimate, or the highest good, or perfection, is to be found in a fully developed humanity, in which the three-dimensional existence of the universe (heaven, earth and humans) has been integrated. Whatever form the ultimate may take, it is always in humanity. Therefore, the ultimate for Confucians is not far removed from the basic elements of humanity. In fact, it is rooted in the same human nature that has been endowed by heaven and earth. One can transcend only in the way that one continuingly pursues learning, sincerely cultivates one's virtues and firmly wills to be perfect; by all this one will become a fulfilled human.[31] A fulfilled human is elaborated in the *Book of Changes* as one who is able to assist Heaven and Earth to complete virtue so that his character is identical with that of heaven and earth, his brilliance with that of the sun and moon, his order with that of the four seasons, and his good and evil fortunes with those of spiritual beings. When such a person acts in advance of heaven, heaven does not contradict him; when he follows heaven, he acts exactly according to the time of heaven.[32] Among the virtues that enable one to be transcendental, the first is that of *jen*, and *jen* is clearly taken as the substance of Confucian ultimate.[33] This is the very reason that the *Great Learning* calls for all the people from ruler to commoners to take self-cultivation as their root.

For Christianity, the ultimate, or the highest good, or perfection, is God and to be in the ultimate is to be living in God's *agape*, by which the universe and the laws of nature have been created and order and peace given. Whatever form God may take, he is always above and beyond human beings. Therefore, the ultimate cannot be found within human beings, but must be sought beyond their existence and activity. Human qualities are to be valued only because they reflect divine qualities. Consequently, human beings cannot reach the ultimate by themselves. They must be led towards it by the ultimate itself. However, this fact should not be taken to mean that Christian men must stay in an absolutely passive state in respect of their pursuit of transcendence. In so far as human efforts are needed in Christian transcendence, Christianity shows certain similarities with Confucianism. Christian theology does not deny that the 'cardinal virtues' are significant both for human life and for Christian faith, so that one can become a good Christian only if one wills to live by moral goodness. Christian theology promotes human virtues as theological virtues so that faith, love and hope become the backbone of Christian doctrine. These theological virtues call for

human efforts in participating in the life of Christ, and demonstrate
that each is responsible for his own destiny, to transcend or to
remain in the temporal, to be in God's love or to be out of it. Faith
is first and foremost understood to be a gift from God. It reveals
what human transcendence is. Just as not all acorns will grow into
oaks, however, not all people will have faith and therefore not all
can transcend their limits of life, both physical and spiritual. Human
transcendence can be realized only by living in God's love. To be in
God's love is to love as God loves. Hope, on the one hand, reveals
that there is no guarantee for one's attainment of the ultimate; on the
other hand, it provides humanity with a guarantee from divine *agape*
as long as one has total reliance on God's mercy. Faith, love and
hope are the three most important things Christians must possess
in pursuing transcendence. Human beings can do so because Jesus
Christ has brought God's grace into the very heart of humanity
by his life and death, and has fundamentally changed the human
tendency of being alienated from God to that of being reconciled
with God. If the salvific significance of Jesus' death is appreciated,
logically it follows that human nature has been implanted with the
seed of transcendence. To let this seed grow is to grow in God's
agape. In this way, Christian transcendence and Christian effort in
attaining transcendence are unified in the life and death of Christ.

Both Confucianism and Christianity take human unity with the
ultimate as their transcendence, although the ultimate means different things in these two traditions. In discussing the transcendental
goal for Christians, Calvin affirmed that the highest goal was
to become one body with Christ. This imagery well illustrates
both the differences and similarities when compared with the neo-
Confucian understanding of the transcendental goal as being one
body with the universe. Calvin says that 'Christ is not without us,
but dwells within us; and not only adheres to us by an indissoluble
connection of fellowship, but by a certain wonderful communion
coalesces daily more and more into one body with us, till he
becomes altogether one with us.'[34] This ideal is similar to the
neo-Confucian ideal that human transcendence is to become one
body with Heaven and Earth. It is different from the Confucian
ideal in the sense that 'one body with the ultimate' in Confucianism
is taken as the goal for which humans can strive, while 'one body
with Christ' in Christianity is taken as the mercy of Christ who
comes down to humanity. This downward movement is essential
for the understanding of the Christian transcendence and of the

Christian approach to the Transcendent, in contrast to the Confucian transcendence that is reached by the upward movement of humans themselves, or more precisely, is attained by returning to one's true self and by manifesting one's originally bright virtue.

Whatever transcendence is taken to mean, a religion must produce and present ways to reach it. Confucian *jen* and Christian *agape* are both the essence of transcendence and the ways to attaining to it. Different conceptions of transcendence need different ways to reach it. As a humanistic principle, *jen* is the realisation of humanity. Therefore, to transcend, one has to develop fully human existence and virtue. According to the first sentence of the *Great Learning*, which was placed as the first book of the Four Books by the Sung and later Confucians, this development is presented in three aspects or stages: to manifest one's character or to illustrate one's illustrious virtue; to love or to renew people; and to have rest or to find peace in the highest good.[35] The highest good is none other than *jen* itself, because only *jen* can give humans peace and rest. It is clear to Confucians that the integration of human existence with the highest good is the transcendental goal; this cannot be attained unless one has manifested those illustrious virtues that are inherent in human nature; one can not do so unless one loves all people and by this love one renews one's own character as well as the characters of others; only by all of these can one find that rest in *jen*, which is the natural result of one's unswerving effort in self-cultivation and love.

The approach to Christian transcendence is different. From the divine point of view, Christian *agape* presents itself in three ways to make human transcendence possible: creating out of self-giving love, bringing back humanity to it by making covenant with them, and unifying humanity and divine love in the life and death of Jesus Christ. From the human point of view, therefore, if we make use of the Confucian formula, we may say that Christian *agape* is realized in three ways or stages, by which human transcendence comes true: to have faith in God and Jesus Christ; to love as God loves; and to find rest in God's grace. To attain transcendence, one has first to have a firm faith in God and in God's creative power. With this faith, anything that seems impossible will become possible. To have faith in God is to follow Jesus Christ who is God's love incarnate. To have faith is to love. In this love, one lives under the protection and love of God, and shares in the life of God. Like all created things, humanity exists in absolute dependence on the divine *agape*, the principle of God's creative activity, the source of human happiness and of human likeness to the creator himself. Therefore, lasting peace is possible only by God's grace.

Because *jen* and *agape* are taken as transcendence itself, on the one hand, and as ways to transcending the temporal, on the other, neither of them is of a passive character. They are active in the creation of a new world and a new people. *Jen* and *agape* are both the character of this new world and people, and the power to create this new world and people, in which the real meaning of transcendence is revealed.

The term 'new' is a characteristic of Christianity and the fruit of Jesus' saving work, as in 'new covenant', 'new commandment', 'new creation', 'new man', 'new name', 'new song' and 'new Jerusalem'. 'New' expresses the Christian belief that God has acted again in Jesus and through him has made a new covenant and gives a new commandment. The basis and symbol of this new covenant is the blood, or death, of Jesus. It is the beginning of a new creation. To be in Christ is to share in the new creation. Because of this new creation, one who is in Christ is renewed day by day, not in one's outer nature which is wasting away, but in one's inner nature (Galatians 4:5). The Spirit of Christ in God is the creative and recreative power, which informs the new way of life. The emphasis is on 'God's gift': humans cannot do anything to renew themselves. They have to rely upon God's grace to transcend themselves. Just as the blind man who was cured by the love of Jesus exclaimed that 'Once I was blind, but now I see'; so the new life of humanity comes from the grace of God's *agape*, and is in complete contrast to the old.

In Confucianism, *jen* is also believed by cultivation of character to bring forth new people. In a short paragraph in the *Great Learning* the term 'new or to renew' [*hsin*] appears five times and describes the complete idea of a new people in a new world in Confucian tradition.[36] Compared with the Christian concept of newness and renewal, the Confucian conception has four distinct aspects.

First, the concept of the new is important for the Confucian principle and its realisation, but, strange to say, it is not explicitly defined or explained, at least not to the same degree as in Christianity, in which the new is a central idea and is explicitly described as the realisation of the divine *agape*. According to Christian theology, there would be no gospel were it not for the divine grace; there would be no new command were it not for the love which Jesus revealed in his life and death; there would be no new life and no new world were it not for the gift of the Spirit of love. Therefore, *agape* is essentially to renew the world. It is emphasized that to be made new is to move from death to life, to depart from the old world and enter the new world. Therefore, the new represents a radical break with the old. In Confucianism too, the first task is to make the old people new through *jen*. But this is not to break with the past, and there is no opposition between the past and the present as far as humanity is concerned. Confucianism does not hold the radical view that the new is in complete contrast to the old. The new is a development of the old. From old to new is understood in terms of the progress of humanity moved by education and enlightenment of the sage and in terms of human self-transformation. The new is significant only in the sense of the new efforts made by humans to integrate themselves with the universe.

Secondly, both stress that the new originates from transcendental power, but the Confucian understanding of transcendence is not as far-reaching as in Christian theology. In Confucianism, *Jen* is not only the principle of humans, but also the principle of *Tian*, the transcendental power because it alone can bring humanity to its perfection. In Confucian classics, *jen* is deliberately identified with *Tian*'s charity and kindness. One poem from *The Book of Poetry* says that 'although the Chou was an old [and small] state, the mandate [of Heaven] that lighted it was new'. When this new mandate was carried out, the Chou was transformed from an old state into a new kingdom. This clearly shows that the Confucian conception of the new depends upon the mandate of *Tian*. It is from *Tian* that the new mandate comes, which will renew the old and establish the new order through human efforts. However, the new mandate in Confucianism is much less connected with creation than with a change of dynastical destiny. When those who have lost the virtues manifested by their ancestry forfeit the support of *Tian*, and their mandate is withdrawn, *Tian* will seek out the virtuous and endow them with a new mandate to rule the earth on his behalf. When the new mandate is given, a new order will be established. However, whether this order can be maintained depends on whether the ruler can 'arouse people to become new'.[37] In this way, the transcendental, the political and the ethical are closely related. The politically new is brought forth by the ethically new; the ethically new is the manifestation of the transcendentally new; and the transcendentally new mandate comes only as an award to the ethically new character. Commenting on this paragraph in the *Book of History*, Mencius asked those rulers who would like to take King Wen of the Chou Dynasty as their example to put into practice *jen* and righteousness, and believed that this would suffice them to make new their states (*The Book of Mencius*, 3A:3). In Christianity, the 'new' is brought in by God through Jesus Christ. Christ sheds light into human hearts. A new people is possible only because Christ has died for them: they have been redeemed from sin and their past has been forgiven. The universe has been recreated and the people transformed by Christ through *agape*. This transformation has nothing to do with political changes. Both its source and its forms are theological. The contrast between the new and the old has thus acquired a creative meaning in Christianity. To renew the people has nothing, or little, to do with the political structure and ethical education. Rather it is a matter of turning away from the sin and to the Holy Spirit.

Thirdly, both stress that it is urgent to renew humans, but they differ over the way to renew them and the reason why it is necessary to renew them. In Confucianism renewal in terms of moral growth is a process of self-cultivation by individuals. The *Great Learning* quotes an inscription on the bath-tub of King Tang, the founder of the Shang Dynasty, to the effect that 'If you can renovate yourself one day, then you can do so every day, and keeping doing so day after day.'[38] The new self is created and recreated by its own efforts. In later Confucianism such self-renewal was taken as characteristic of Confucian doctrine. According to Confucian understanding, three elements are significant in self-renewal: (1) The most difficult thing is to start one's self-cultivation here and now. Human activity is often carried on by force of habit. Few people realize that the source of a new life lies in their own self. As soon as one realizes this and puts *jen* into practice, a new process of life begins; (2) One day's effort cannot make a new person. One has to keep on persevering everyday because the renewal of oneself takes the whole of one's life; (3) To renew oneself is a gradual process in which each day will see the change of a bit of one's character. The accumulation of these changes will at last enable one to become a completely new person.[39] Central to the mainstream of the Confucian concept of renewal is the belief that everyone has a seed of *jen* in his nature. When preserved and nurtured, the seed will grow up and mature as the great tree of humanity; or in other words, one will become perfect through learning and the practice of human virtues. Self-renewal is not only the character of humanity, but also the principle of the universe. *The Book of Changes* takes 'daily renewal' as the 'glorious virtue' (*sheng*

te) and identifies 'production and reproduction' with the principle
and essence of change.[40] The idea of self-renewal is foreign to the
thinking of the majority of Christian theologians. In accord with its
theological understanding of *agape*, Christianity sees the renewal
as wholly an act of the divine. *Agape* is not originally part of
human nature. It comes from God and needs to be initiated by
divine grace. Therefore, the new comes from grace and is a fruit
of the self-sacrifice of Jesus. Nor is the new a process by which
one accumulates virtue. It begins and ends with participating in
Christ: 'If anyone is in Christ, he is a new creation. The old has
passed away, and the new has come' (II Corinthians 5:17). There
is a role for Christians to play in being in Christ, and so the call
to discipleship and the need to follow become part of Christian
renewal. In this sense, to be new is to grow in grace, in which
Christian response participates. However, since this participation is
possible because of Jesus Christ, human efforts play only a limited
role in human renewal.[41]

Fourthly, the necessity for renewal stems from human corruption.
For most Confucians, humans are innately good, or as Mencius
puts it, humans possess shoots of goodness which will grow into
virtues when nurtured and cultivated. However, this good nature
is believed to be vulnerable to human circumstances and selfish
desires. To guard against corruption, preservation of a good nature
in the heart and pursuit of righteousness in social interaction are of
primary significance for *jen* to grow. Therefore, the heart plays an
essential part in the Confucian idea of self-renewal. The heart is the
microcosmic entity and is related to the Transcendent; anyone who
has fully realized his heart understands his own nature, and anyone
who has understood his own nature knows *Tian*'s nature (*The Book of
Mencius*, 7A:1). When the moral and spiritual propensity inherent in
human nature is frustrated by a complexity of internal and external
causes, the human heart will be spoiled. While it is important to
remove these causes, most Confucians insist that it is more urgent
to start this work from within – to seek one's good heart – because
it is believed that 'seek, and you will get it; let go and you will
lose it'. For Christians, the heart also plays an important role in
their renewal. To be new, one first has to have a new heart and a
new spirit. Jesus praised those who had a 'pure heart' (Matthew
5:8). Paul spoke of the 'circumcised heart' (Romans 2:5, 29) and
bade his readers: 'Have this mind in you which was also in Christ
Jesus' (Philippians 2:5). Therefore, 'to repent and to turn to God'

is to be understood as having 'a change of heart'.[42] The difference
between the Christian idea and the Confucian idea of heart is that
for Christians the good heart is a gift from the Spirit, while for
most Confucians it already exists in human nature. In recognizing
that one's true heart is also that of the sage or of Jesus, Christians
and Confucians seem to possess a common ground. However, for
Confucianism it can be cultivated by oneself, while for Christianity
it must be received through faith in Jesus Christ.

The 'new man' attains to fulfilment in the sage of Confucianism
and the saint of Christianity respectively. In one sense, a sage or
a saint may be taken as an embodiment of Confucian or Christian transcendence. Thus, the similarities and differences between
Confucian humanism of *jen* and Christian theism of *agape* are clearly
to be seen in their different portraits of a sage or a saint.

While Confucius believes that humans are perfectible and sets
sagehood as the ideal for his followers, he hardly envisages a real
possibility for an ordinary person to become a sage. The difficulty
for a person to become a sage lies not only in natural weakness, such
as preferring sexual enjoyment to the cultivation of moral character
and in the unwillingness to pursue learning, but also in the social
inability to benefit all people. However, the caution of Confucius in
discussing sagehood was mostly overlooked or disregarded in the
writings of later Confucians. The emphasis on the possibility that
everyone can become a sage is so strong in their arguments that the
difficulties in doing so do not appear as great as they in fact are.
This possibility is explored not only by Mencius, who proclaims
that human nature is innately good, but also by Hsun Tzu, who
believes that human nature is innately bad. For the former this is
possible, because humans can develop their innate good capacities
to perfection; while for the latter it is possible because there are the
moral laws which sages have laid down for human education and
training. In their theories, sages are less salvific than they are in
the conversations of Confucius, in which a sage seems to be taken
as the creator of the golden past and the saviour of the people.
Sagehood, rather, becomes the achievement of restoring the ideal in
contemporary society and in one's own life, and this can come about
through self-cultivation, including the study of the classics and the
practice of the moral virtues, of which the first and foremost is that
of *jen*. Sagehood and its attainment again became a central theme in
the neo-Confucianism of the Sung and Ming Dynasties. Generally
speaking, the majority of Confucians during this period had the

firm conviction that everybody is perfectible and that sagehood can be 'learned' by everyone. Different understanding of this 'learning' led to the growth of different schools. Some believe that to be a sage is to engage in the study of the ancient classics; others insist that it is to explore one's own mind, which is also the mind of the sage. For example, Wang Yang-ming developed Mencius' theory that the human heart contains everything needed for attaining to sagehood and claimed that sagehood was the original state of every human being.[43] Everybody has an original mind of sagehood, the mind of *jen*. The problem is simply that not everybody can realize this. Instead, ordinary people are led away from their mind of sagehood by selfish desires. Therefore, for him to learn is to correct. Sagehood can be realized and the original mind can function freely as soon as one has eliminated these desires. Since the classics were written by sages who had the same mind as our own, one can find in exploring one's own mind as much as one can in the study of these classics. Further, since the classics and their authors were all historical, the more efficient way to look for sagehood is to reflect on one's own mind rather than to read these ancient books. Furthermore, too much attention paid to learning the classics leads one away from exploring one's own mind, where sagehood is to be found; the sages of the past and the classics may even become obstacles to the goal of attaining one's own sagehood, if they are overemphasised.

In Christianity, the conception of a saint is rooted in the concept of the holy and divine. Therefore, a saint is not so much a perfect person, who possesses the ethical virtues, as one of the 'called', 'elect' and 'faithful' (Romans 1:7; 8:33; Col. 1:2). He is someone filled with the Holy Spirit. In the O.T. we read that the people of God were holy because God had selected them, i.e. they belonged to God. In the N.T. this understanding of holiness or saints is maintained: Christians are regarded as holy or 'a holy people' because they were called. Holiness or saintliness is fundamentally a gift from God. The downwards movement of divine *agape* makes it possible for people to grow in God's grace, therefore those who have shown special marks of grace are recognized by the Church as holy persons or saints. Thus saints have been playing a double role in the Christian church. 'As a type of religious person, the saint in Christianity suggested characteristics of both "otherness" or inimitability, associated with the veneration of the saint, and exemplariness or imitability, resulting in the emulation of the saint by his followers.'[44]

Both Confucian sages and Christian saints are venerated as
'above' ordinary people, as exemplars for others in showing them
the path to salvation, and as the embodiment of the Way. However,
despite these similarities, we must admit that the differences are
more striking. The first difference between a Confucian sage and
a Christian saint lies in their nature. Sagehood is the perfection of
humanity, which comes as the result of self-cultivation. A sage is
essentially a perfect man who, by exerting his *jen*, penetrates and
understands all things and makes the Way prevail in the world:
'The sages and ordinary people are the same in kind. But they stand
out from their fellows and rise above the level . . . ' Therefore, 'the
sages are the perfect embodiment of human relations' (*The Book of
Mencius*, 2A:2; 4A:2). To be a sage is the ultimate goal for Confucians.
Therefore, a sage is both the fulfilled human and the transcendental
manifestation. Although Confucius believed that he was far from
being a sage, he was nevertheless placed at the summit of the
Confucian world and identified with the sage, and it is believed that
'He is in harmony above with the heavenly seasons, and below with
[the elements] of water and land. He may be compared to heaven
and earth which contain and support . . . all things, to the four
seasons in their cyclical progress, and to the sun and moon in their
alternative task of giving light' (The *Doctrine of the Mean*, chap. 30).
Compared with this understanding of the Confucian sage, a saint
occupies a much lower position on the Christian ladder. A saint is
essentially a chosen man who, by the grace of God, understands the
will of God and acts on his will. Saintliness is sometimes identical
with 'perfection'. However, this perfection is not the same as ethical
perfection. The marks of saintliness are those associated with the
presence of grace and the power of the Holy Spirit. Therefore,
although saints are venerated in the Christian tradition, it is not
the goal of a Christian to become a saint. Concentration on one's
own person cannot result in sainthood. Only those who concentrate
on God and have faith in and love towards God can be saved and
only those who are saved can become Christian saints.

The second difference between them is that sagehood comes from
one's own self-cultivation, while sainthood comes from enlightenment by the Holy Spirit. *Tian* plays an important role in human
attaining to sagehood. However, a person is not **raised** by *Tian* to
be a sage. He promotes himself through his own cultivation. Perfectibility is an essential characteristic of human nature, and to be
a sage is to learn how to be a true, or a great, human. Since Mencius,

the unity between *Tian* and humanity has been used to justify the belief that human nature contains everything potential for perfection and one can become perfect, that is, a sage, by developing these potentials to the utmost. Mencius admitted that there are two parts within the human person: the great part and the small part, or the transcendental self and the experiential self. To be a sage, one must first make a correct choice between them: those who have chosen and followed the transcendental self will become great humans, while those who have chosen and been guarded solely by the experiential self will become 'small men' (*The Book of Mencius*, 6A:15). To be a sage, one must then make efforts in developing the great part inherent in human nature. Without being cultivated and nurtured, seeds remain seeds and cannot become power of human perfection. Mencius took the five grains as an example: 'The five grains are the best of plants, yet they would be even worse than the wild plants should they not ripen. The beauty and greatness of *jen* also lies in its being cultivated to maturity' (6A:19). Some schools of neo-Confucianism went even further to claim that sagehood is none other than a conscious realization of unity and harmony with all things. This unity already exists in human nature. What one has to do is to enlarge one's mind so that one can enter into all things in the world, or that one can include all things and beings in one's own mind. Neither bringing one's *jen* into maturity nor enlarging one's mind to include the world is the same as destroying one's experiential self. On the one hand, Confucians believe that sagehood cannot be developed unless one's experiential self is transformed. On the other hand, they emphasize that one's biological, psychological or even sociological conditions are necessary because self-transformation must be made through experiencing one's social condition and regulating one's physical needs. Since everybody has within himself the root of sagehood, there is no need for him or her to adopt a special life-style in order to become a sage; since one's experiential self is a way to one's transcendence, the motto for one thus becomes: 'To be a sage, first be a true human'.

By contrast, sainthood is determined by the Holy Spirit. Although Christianity insists that before the Fall human beings were created in the image of God, and therefore agrees that relationship with the divine is an essential aspect of human nature, this does not lead to the conclusion that humans can raise themselves to the level of God. Christian theology holds that a person cannot be a saint in his own power, whatever efforts he may exert. However, he may become a saint if and when God bestows his grace on him. The veneration given to a saint is not to glorify the saint himself nor his person, but to glorify God. Since sainthood is essentially a gift of God, there has been a tendency in some forms of Christianity to hold that to become a saint means to abandon one's natural self and all that one is biologically, psychologically and sociologically, since here there is no trace of *agape*. Consequently, emphasis is laid more on escaping from worldly affairs than engaging in the world. The outward process cannot start until one has resolved to leave behind all secular and worldly considerations. This is why in some traditions the monastic life became so important for the conception of the Christian saint. For other traditions, however, the argument develops in another way. God is love, which has been bestowed on humanity. The divine and the human co-exist in human life. Human nature was corrupted by sins. However, humans are still responsible for their own salvation, although they are unable to do so by themselves. The restoration of the corrupted nature cannot be achieved without human efforts being involved, and without human engagement in worldly affairs. Therefore, for them to search for sainthood and to lead a good life in human community are by no means contradictory.

The humanism of Confucianism enables its conception of sage to be related to almost anybody and anywhere, whereas the theism of Christianity means that sainthood is possible only when grace is bestowed upon humans. From these facts it would seem to follow logically that there should be more sages in Confucianism than there are saints in Christianity, since it should be easier to be a sage than to become a saint. However, this is not the case. In Confucianism, everybody is said to be perfectible. On the other hand, however well one may do, one is very unlikely to be said to be perfect. In fact, very few are given the title of sage within the Confucian tradition. By contrast, in Christianity it is denied that humans are perfectible by themselves. Nevertheless, images and pictures of saints with halos are widespread in churches and outnumber statues of sages in Confucian temples. This again demonstrates that Confucian sages and Christian saints are not parallel in respect of their nature, role and function.

The third difference lies in their different understanding of how important learning is for attaining sagehood or sainthood. Confucians believe that, in order to attain sagehood, one has to go through a process of learning. Confucian sagehood, it appears, is the result of internalizing the external Way. Learning for most Confucians is not a mere study or accumulation of knowledge. It starts with an understanding of one's existential conditions. To understand is not primarily a process of cognitive grasping, but of reshaping oneself by returning to one's true self. It is a process of integration between the universal and the particular, and therefore it is practical in nature.[45] Mencius believes that when one exerts one's own mind to the utmost, one knows one's own nature; when one knows one's own nature, one knows the will of *Tian*. When one knows the will of *Tian*, one can serve it, and in serving *Tian* one is becoming a sage. Cheng I of the Sung Dynasty puts it directly: 'The way to learn is none other than rectifying one's mind and nourishing one's nature. When one abides by the mean and correctness and becomes sincere, one is a sage.'[46] Therefore, the attainment of sagehood is entirely in one's own hands and is seen as the extension of *jen* in one's self-cultivation.

In practice, Christians insist that to be a saint, one has to go through a process of prolonged learning and discipline. Whether Paul, from the persecutor of Christians to Christian saint, or Augustine, from playboy and debaucher to devoted bishop, each came to the truth of their Lord only after a great deal of effort and painful experience. This fact appears to show that sainthood is also a process of internalizing the external Way. However, the primary emphasis here is not on one's own effort in grasping and understanding, but on the enlightenment of the Holy Spirit. Without grace, nobody can attain to the ideal. Those who became saints were seen as the proofs of God's *agape* and of the power of the Holy Spirit, rather than as the product of their own achievement.

We may now conclude that the fundamental differences between *jen* and *agape* lie in the aspect of transcendence, the one rooting in humanity and the other rooting in God's grace. *Jen* and *agape* come from different sources, are orientated in different directions and therefore need different ways to be manifest. Because of the identification between *jen* and humanity. Both the Transcendent and human transcendence must be understood in terms of humanity, and Confucians lay the responsibility of one's transcendence primarily upon one's own self. On the other hand, there is a separation between divine *agape* and human nature in Christian tradition so that not only the Transcendent but also human transcendence can be appreciated only in terms of divinity, and Christians hold hope of human transcendence on God's mercy. Although it is not denied that humanity has a role to play in their reconciliation to God, this role is predetermined by God's grace and can be actualized only in their faith in God. In this sense we may say that in regard to human communication with the Transcendent, Christianity places more emphasis on having faith in, and hope on, God, than human own responsibility, while Confucianism places more emphasis on exploring human nature and human life in which human transcendence is attained. However, this contrast must not be extended to imply that it is less significant to grow in *agape* for Christians than to be in *jen* for Confucians. Both humanism and theism carry within themselves the concern for human transcendence, individually as well as collectively, and *jen* and *agape* are taken not only as the transcendental ideal but also as the power moving humans to this ideal, by penetrating into the human heart. Whatever form the Transcendent may take, it is always the ultimate goal for humanity. In the last analysis, Confucian *jen* and Christian *agape* are both the embodiment of, and the ways to, human transcendence, and they are different only in their implications of what human transcendence is and how human beings can attain to transcendence. This is what we are going to examine in the next chapter.

5

Jen as Virtue and *Agape* as the Human Response of Love for God

A religious principle is a transcendental calling and a necessary guide for people to the ultimate. However, it should not be reduced to an external action-guiding rule. It penetrates a person's heart and become part of his or her nature or self. Without this 'subjectivization' of the transcendental commandment, a principle could not function as a truly religious and moral principle, indicating, and motivating people to, the path of transcendence. Therefore, *jen* and *agape* not only have their roots in the conception of transcendence, but also have their application in the subjective consciousness and its orientation to the ultimate, although this process of internalization of the ultimate takes on different forms, due to differences between Confucian transcendence and Christian ultimate. On the one hand, both are a unity of the ultimate and the internalization of the ultimate, and therefore are both objective and subjective. On the other hand, the unity between the ultimate-objective and the ultimate-subjective is manifested in different ways. From the humanity that is the root and essence of Confucian *jen*, *jen* manifests itself directly both as the transcendental calling within humanity and as the inner quality of human beings, so that the religious subject and the religious object are originally united in *jen* as one body, without further mediation. From the divinity that is the root and essence of Christian *agape*, however, *agape* cannot be internalized in human nature without divine assistance, and the human attainment of divine *agape* appears only in the form of human response to the divine calling or command. Thus comes the second contrast between *jen* and *agape*: within *jen* there is no difference between

religion and ethics and transcendence is taken as the ethically good
so that *jen* takes the form of virtue, while within *agape* the religious
is differentiated from the ethical and human virtues are important
only when they are taken as a response to the command of loving
God. However, as far as the relationship between religion and ethics
is concerned, there is a kind of convergence between Confucian
way and Christian approach. As in Confucianism virtue is not
only meant in the moral sense, but also in the sense that it is a
way to transcendence, so in Christianity response is not only taken
as a divine penetration, but also as a positive application of divine
grace by human beings. The division between transcendence and
ethics is not appreciated in Confucian *jen*, nor does it assume its
absolute form in Christian *agape*.

JEN AS VIRTUE

Jen originates in the humanity that is the integrating power and
unifying substance of the universe, and this power and substance
has its most active form in human existence and activity. In human
existence and activity *jen* refers not only to human existential form
but also to human transcendental quality. Therefore, humanity
needs to be understood in both metaphysical and ethical senses.
In its ethical sense, *jen* manifests itself in humanity as virtue.
Confucianism is more concerned with the moral than with the natural order. Consequently, more has been said, within the Confucian
tradition, about *jen* as virtue than about *jen* as humanity itself,
although these two aspects are always related. *Jen* as virtue overlaps
with another Chinese character for virtue: *te*. In Confucius, these
two terms are used interchangeably in most cases, both the power
of humanity and the seed that can grow into full humanity. On the
metaphysical side, while both are the root of virtues, their difference
is that *te* refers more to the potential of this power while *jen* more to
its content, or *te* refers more to the seed itself while *jen* more to its
growing power. On the ethical side, while both describe the quality
of good life, *te* refers generally to goodness and desirability but *jen*
manifests itself in the form of particular qualities in life. When the
potential of humanity is realized, the content of *jen* obtains its forms
so that *jen* becomes virtue. As virtue, *jen* functions at four levels: as
a moral quality, which everybody, or at least every respectable person, should possess; as a specific virtue, which reveals a particular

aspect of human goodness and nobility; as the highest virtue, or crown of virtues, which is an embodiment of perfection; and as the ground of all virtues, a summary of human life that gives meaning to virtue as a whole.

Jen as moral growth is closely related to the concept of *li* (propriety or moral codes). To be *jen* is to acquire the moral quality of human beings, and one of the most efficient ways to acquire this quality is to observe *li*. *Li*, which was originally a concept referring to religious rituals, became a complicated concept in Chinese culture and in Confucianism. As far as *jen* is concerned, the value of *li* for Confucians is that *li* provides a kind of moral code which encourages people to cultivate *jen* through doing right and avoiding wrong, and provides the rites of passage which lead human beings through the whole process of life. Through *li* a system of moral standards that can guide social life both legally and morally, and an elaborate series of religious and moral prescriptions for various personal or social ills, are established, so that in seeking after *jen* human beings are provided with a necessary route, or guide. When one of his disciples asked him how to attain to *jen*, Confucius replied that 'to control oneself and return to *li* is the way to *jen*'. When the disciple asked for more details, Confucius added that to be *jen* was 'to look at nothing which is not in accordance with *li*; to listen to nothing which is not in accordance with *li*; to speak of nothing which is not in accordance with *li*; and to do nothing which is not in accordance with *li*'.[1]

Defining the attainment of *jen* by *li* was not an innovation of Confucius. In *Tso Chuan*, we read that 'An old book tells us "to overcome oneself and return to propriety [*li*] is the way of benevolence [*jen*]"'.[2] However, Confucius expanded this saying in every possible dimension. In the paragraph quoted above, Confucius defined the attainment of *jen* and described how a person could become a person of *jen*. To become a person of *jen*, one should do two things: control oneself and return to *li*. Literally translated, as we quoted from Watson's translation, the first is 'to overcome or subdue oneself'. However, as many scholars have pointed out, this translation is misleading, or at least does not reflect the full meaning of its Chinese counterpart (*ke ji*). *Ke ji* in a Confucian context is not to suppress all one's desires and interests, but to guard against being overcome by *extreme* motives, emotions or instincts. It is concerned more with how to control oneself than with how to suppress oneself. As he looked for the right way to control oneself, Confucius concentrated on the concept of the middle way. He advised people that neither too much nor too little was the way to lead one to *jen*. In itself a desire was not wrong, but when it was aroused at an inappropriate time, or when it exceeded its proper limits, it could result in disaster. For example, Confucius once spoke of three highly dangerous desires in three respective stages of life, which required careful regulation. He said that when one was young and one's 'blood and breath' [physical powers] had not settled down, one should be on one's guard against sex; when one matured and one's physical powers were vigorous, one should be on one's guard against fighting; and when one was old, and one's physical powers were diminishing, one should be on one's guard against greed (*Analects*, XVI, 7). The key to understanding these three occasions of 'guarding against' is that they serve to correct excess of desire, and 'excess of desire' is relative to one's physical and social conditions. In this way, 'to control oneself' is understood as 'following the middle way' rather than a sheer negative attitude towards oneself.

The same is true of the term 'to return to *li*'. In one sense, *li* is a recognized moral code. However, to return to *li* is neither a passive submission to external requirements, nor a negation of one's self-cultivation. External norms are necessary only because they can help one find the middle way conducive to self-cultivation. *Li* as moral rules should not be allowed to dominate or transgress human nature; rather, *li* must be in harmony with *jen*. It has been observed that there is both harmony and tension between *jen* and *li*. As regards harmony, *li* is the externalization of *jen*, and *jen* is the internalization of *li*. *Li* would be void without *jen*, and *jen* could not find expression as virtue without *li*. As regards tension, *jen* is, in Buddhist terminology, one's self-nature and *li* is one's other-nature. For example, Tu Wei-ming firmly believes that *jen* is above *li*: '*jen* as inner morality is not caused by the *li* from outside. It is a higher-order concept which gives meaning to *li*. *Jen* in this sense is basically linked with the self-receiving, self-perfecting, and self-fulfilling process of an individual.'[3] While we may agree that *jen* is a higher-order concept in Confucianism, it is a mistake to separate *jen* as a principle of inwardness and *li* as a principle of outwardness. *Jen* involves both the inner world and the outer world of human beings. It is both a transformative force within one's personality and an integrating power in one's social and cultural environment. Only when the encompassing power of *jen* is considered can the harmony and tension between *jen* and *li* in Confucianism be appreciated, not in the sense of a contrast between autonomy and heteronomy as in Kantian ethics, but in the sense of a harmony in tension as with *agape* and law in Christian tradition.

To follow the middle way and to be guided by *li* provides Confucians with the practical means of being virtuous, by which a person may attain to *jen*. Thus the true meaning of 'to control oneself and return to *li*' is that it is a means to transforming oneself from what one is to what one should be. This transformation proves to be extremely difficult and needs courage and a strong will. For Confucius, the world remained below the moral standard because there were not yet many people of *jen*. The reason why there were not yet many people of *jen* was that they lacked the will to raise their own existence from the natural state to the moral state. Of course, to raise oneself from being subject to physical needs to being above these needs is not to disregard totally one's needs and desires. For example, to be wealthy is taken as one of the most urgent needs. There is no reason that we must reject it. Rather, if possible everyone is justified in pursuing it (*Analects* VII, 12). However, one remains subject to one's physical needs if one knows nothing but the satisfaction of one's needs by any means. By contrast, those who strive to promote themselves to moral being accept or pursue wealth only if it is obtainable through righteous means. The wealth and rank that comes through immoral means is taken only as floating clouds, which have nothing to do with one's being (VII, 16). In adopting different attitudes towards different kinds of wealth, one's character is cultivated and *jen* is manifested.

Since *jen* must be cultivated by, and obtained through, conformity of life and conduct with the principles of morality, it is not unlike the ancient Greek understanding of *arete* (virtue). In Greek philosophy, virtue is connected with human nature, and for Plato and Aristotle, human nature has a determinate form. For Aristotle, virtue is understood as a mean between two extremes. Such ideas can also be found in the Confucian theory of *jen* as virtue. However, *arete* in Greek is a 'word which by itself is incomplete'.[4] Even after Socrates, Plato and Aristotle had rescued its meaning from the 'valour' of Homeric society and had used it as a specific term for human excellence, *arete* was still too general to be defined. Its 'central meaning in Greek philosophy was excellence of any kind, but from the beginning it was also associated with the idea of fulfilment of function: excellence, whether in animate or inanimate objects, consists in the fullest performance of the object's function or its power to achieve the fullest performance.'5 For Greek philosophers, *arete* is a fulfilment of one's function and so a kind of 'efficiency'. It is true that Aristotle tried to attach to *arete* a specific idea of humanity. However, it is not clear to what extent he could be said to have succeeded. For most Greek philosophers, *arete* of human beings combines aspects of human physiology and social ethics. Since *arete* is human excellence, it must include beauty and strength of body. For the Greeks this was so important that they instituted the Olympic competitions to encourage people to attain their ideal. They believed that there was an unbroken tie between beauty of body and goodness of soul, and the ladder of virtues culminated in physical beauty as well as in moral goodness. When they granted the title of *arete* to victors in the games, either they were restricting the concept of *arete* to a limited sphere or they were expressing the naïve idea that 'good at something' implied 'good at everything'.

Turning now to the Confucian understanding of *jen,* we find that the idea of virtue as efficiency also appeared in the conversations of Confucius. When Confucius required his disciples to show filial regard to parents, to be respectful to brothers, to cultivate friendship with the good, and to love the people, what he stressed was the need to perform one's duties to the utmost and to carry out human works most efficiently. The difference between Confucius' *jen* and Greek *arete* lies in the range and order of their application. The ancient Greeks understood *arete* as a concept applicable to the performance of any object, so that for them *arete* was primarily a metaphysical concept, while its application to human virtue was only secondary. However, Confucius believed that *jen* as virtue was concerned firstly with humanity, and only then was it to be extended to the metaphysical level. Although all beings participated in *jen,* it was human beings who could fully realize it. In the unity of humans and the universe, the former were always given primary position and were held responsible for the proper order of the latter. Thus comes another difference between *jen* and *arete. Arete* starts with metaphysical existence and ends as a philosphical term. This fact demonstrates that *arete* is essentially a philosophical concept. However, *jen* starts with humanity and ends in the integration between humanity and the universe. This fact demonstrates that *jen* is not only an ethical concept, but also a religious ideal. To be good thus obtains a meaning more than being moral. 'To be good' is a way to transcendence, or is itself the process of self-transcending.

Since *jen* is both ethical and religious, in describing the human ideal it is itself independent and complete. It is not necessary to add other qualities to *jen*, since there is nothing that *jen* has not yet included in itself. Although in the *Book of Poetry jen* is also used together with the word 'handsome' to mean a perfect person, and in this instance refers to a specific virtue, i.e. beauty of mind, as opposed to beauty of body,[6] this usage did not appear again in other Confucian classics. The Greek identification of physical beauty and ethical goodness does not occur in the Confucian tradition. *Jen* as virtue was sufficient for human perfection, and as a moral quality it was different from, and preferred to, strength of body. Physical things could not be given the status of the good unless they were steps towards moral goodness.

Concerning the nature and yardstick of virtue, one of the main similarities between Confucius and Aristotle is that both regard the mean as a criterion of virtue, and following the middle way as one of the essential characteristics of a good person. For Aristotle, 'Virtue is a state of character concerned with choice, lying in a mean, i.e., the mean relative to us, this being determined by a rational principle, and by that principle by which the man of practical wisdom would determine it.'[7] The mean is also essential for understanding the Confucian concept of *jen*. Human beings, though possessing a good nature, can very easily go to extremes if they are not regulated by *li*, the performance of the mean. Without a proper sense of the middle way, without being regulated by *li*, even behaviour which was normally good would appear ridiculous and become inappropriate. For example, 'Courtesy not guided by *li* becomes tiresome; caution not guided by *li* becomes timidity; daring not guided by *li* becomes turbulence; and frankness not guided by *li* becomes effrontery' (*Analects*, VIII, 2). On the contrary, a person of *jen* is not a person of rigid dogma, because he would always regulate his own attitude and behaviour according to *li*. Therefore he does everything exactly right, no more nor less, because he would always follow the middle way, neither going too far nor falling too short (XI, 16). A person of *jen* is also a person who has achieved a balance between his natural attributes and his acquired character, because 'when nature prevails over culture, a person will be a boor; but when culture prevails over nature, a person will be a pedant' (VI, 18). By following the middle way, a person of *jen* can be 'generous without extravagance, get work out of people without arousing resentment, have desires without being greedy, be proud without being arrogant and majestic without being fierce' (XX, 2). One poem from the *Book of Poetry* begins with a description of a lover's grief at being separated from his lady love and ends with a description of their joyful reunion. Confucius saw in it more than a mere poetic artifice. He insisted that the principle of the poem, 'pleasure, but not carried to the point of debauch; grief, but not carried to the point of self-injury',[8] should be a general guiding principle for the whole of life, whether at home or in the state or in the community. Confucius himself embodied the mean so completely in his own life that it became the mark of his character. His disciples described him in this way: 'The Master was cordial yet stern, awe-inspiring yet not fierce, respectful yet at ease' (VII, 38). Since *jen* and the mean were closely connected, and the mean was taken as the only way to *jen*, it was very natural for Confucians to identify them or to use them interchangeably. The mean for Confucius was the virtue which people needed just as they needed fire and water (*Analects*, VI, 29). In the *Doctrine of the Mean* and the later form of Confucian philosophy, the mean was promoted to be the universal virtue which governed every operation in the universe.

By *li* one would follow the mean, and from the mean one could attain to the moral good, that is, *jen*. The close relation between *jen* and moral goodness has led many sinologists to translate *jen* as 'Good' or 'goodness'. Indeed, to be *jen* is to be a good ruler, a good citizen, a good parent, a good child, a good husband, a good wife, and a good neighbour. However, there is something in *jen* more than merely observing moral rules. To be *jen* is a process of self-transformation. One cannot attain to *jen* if one's endeavour is aiming at anything else other than one's own moral growth. This is why Confucius stressed that one practised *jen* for oneself rather than for anybody or anything else.[9] Only out of one's own power and for one's own growth can one transform oneself. Therefore, Mencius calls for 'practising *jen* and righteousness out of one's own heart', while rejecting the principle of putting *jen* and righteousness into practice merely for the sake of following moral rules (*The Book of Mencius*, 4B:19). Although both involve the observation of moral rules, the former is essentially a self-transformation, which may result in one's transcendence, while the latter is a conformity to the moral requirements, which can bring to oneself only a good reputation.

Like the Greek *arete*, which is a relative term and to which it is always possible to ask such questions as what *arete* is and whose *arete* it is, there seems to be no fixed model for *jen* in Confucian conversations. It was described differently in different cases and for different people, and some descriptions even contradicted themselves, as Wing-tsit Chan has discovered.[10] It is true that *jen* is itself a complex concept and that it embraces many aspects of a virtuous life, by which the comprehensive meaning of *jen* is manifested. In discussing this variety of the manifestations of *jen*, Confucius purposely revealed different aspects in different conversations with different pupils, so that his audience could grasp what was the most important for them and the most useful for guiding their own lives. To further our inquiry into the variety of *jen*, we must see that *jen* is the power of self-transformation, raising one's natural existence to moral and therefore transcendental existence. Since this transcending must be made by oneself and there is no other power except *jen* one can rely on, one has to find one's own way to attain *jen*.

For some people, the first thing that must be done for self-transformation is to keep themselves from bad habits, because these habits would wreck their efforts to transcend the limitation of life. One such habit is a show of sincerity in good words rather than in good behaviour. Confucius denied that a person like this could ever be a person of *jen*: 'It is rare for a person with cunning words and a pretentious manner to be *jen*' (*Analects*, I, 3). On the contrary, 'To be firm, enduring, simple and modest', though still short of *jen*, is 'near *jen*' (XIII, 27), because all such attitudes and behaviour represent one's true self and are the opposite of hypocrisy and self-indulgence. To be a person of *jen* requires the practice of virtue, and the constant practice of virtue can enable one to attain to *jen*. Therefore, the constant practice of what is required by *jen* was also regarded as 'being near *jen*'.

For others, the most urgent task is to engage actively in human interaction. Human beings cannot completely isolate themselves from their fellow men and women. Both in practice and in theory, there is a need to find a proper way by which one can balance one's own cultivation and one's interaction with others. Confucius disagreed with Taoists who insisted that the only way to reach the ideal was to cut oneself off from the corrupt world. Anyone who devoted himself to *tao* must live in community and perform his duties. In order to walk on the path to *jen*, one should carefully choose one's living quarters, keep away from those who have bad character and keep in close touch with those who have manifested

the virtue of *jen.* Confucius compared the choice of good circumstances by a person who wished to be *jen* with the sharpening of
a tool by a craftsman who wanted to do good work. Although
a good tool did not necessarily lead to good art, nevertheless it
was very important for doing so. 'Tzu-kung asked about how to
be *jen.* The Master said: A craftsman who wishes to work well
must first sharpen his tools. Whatever state you are living in, take
service with the most worthy among the great officers, and make
friends with persons of *jen* among scholars' (*Analects,* XV, 9; XIX,
7). Contact with, and service of, the worthy and virtuous, although
not necessary to enable one to be a person of *jen,* was regarded as an
effective means of living the good life. From this paragraph we can
see that Confucius believed that one's social circumstances could
influence one's personality and one's moral growth, a theme which
was finely developed later by Mencius.

Still for others, to be *jen* is to have a good character. A person of
jen has no anxiety and enjoys a peaceful, quiet and long life, so that
he can rest content with his virtue, in which he has found complete
harmony and happiness (*Analects,* IX, 29; VI, 23; IV, 2). To attain
jen, one must work hard before one achieves the goal. One must
be diligent in the performance of all his duties: in private life one
must be courteous and sincere; in serving the state, respectful and
punctilious; in providing for the needs of the people, graceful and
generous; in requiring service from the people, just and righteous
(*Analects,* V, 16). When so doing, one not only cultivates one's
character, but also bring benefits to others and harmony to the state,
which is the manifestation of one's virtue. The moral strength of *jen*
enables one to exert a much greater influence than seems possible.
One day Confucius said that he would go and settle among the
Nine Barbarian Tribes in the East. His disciples asked in surprise
how their master could put up with the people there, since they
were notoriously rude and uncivilized. Confucius quietly replied
that 'if a *chun tzu* lived there, what rudeness would there be?'
(*Analects,* IX, 14). In order to exert moral influence, one must practise
the Five Virtues in one's dealing with the world: respectfulness,
liberality, truthfulness, diligence and generosity (*Analects,* XVII,
6). In practising these virtues, one may make mistakes, but one
should be never too ashamed to admit one's mistakes, and one
must correct them as soon as one realizes them. Admitting and
correcting them does not reduce the worth of one's personality
but makes one even more worthy of respect (*Analects,* I, 8). To

attain to *jen,* one must be careful about one's words and action, such as 'acting before speaking and then speaking according to one's action', 'being ashamed if one's words exceed one's deeds', and 'from every attitude, every gesture that one employs, removing all trace of violence or arrogance; in every look that one composes on one's face, betokening good faith; from every word that one utters and from every intonation, removing all traces of coarseness or impropriety' (*Analects,* II, 13; XIV, 27; VIII, 4). Good attitudes, gestures, looks, words, intonation, all are necessary parts of *jen* and therefore are taken as efficient ways to *jen,* although none of them can be identified with *jen* itself.

Jen manifests itself as virtues and shows people how to transcend their limitation. However, *jen* is not an ordinary virtue. *Jen* is a higher virtue than others, indeed, the highest virtue among all the virtues. When Confucius said, 'Love of knowledge is near wisdom; keeping practice is near *jen;* and sensitiveness to shame is near courage', and 'The person of wisdom has no perplexity; the person of *jen* has no worry; and the person of courage has no fear' (*Analects,* IX, 29; XIV, 28), he seemed to be contrasting *jen* with other virtues like wisdom and courage. However, there can be no doubt that he regarded *jen* as a higher virtue than wisdom and courage. In Book IV, Confucius made this contrast very sharply: without *jen,* a person, though wise and brave, could not for long endure poverty and hardship, nor for long enjoy prosperity. A person of *jen* pursued *jen* because he felt at home in *jen,* whereas a person of wisdom pursued *jen* in order to benefit himself.[11] *Jen* was also higher than courage: 'A person of *jen* will certainly possess courage, but a brave person does not necessarily possess *jen'* (*Analects,* IV, 2; XIV, 4). Confucius expressed his doubts on many occasions as to whether a particular good action or a particular good talent could earn one the virtue of *jen.* Confucius appreciated the talents of his disciples, such as skills at administering a big state or the ability to command a large army, but he could not agree that there was any necessary connection between these talents and a person of *jen* (*Analects,* V, 5; V, 8). Confucius fought against moral ills and called for the elimination of bad habits; nevertheless he declined to ascribe *jen* to a person who had avoided such vices as aggressiveness, boasting, resentment and covetousness, because the conquest of these undesirable characteristics, though very difficult, was still short of *jen* (*Analects,* XIV, 1). *Jen* enables one to be a person of uprightness and perfection. For an upright and just person, only the truth and the Way should be taken as his standard, and his desires and decisions must be examined in the light of *jen*. As Confucius said: 'Wealth and honour are what everybody desires. But if they are to be obtained in violation of *tao*, one should refrain. Poverty and a lowly social status are what everybody dislikes. But if they are to be avoided by violating *tao*, one should not avoid them' (*Analects*, IV, 5). In order to be a person of *jen*, one should be ready to give up one's life so that one can keep in harmony with *jen*.

That *jen* is higher than all other virtues is also due to the fact that *jen* is taken as the basis on which the other virtues are built and the root from which the tree of virtues gets its nutrition. *Jen* is not confined to any single virtue but penetrates all virtues. As the basis of all the virtues, *jen* gives meaning to filial piety (XVII, 21), to wisdom (V, 8), to *li* (propriety XII, 1), to courage (XIV, 5), and to loyalty (XVIII, 1). As the totality of virtues, *jen* precludes all evils: 'If you set your mind on *jen*, you will be free from evil' (*Analects*, IV, 4), because evil is the opposition to *jen* in the sense that it arises from the frustration of *jen's* growth. Freedom from evil and abundance of goodness can easily lead one to exert one's humanity to its utmost and so to reach the human ideal.

Whatever one needs to do in order to attain to transcendence, it is always associated with the exploration of *jen*, which is the master of all virtues. This argument was further developed in later Confucianism, and *jen* is understood as the root and basis of all virtues, like righteousness, propriety, wisdom, and faithfulness, which are only different expressions of *jen*. If these virtues are compared with one's four limbs, then *jen* is one's body. All learning and all practice are to be related to *jen*: what one has to learn is the essence of *jen*, and what one has to practise is the nurture and expression of *jen*. In *jen* human virtues are developed to the ultimate, and by *jen* human beings achieve their ideal: a harmonious identification not only between oneself and others, but also between human beings and nature.[12] Although Confucians speak of four virtues, nevertheless, 'Spoken of separately, it [*jen*] is one of the several, but spoken of collectively, it embraces all four.'[13] Chu Hsi developed the earlier concept of *jen* as the root of all virtues into his concept of *jen* as the Vital Force. As Vital Force, *jen* is flowing in human beings as well as in the universe. By *jen* human beings become the noblest creatures in the world, and by possessing *jen* humans harmonize their own lives and enrich the world. Therefore, *jen* not only illustrates goodness and perfection, but also produces all the virtues and is indeed the 'parent or master of all the virtues'. Therefore, *jen* is the principle of love and the way of growth. From *jen*, the principles of reverence, wisdom and righteousness are produced. Therefore, 'from the point of view of priority Love [*jen*] is first; from the point of view of greatness Love [*jen*] is greatest'.[14] The highest virtue, however, is not only a virtue, but a summary of human life. Moreover, it is not only a summary of human life, but also a fundamental principle of the universe. *Jen* as the highest virtue transcends the limitation of human morality and links to the power of the cosmos and the life of the universe. In this sense, *jen* as virtue enters the realm of religion, a humanistic transcendence.

AGAPE AS HUMAN RESPONSE: LOVE FOR GOD

Like Confucian *jen*, which offers the means to transcend human limitation, Christian *agape* is taken as the only hope for human salvation. Unlike Confucian *jen*, which is both a human quality and a universal substance, Christian *agape* is essentially divine and humanity cannot initiate it by themselves. *Agape* must be infused into the human heart from the divine. Humans are to respond to this infusion and thus *agape* obtains its human form. However, this response is not like the reflection of light by a mirror, such that it does not enter into the inner being of the responder; rather, the human response to the divine calling involves a positive process of reception and appropriation, in which *agape* is incorporated into the human self. Without this subjectivization of the objective command, *agape* would fail to be the Christian principle and human *agape* would not come into being.

Human *agape* is basically applicable to two kinds of love, love for God and love for other humans. These two forms of human love are distinct but inseparable. One of the most important features of Christian doctrine is that it does not recognize a separation between love for God and love for men. Jesus saw all the commandments as a single comprehensive commandment which had its source in God, and 'refused to play off the command to love God against the command to love men'.[15] Thus, human *agape*, which comes from God's command, must be taken as a unity of two commands: love for God and love for humans; and both forms of love are the same response to God's command. However, in order to explore human *agape* and compare it with Confucian *jen*, it is necessary for us to discuss them one by one. In this chapter we shall consider *agape* as the human response in which it takes the form of human love for God, and in the following chapter, *agape* as the human response in which it assumes the form of human love for one another.

The theistic character of human *agape* means that it must be understood in the light of divine command. As command, *agape* is first taken as a calling from God. To this calling, humans must respond with love, whereby communion between God and humans is established. The command of God to love is manifested in the covenant which God made to communicate his words, his will and love to humans. The covenant requires a faithful human response, just as God faithfully adheres to the covenant. In order for the covenant and its consequent duties to be observed, there needs to be a system of law, regarded as the express embodiment of the covenant. In the Bible, this work of law-giving is credited to Moses, who explicitly promulgated the commandments of God. The law is not only, or not primarily, understood as a system of legal codes, but as the underlying natural and moral law, coming from God and applicable universally. However, according to the writers of the N.T., the proper understanding of the law revealed by God was gradually replaced by the dogmatic concept of a legal system, and law was revered, not as the means of communication between God and humans, but as the historical and religious enactment of priestly privilege. Jesus and his followers blamed this corruption for the failure to carry out the true mission which God had laid upon his people. Thus, on the one hand, they too were committed to the law until the day when the new creation should be revealed in glory; on the other hand, they tried to renew the true understanding of the law and of the true human attitude towards it. The heart of this understanding, according to Jesus, was that the law acts as a bridge between God's command and human response, but that it is not the command itself. Thus human obedience to the law is first of all obedience to God's command, not to human authorities. Obedience to God's law not only leads to faith in God, but also to the virtues that are essential for Christian community. Consequently, *agape* as human response to God's command brings forth, and reveals itself in, three excellent qualities of human life: sincere love, insistent faith and comprehensive virtue. These three qualities are essentially manifestations of a human attitude to God. As a response to God's command of love, they are a form of religious piety. However, they are also the sum of the good qualities which human beings should strive for, and they carry in themselves the clear mark of ethical requirements, making a deep impression on the life of Christian communities.

As in many other cases, the Christian concept of *agape* as human response to God's command originated in the Israelite tradition. Clearly, the command stems from the authority of God over all other beings and affairs. The universe, humans, history and human affairs are all under God's control and command (Psalms 33:9). The aim of this command is not to separate God from his creatures, but to bring his creatures, namely, humans, to God. 'The ultimate purpose for which this effective control is exercised is to create a community which, in all the detail of its life, will show the characteristics of the people of God, and thus bring credit to him.'[16] What are the characteristics of the people of God? How can the people develop these characteristics? The Hebrew approach to these questions was through 'the guidance or instruction which comes from God through the oracular utterances of the priests or through the prophets; it [*torah*] is the whole content of God's revelation of his nature and purpose, which incidentally makes clear man's responsibility before God.'[17] Later, this guidance and instruction gradually gave way to a detailed legal code, and became the basic system of rules and regulations for the whole Israelite community, religious and secular.

Historically, it was Moses who was credited with being the mediator, through God's commandments, of the Israelites' communication with God. As a term, 'commandment' is synonymous with 'statutes', 'judgements' and 'ordinances', and denotes edicts or decrees from a person possessing authority. The commandments from God were taken as the basis of those from human authorities, or, as we should say, there could be no human authority without God's command. God's command is expressed on many different occasions and in many kinds of commandments, each issued for a particular case or time. However, the term 'commandment' in the Judeo-Christian tradition is specially used for the Ten Commandments promulgated by Moses. Among these ten commandments, the first four are concerned with relations with God, and the other six with human relations.

The Ten Commandments were later developed and extended into a complicated system of more detailed commandments, which were all claimed to come from God. Although there are so many commandments, it is assumed that one commandment underlies all the others. This is the chief commandment both for Jews and for Christians. It is the commandment to love God: 'Love the Lord your God with all your heart and with all your soul and with all your strength' (Deuteronomy 6:5). This love, itself rooted in God's love for his people, is a response to, and an imitation of, God's love. To love God, one must walk in God's way, serving him (10:12), honouring him and following all the requirements of God's law (17:19). This love cannot be produced from within the human heart itself; it must have first come from God's grace. As God himself speaks through the prophet: 'I have loved you with an everlasting love; I have drawn you with loving-kindness' (Jeremiah 31:3).

According to Matthew, Jesus did not come to abolish the Law or Prophets, but to fulfil them (5:17). In fulfilling the commandments, however, he radically extended the notion of love and pointed to a deeper relation between love and commandment: the essence of the commandments is love, and love itself is commanded. This commanded love was not to be based on the fear of punishment, but on the promise of forgiveness, which Jesus had come to bring. So, according to the writer of Fourth Gospel, Jesus brought with him both the commandment and the love, whereby humans might find eternity: Jesus' 'commandment is eternal life' (John 12:50). To remain in Jesus' love, which comes from the Father, is to obey his commands, which are God's commandments. Through this obedience Jesus is said to have found his joy in humans, and human joy is promised to be complete. When one does what Jesus commands, one becomes his friend rather than his servant. A servant does not know the master's love and mission, while a friend does. Fellowship between humans and Jesus enables humans, whether rich or poor, humble or noble, to share all God's gift, the greatest of which is love (John 15:9–15). Recipients of God's love, the only response humans should make is to return love to God. In this context, while obedience to the commandments is also emphasized, love and command are fully integrated. For Paul, too, this response of humans to Christ is of fundamental significance, although he prefers to refer to this response in other ways, especially in terms of faith. Whatever words he uses, however, love is always their context and content. Faith is active in love: 'God's love makes faith possible and man's love gives it visibility and effect in the world'.[18]

The greatest theologian of his time, St Augustine, followed this line and continued to affirm the integrity of love and command. For him, human reason is unable to grasp the divine grace. However, three texts of Scripture reveal what humans need to know and give them a chance to respond to God's command. The first, Augustine said, is a saying of Jesus Christ: love God with all your heart and all your soul and all your mind. This command imposes upon humans an absolute obligation. To respond to this command, humans must devote themselves to Jesus Christ, whose love comes from God's love. The second text, which is taken as guidance for life, is Paul's word that love for God works everything for human good, and Augustine affirms that God is not only the Supreme Good but also the 'sum of all our good things'. In response to this text, loving God and pursuing the Good become one. And the third text, also from Paul, declares that nothing can separate us from the love of Christ.[19] For Augustine, these three texts constitute a unity of command and love which originates from love for God, culminates in the fulfilment and happiness of union with God which result from this love, and is bound together in the love of Christ. The only adequate response to God's love and to the divine command is a deep love for and devotion to Jesus Christ who is himself love.

For Augustine, the proper human response to God is to love God faithfully and sincerely. However, humans are finite while God is infinite and unknowable to human reason. How, then, can humans love God of whom they have little or no knowledge? Augustine did not believe that human love can bring us to know God, nor that we can come to know God through loving our neighbours. He argued that the only way in which we could know God and therefore love God was through God himself, by God giving his presence to the human soul as fire enlightens what it kindles. This doctrine that human communion with God is possible only through God's self-giving deeply influenced Western Christian thinking concerning human response to God's love and was a contributory cause of the Protestant Reformation.

As a response, love is in some ways similar to faith. Faith in God and in Jesus Christ is the primary expression of human *agape*. To follow Jesus and to be with Jesus is taken as evidence of loving God and the basic condition for being called a Christian: 'He who is not with me is against me, and he who does not gather with me scatters' (Matthew 12:30). This declaration directly points to a bond that unites humans with Christ in a relationship of love. Paul linked love for God with love for Jesus on the cross, and thus love becomes a response to the sacrifice of Jesus who died for humans and brought new life to the sinful world. Human love for Christ entails faith in him and the willingness to carry the cross with him. Being united with Christ, humans have died with him and been raised with him, so leaving the world of sin and entering God's eternal kingdom. Therefore, 'love is both the context and the content of faith; God's love makes faith possible and *man's* love gives it visibility and effect in the world'.[20] Jesus becomes the way and the truth and the life, and no one can come to God the Father except through Jesus the Son. Therefore, both God's own love and love for God are united in Jesus. Identification of love of Jesus with love for Jesus can be seen clearly in Jesus' washing his disciples' feet (John 13:5), whereby he shows them the full extent of his love for them while at the same time giving them an example of how to respond to his love. To respond to this love in action, humans should also exercise love in action and devote themselves to the mission to which Jesus calls them.

Love as command and love as response to command are the same in content but are different in form. For this reason, some Christian theologians feel it necessary first to differentiate them and even to separate them, although they admit that these two kinds of love are associated and linked together. The divine love is, in the words of C. S. Lewis, pure Gift-love, while human love is essentially Need-love,[21] and these are two different kinds of love. God's love becomes the model for human love, while human love is an extension of God's self-giving love in the form of a loving response. 'God, as Creator of nature, implants in us both Gift-loves and Need-loves. The Gift-loves are natural images of Himself; proximities to Him by resemblance which are not necessarily and in all men proximities of approach.' In contrast, the Need-loves 'have no resemblance to the Love which God is. They are rather correlatives, opposites; not as evil is the opposite of good, of course, but as the form of the blancmange is an opposite to the form of the mould.'[22] Anders Nygren distinguishes God's love and human love for God, and rejects the concept of human *agape*: the former is called *agape* because it is spontaneous and self-sufficient, while the latter is called faith because it has the character of a response and its keynote is receptivity.[23]

As many critics have pointed out, the distinction between God's love and the human response to God has its value in clarifying the terminology and in protecting the purity of Christian faith. However, they have also challenged its legitimacy, because they believe that this distinction destroys the unity between God and human beings which is characteristic of the Christian doctrine of love. In fact, the artificial distinction between faith and *agape* agrees neither with common sense nor with the scriptures. Neither the prophets in the O.T. nor Jesus nor the writers of the Gospels hesitated to use 'love' to indicate the proper human response to God's love: you shall love God with all your heart and strength. They did not, like Nygren, replace love in these contexts with a phrase such as 'have faith in God', because they could not see any contradiction between these two expressions. To have faith in God is to love God. These two attitudes are the same, but with different names. Love for God is indeed a response. However, this love, imitating God's love, is able to share its self-giving and self-affirming. Human love comes from God's love, but it also comes from one's own heart. Spontaneity and receptivity are not as distinguishable in respect of love as Nygren suggests, and the need-love and the gift-love of the human response to God are not as separable as Lewis sometimes implies. It is true that, as response, human love has to wait for its initiation from God. However, the responsiveness of human love should not reduce its value as a person's own devotion. Without a measure of spontaneity, human love for God would be compelled rather than evoked. Compelled love is something that Christianity has opposed since its very beginning.

We have shown that love for God is a response to God's love. However, the question remains: what is the content of a Christian response? To answer this question, we return to the doctrine of the covenant in Israelite tradition, because the response to God's love is clearly revealed in the human attitude adopted to the covenant with God. As far as love is concerned, the Covenant does not differ much from the Commandments. Both are given by God, and both are particular manifestations of God's command and of God's love. As we have discussed in the last chapter, God is the maker and sustainer of the covenant. Without God's grace and love, there would be no covenant at all. Because of God's unswerving love, the covenant remains secure and is not broken by the sins of the Israelites. How, then, should humans respond to this sustaining love? The prophets called for the imitation of God's faithfulness and for complete devotion to God's covenant. That is to say, the human response consists of faithfulness, loyalty and piety towards God.

To enact the Covenant it was necessary to establish the requirements of the Covenant in a written code or the Book of the Covenant.

In this way a legal and moral code developed which eventually established the law as the norm of daily life for the post-exilic community. The Israelites were required to reverence and obey the laws, which included not only the Ten Commandments but also many other rites and rules, prescribing what must be done and what must not be done. When Jesus proclaimed his message, he needed to explain the relation between the commandments of the law and the spirit of love. He rejected the established teaching, in which the commandments were understood dogmatically and impersonally, because such an interpretation of law had lost the spirit of love and become an oppressive instrument of the establishment. Paul showed how, because of human nature, the law and commandments had come to play a contradictory role, by creating opportunities for sin to thrive among humans. Thus 'the very commandment that was intended to bring life actually brought death' (Romans 7:10). Nevertheless, the law and commandments were, for Paul, holy, righteous and good. They made humans struggle against sin within and search for the gospel of redemption. In the love of Christ humans found their salvation and peace, and in his new life the externality of the law and commandments was replaced by the internality of the human response of love. Through the cross 'a new humanity' was created (Ephesians 2:14–16).

What is this internality of human response? In answering this question, Christian theologians shed light on human nature and virtue. In the O.T., human nature is seldom discussed directly, except for the claim that humans were made in the image of God and that they had fallen from a state of primeval innocence, acquiring knowledge, and a sense of right and wrong, but losing the life of paradise. Christianity formulated a new doctrine of human nature in the light of the salvation brought by Jesus Christ and his God-given power to redeem humans from their sin and give them everlasting life. Paul, for example, speaks of a constant struggle between the 'sinful I' and the 'spiritual I'. The spirit wills to do what is good, but the sinful flesh makes the will impotent. Hence the wrong that is done is done by the sin which dwells within humans. The good will cannot bring forth good acts because of sin, and the painful split that results is such that 'What I do is not the good I want to do; no, the evil I do not want to do – this I keep doing'. In their inner being, humans may delight in God's law, but the law of the body wages war against the law of the mind, so that they become slaves of sin (Romans 7:19–23). Because of this split, the only hope for humans lies in Jesus Christ, who delivers humans from sin by his death and resurrection. Christ will raise those who are his from life on earth to life in glory. The life that is raised by God is not the life that is sown. 'What is sown is perishable, what is raised imperishable; it is sown in dishonour, it is raised in glory; it is sown in weakness, it is raised in power; it is sown a natural body, it is raised a spiritual body' (II Corinthians 15:42–44). As in many other cases, the resurrection of humans must be understood in the context of the love of God, which is revealed in Jesus Christ's saving work (Romans 5:8; 8:35). However, the human response to God's raising to new life is also very important. Those who are loved by God and Jesus Christ will respond with love; and those who have responded with love will enter the sphere of God's love and attain to eternal life. Although the human response to God's love is mostly described by Paul as faith (*pistis*), or even knowledge (*gnosis*), it is also set forth as love (*agape*).[24]

Since everything that is good in humans must be understood in the light of God's love and the proper human response to God's command, virtue (in Greek, *arete*), or goodness, does not play a significant part in the vocabulary of either the O.T. or the N.T. 'Virtue' is, first of all, a term used of the praiseworthy acts of God (Isaiah 43:21 and I Peter 2:9); but it can also be used to signify God's attribute of perfection. Through his manifestations of power (*dynameis*) God has granted gifts to men, by which they in their turn may become partakers of the divine nature (*theias physeos*), i.e. share in the divine virtue of perfection (II Peter 1:3–4, and Matthew 5:48).[25] In this usage divine love and human response are again related. As a response to God's perfection, virtue is the appreciation of 'whatever is good, whatever is just, whatever is honourable and whatever is lovely' (Philippians 4:8). As response, the virtues are themselves good. However, all the virtues, whether affection, friendship, patience, kindness, faithfulness, gentleness and self-control, or goodness, 'are brought under the main concepts of love (Galatians 5:22; Ephesians 4:32, 5:2; Col. 3:12) or of faith (Ephesians 4:2 ff; I Peter 1:5) and are controlled by these'; and therefore, the Christian conception of virtue is essentially understood as the human response to God's love and is different from the Greek understanding of virtue as excellence. The Greek philosophical notion of the virtues as secular and autonomous qualities was, in Paul and reformed theology, taken up 'by the Spirit-given freedom of the Christian, which is both developed and maintained in love'.[26]

The concept of virtue as the response of human *agape* raises another question for Christian theologians: how to reconcile the grace which controls human destiny with the human freedom to choose between doing good and doing evil. Augustine was the first theologian seriously to explore the Christian doctrine of free will and, correspondingly, the idea of merit and virtue. He believed that Christ did not extinguish the individual will and that God's working in human hearts was never a matter of compulsion. However, what free-will could accomplish is not a matter of obedience to human commands or the attainment of human goals, but a matter of response to God's command or Jesus' calling. Therefore, a proper response of humans to the perfection and love of God takes the form of human merit, since it is a human achievement through God's gifts: both the fact that we believe and the fact that we perform what is good 'are ours, because of our will's free choice, and yet both are given, through the Spirit of faith and love'.[27] Therefore, merit and virtue are possible in the sense that they arise from a proper human response to God's grace; they are also necessary, in the sense that they are the path to ultimate happiness and to the love of God itself. 'Virtues prove nothing but the perfection of love to God,' and therefore they themselves are forms or manifestations of love. This love is not an affectionate emotion, but a devoted resolution of love for God, with the goal of union with God. Love for God as a response to God's love is the whole of human life and includes all forms of love: love of the human mind, of the heart and of the lower soul. The love of the mind is the Platonic *eros*, which desires and yearns for union with God; the heart offers love to the neighbour, and is part of the love for God; and the love of the lower soul is to care for oneself, which means to give one's self to God. There are three theological virtues. However, according to Augustine, love is more important than the other two. For him, faith is important, because it can bring knowledge and growth. But knowledge and growth must be controlled by love. Christian communities, or churches, are means by which one can find the path to life and the love of God. 'The life of virtue is the life of love, and eternal life is its reward'.[28] Since love is a gift from God's love, virtue is firmly based on the ground of human response in the form of love for God.

Unlike Augustine, who was deeply influenced by neo-Platonism, Thomas Aquinas (1224–74) successfully integrated Platonic and Aristotelian philosophy with Christian theology and explored thereby the human response to God's love in the form of virtue and goodness. Aquinas insisted that God's life was beatitude, and that human participation in it exceeded all natural powers. By sharing in God's love, it was possible to recover the 'super-nature' that characterizes the 'New People'. Human love for God does indeed derive from God's grace, which spreads abroad in human hearts through the Holy Spirit given to them. However, this does not reduce the freedom of human love, or *caritas*. In his own words, 'grace does not abolish nature, but perfects it'. Like Paul and Augustine, Aquinas insisted that love was the most excellent of the theological virtues. In faith, humans look for truth in God; in hope, humans search for the good in God; therefore, both are a process from the outside to the inside of their object. In contrast, charity attains to God himself, 'in order to rest in Him, and not that something may accrue to us from Him', and so love is in its object.[29] Thus, love for God is in an immediate unity with God and in a complete rest in God. Human love for God is a response to God who 'is the good which of its very nature beatifies all with supernatural beatitude; he is loved with the love of charity'.[30] God endows humans with creaturely perfection. However, humans strive for ends which oppose God's will, and thus they have lost their direct communion with God and the unity of God's love and the human response. In order to restore this communion and unity God, out of his mercy, has revealed himself in the life and person of Jesus Christ, and has called the sinner out of his mercy and established a 'spiritual fellowship', so that sinners can once again be called the friends of God.[31] In this fellowship, humans gain their virtues and merits, which are cultivated in response to God's love and, indeed, are the divine rewards for human faith in Jesus Christ. In this sense, Nygren is correct when he says that 'Agape opens the way of fellowship with God.'[32]

There is no doubt that for most Christian theologians human *agape*, as response to the divine, is the most important theological virtue. Our discussion of Christian doctrine has supported the statement that among faith, love and hope, love is the greatest. The question we have still to ask is whether it can be a general virtue, ethical and theological alike.

In Christian ethics, human *agape* is commanded. Any command that is to be fulfilled must receive a response. God did not and will not implant a fixed response in human hearts, although a response is possible because of God's will and creation. Neither is a response simply an echo, nor is it an instinct of animal nature. A proper response is a combination of obedience to the commandment and conscious will and emotion. As obedience, the response is passive compliance. However, as conscious will and emotion, it is a spontaneous action, the expression of a deliberate attitude and intention. A spontaneous action is a consciously accomplished piece of behaviour, and it should therefore be treated more as a virtue or vice than simply as the act of a good or bad will. To be a general virtue, the response to the divine command must appear in two forms. It must be a response to the divine love with a sincere love that is intentionally directed to One who commands: this we call a theological virtue. Or it must cultivate the will and intention of love, and then express them in action that corresponds to the divine command: this we call an ethical virtue. In so far as it is commanded by the divine love and based on the divine command, the second form is a theological virtue. In so far as it is not controlled by the command but formed by the combination of command and choice, it may be taken as a general virtue. It responds to the command, not only by returning love to God, but also by offering love to all other beings. It is also a general virtue because it is an affectionate relationship with its object, either with God himself or with other beings or things. In the first case, it is a theological virtue, while in the second and third cases, it appears as an ethical virtue.

As is the case in its form as a theological virtue, in its form as an ethical virtue human *agape* is endowed with a much higher position in Christian ethics than other virtues, and it is seldom taken as only one virtue alongside many others. According to Gene Outka, there are two claims in modern Christian theology concerning the relationship of love with other virtues. One is the weaker claim that love has priority over other virtues only when there is a conflict. The other is the stronger claim that love is the basis of all the other virtues, providing the fundamental justifying reason for their existence and explaining the value and meaning of all other virtues.[33] It is not only a supreme virtue above all others, as, in the words of Dietrich von Hildebrand, 'the most total, central and intimate of all value responses';[34] it is also the foundation of the virtues, so that all other virtues must be explained in terms of human *agape*. The significance of human *agape* is that it is the source of all virtues, the 'bond' which unifies and perfects all virtues: 'And over all these virtues put on love, which binds them all together in perfect unity' (Colossians 3:14). As source and bond of the virtues, love is indeed understood as the core and summary of the meaning and value of the good life of a Christian. For example, in Augustine, virtue is an art or a harmony between extremes, and therefore it may be identified with the love with which what should be loved is loved: 'A concise and accurate definition of virtue is: the order of love'.[35] Love as the definition of virtue makes it possible for all human goodness to be called virtue. Therefore the following paragraph can be used to refer to the relation between love and virtue in general. 'Temperance is love keeping itself entire and incorrupt for the beloved; courage is love bearing everything gladly for the sake of the beloved; righteousness is love serving the beloved only and therefore ruling well, and prudence is love wisely discriminating between what helps it and what hinders it'.[36] While we may agree in principle with the stronger claim that love underlies all other virtues, we should also give attention to the fact that love does not preclude or replace them. Love is the principle or central thread running through all forms of virtue and is embodied in different aspects of a virtuous life. This does not, however, detract from the value of any particular virtue, because 'a virtue has an intrinsic excellence of its own'.[37]

WAYS TO TRANSCENDENCE: VIRTUE AND RESPONSE

Having originated from different sources, *jen* from humanity and *agape* from divinity, both become effective ways to transcendence. The way in Confucianism is essentially the way of self-transformation, by which one transcends one's limitation and attains to *jen*. The way in Christianity is essentially the way of turning to God, by which one responds to the divine calling and is reconciled with the divine *agape*.

Virtue plays an important role in Confucian and Christian searching for the ways to transcendence. Both *jen* and *agape* are the fountain-head of moral virtues. Confucian *jen* is not only a virtue, or even *the* virtue; it is the virtue of virtues, the basis of moral qualities and the root of moral goodness. It is *jen* that gives moral virtues their meaning and value, and it is *jen* that unifies the various aspects of a virtuous life. Similarly, Christian *agape* embraces all the virtues of human life, is the bond of virtues and the meaning of righteousness. Human *agape* is the proper response to God's love, which creates the important virtues in the human heart. All virtues are believed to be merely different manifestations of human *agape*, and humility, patience, honesty, gentleness, justice, chastity and forgiveness are taken to be the functions of Christian love. They are good because they have manifested Christian *agape*. In this sense, the root of Christian ethics is its concept of *agape*, just as that of Confucian ethics is its concept of *jen*.

As the virtue of virtues, neither Confucian *jen* nor Christian *agape* is simply a theoretical idea. They are active and generate the strength and power in humanity to fight the moral sickness that is destroying human community. However, divergences arise over what the sickness is and what are the ways in which one can fight it. For Confucianism, moral sickness is caused by the lack of *jen* in the heart. To cultivate or to restore *jen* in the heart and in society it is necessary to re-establish the authority of *li* and to reconfirm that moral rules are the externalization of *jen* rather than the arbitrary restrictions of institutions. For Christianity, moral sickness is the result of alienation from the Creator and corruption through the sin of original nature. Having lost their harmony with their Lord, humans have also lost their ability to reconcile themselves to God. They cannot overcome their condition of alienation by themselves. God, however, is the God of charity and forgiveness, who has sent to humans his only Son with the good news so that peace and harmony between the divine and the human can and will be restored. The welcome afforded by this good news marks it off from the impersonality of the traditional laws but cannot be separated from them. Thus, the relationship between love and law in Christianity bears a hallmark similar to that between *jen* and *li* in Confucianism, and the problem of dealing with the conformity and conflict between the fundamental principle and its externalization becomes the common concern of both Confucianism and Christianity.

The disorder and chaos created by rejection of God was evident in the time before Jesus when the prophets condemned sinful Israel: 'There is no faithfulness, no love, no acknowledgement of God in the land. There is only cursing, lying and murder, stealing and adultery; they break all bounds, and bloodshed follows bloodshed' (Hosea 4:1–2). The situation was no better when Jesus began to call people to repent. Moral corruption was condemned because it went against the divine will and human *agape*. To restore *agape*, it was necessary to correct these moral wrongdoings. However, Jesus did not simply condemn the people. Rather, he brought hope to the despairing, blessing to the outcast and light to the blind, fulfilling what had been said through the prophet Isaiah: 'The people living in darkness have seen a great light; on those living in the land of the shadow of death a light has dawned' (Matthew 4:14, 16).

In resolving the problems of social life, the Israelite establishment by the time of Jesus had created a tension between some of the many commandments which had accumulated in the course of its history. On the one hand, Judaism rightly attempted a systematization of these commandments, so that the people could follow the right path to their goal. On the other hand, this attempt was criticized as a wrong turn in seeking to construct a hierarchy between the lesser and the greater commandments. Jesus ascribed this division among the commandments to 'the tradition of men' (Mark 7:8), which had turned the command to love God into an empty rule and the command to love one's neighbour into an exclusive legal code. Instead, Jesus' approach was to bring the commandments together, and especially to join the two greatest commandments into a single unity, both setting forth the truly human response to the love of God and both offering new life to those who obeyed them. By integrating these two commandments and making the love of neighbour a God-given opportunity to love God, Jesus removed the tension within the tradition. A further integration of love and law was made by Paul when he affirmed that love itself was the fulfilment of law because it was out of love that Jesus had died for sinners. John completed this integration, when he affirmed that to love was to obey Jesus' teaching and to keep his command (John 14:23–24).

Another tension in the Jewish tradition existed between command and response. During their history the number of the commandments had grown. By the time of Jesus it had reached 613, with 365 negative and 248 positive. In Christian experience, however, the more commandments there are, the less clearly is one aware of their significance and therefore the less actively does one respond to them. While insisting that he had not come to abolish any of these laws, Jesus nevertheless grasped the essence of the commandments and called for a response of love with all one's heart and all one's understanding and strength. However, neither Jesus nor his followers took this response as forced or mechanical. Rather, they believed that it must be fulfilled with a sincere will and deliberate action. The rich young man would certainly have wished to listen to the divine command and follow the tradition. However, he could not respond to the command of love because he was possessed by a desire for possessions (Mark 10:17–31). A true response to the command is a restoration of heart-felt faith and a renewed devotion to the source of all human institutions. For example, everybody acknowledged the duties of husband and wife, so that divorce was a breach of the legal bond. However, Jesus grounded marriage in the faithfulness of the heart and made husband and wife responsible, not only to each other, but also to the source of life. 'What God has joined together, let man not separate' (Mark 10:9). By this remark Jesus tried not only to express his disapproval of divorce, but also to base the marriage commitment on the divine commandment. In this way, Jesus harmonized, in God's eternal love, the commandment and the human response.

The third tension in the Jewish tradition was said to have existed between word and action. The teachers of the Law and the Pharisees were accused of separating their moral teaching from their actual behaviour. Jesus criticized them for appealing to the divine commandments and in doing so claiming to be an authority that should be obeyed while themselves failing to practise what they were preaching. Therefore, the commandments became burdens to be loaded on to other people's shoulders, so hindering human communion with God (Matthew 23:2–4). In contrast, Jesus condemned their example, while calling for obedience to the true source of their authority. As a unity of word and action, the true response to the commandment cannot simply be a repetition of the commandment, but the actual practice of what it commands. For example, one must love each other as brothers. Nor must one forget to show hospitality to the poor and to strangers. In harmonizing word and action, love is no longer a burden but a glory, and one's response is no longer a forced duty but a constant consciousness and deliberate action, treating others as oneself and trying one's best to relieve others' sufferings. 'Remember those in prison as if you were their fellow-prisoners and those who are ill-treated as if you were suffering' (Hebrews 13:1–3). Jesus Christ himself is believed to be not only the Word but also the Action: in his sacrifice the word of love is enacted and the action of love is expressed.

In dealing with these man-made tensions, Jesus was said to have given 'a new command', to love one another as he had loved them (John 13:34). Although the actual words speak of 'loving one another', they have been understood more generally and universally. The new command was to create a new world in which the loving human response to God's love is made real, the broken bridge between the divine and the human is restored, and the difference between word and action is removed. In a word, command and response are harmonised, and humanity is being brought to the eternal.

Love as human response to the divine command is manifested not only in one's faith in God but also in one's love for one's neighbour. Loving one another without any motive of self-interest is, like loving God, a response to the divine command. Paul speaks of this response as if Christians are 'predetermined by God to love one another'. This causes some theologians to deny that the response is a virtue, insisting that love can be understood only in the light of law and demand. However, this is not entirely true. There is a much more complicated relationship between demand and response, and this is illustrated in Paul's teaching concerning law and love. For him, love is the way of salvation, but law is not. Law is only a norm for the conduct of one's life. However, love as human response, either in the form of loving God or in the form of loving one's neighbour, is none other than the fulfilling of the law. Since faith can work only through love, the law of faith functions only in love, to be bound to Christ means to be bound to one another in a love that cares and that serves. If we say that the old law *forces* one to love, then we have to say that the transformed, or internalized, law gives one freedom to love, or that one is 'freely bound' to love others and serve others in freedom. The key to understanding the unity of freedom and love lies in that transformation of law from formal compulsion to the power of love. This transformation itself, as in the Confucian transformation from *li* to *jen*, results in new inward attitudes, which are the 'fruit of the Spirit', namely, love, joy, peace, patience, kindness, goodness, faithfulness, gentleness and self-control. In contrast to immorality, impurity, debauchery, idolatry, hatred, discord, jealousy, fit of rage, selfish ambition, dissensions, factions and envy and so forth (Galatians 5:19–23), these qualities are manifestations of love and therefore can properly be called 'virtues', although they are motivated by, and nurtured in, Christ's love rather than in and by social convention.

In one sense, the Confucian attitude to *li* is not very different from the attitude to law in the Jewish religion. Ninian Smart has seen the similarity, pointing out that 'The inwardness of religion is the vital essence of it. Later Judaism always had something of this polarity: the very complexity of the Law meant that there were many, many externals in the Jewish religion, but like ancient *li* they were useless without the sincerity of inwardness.'[38] However, as we have said above, in dealing with the problems of the conflict between inwardness and outwardness, Confucianism arrives at a position some aspects of which are more similar to those of Christianity, in the sense that both are working to reduce tensions and to harmonize what is internal and what is external.

Confucian harmony is achieved in their struggle to reduce the tension between *jen* and *li,* between the inward and the external, and between substance and function. Looking for unity between inward motivation and external manifestation, Confucians first searched for the right solution in the proper performance of traditional requirements. *Li* must be followed and taken as guide for one's life. In this sense, *li* is the absolute in a Confucian context. Confucian learning consists for the most part in acquiring ever more knowledge of *li,* and Confucian practice consists essentially in the performance of *li.*

However, Confucians do not rest content with the absolute observance of the external rules. They go on to find more important ways by which harmony can be realized. Confucianism stresses the fact that it is essential to have a proper inward motivation for conforming with propriety or performing the rites. Whatever one may do or avoid doing does not qualify one for the title of a person of *jen.* To attain to harmony in one's heart, one must find ways of making accord between performance and motivation. One cannot become a moral agent without a commitment to *jen,* nor can one become virtuous only by observing rules. In fact, Confucius believed that those 'village honest men' had nothing to do with virtuous life; rather, they were the enemy of virtue because they followed every rule so that their reputation would be maintained and nothing could be blamed on them (*Analects,* XVII, 13; *The Book of Mencius,* 7B:37). For Confucius and Mencius, *li* should not be insisted on dogmatically. When it is necessary, it may be adapted as Confucius puts it: 'A *chun Tzu* in dealing with the world is not definitely for, nor against, anything. He does whatever is righteous' (*Analects,* IV, 10). That is to say, moral rules are considered important only if they are conducive to one's attainment to *jen* and to one's endeavour to bring righteousness to the world. Therefore, although Confucius holds in high regard the proper performance of *li* and music, he nevertheless gives priority to the heart of *jen* and makes performance subject to *jen* (*Analects,* III, 3).[39] He does so, not only because *jen* is an inner quality, while *li* is an external requirement, but because *jen* is the summary of all aspects of the good life and the basis of the performance of *li* and music. *Li* is important in leading one to *jen*. However, in the last analysis, it is *jen* rather than *li* that can guarantee one's transcendence. In this sense, Herbert Fingarette is inaccurate when he contrasts *li* and *jen* by saying that '*jen* is surrounded with paradox and mystery in the *Analects*. *Jen* seems to emphasize the individual, the subjective, the character, feeling and attitudes; it seems, in short, a psychological notion.'[40] There is no doubt that Confucius concentrates on *jen* as an inner quality, which needs to be explored by learning. However, any attempt to understand it solely in psychological terms would fail to reveal its ethical, social and religious true nature and function.

In harmonizing the internal and the external another similarity between Confucian *jen* and Christian *agape* is revealed. On the one hand, both emphasize that the ultimate goal must include the internal and the external, embracing a new world as well as a new humanity in Christianity and sageliness within and kingliness without in Confucianism. The Confucian external includes taking social responsibilities upon oneself as well as observing moral requirements, while the internal refers to cultivating one's nature and developing one's spirituality. Just as Christianity emphasizes that salvation cannot be attained except through *agape*, Confucianism believes that the unity and harmony between internal motivation and external manifestation cannot be attained until *jen* has been cultivated. *Jen* as self-transformation is both inner motive and external performance. *Jen* manifests itself in the combination of the internal feeling of compassion and the action of doing good to others. A person who is seeking for *jen* not only has to establish his own character, but also has to establish the character of others. To establish one's own character is internal, while to establish the character of others is external. However, they are one in *jen*, and they are both needed for bringing *jen* to maturity and for attaining to the ultimate goal. On the other hand, both Confucian *jen* and Christian *agape* interpret external rules as the path to the ultimate goal, and insist that the external rule (law or *li*) is only secondary to one's attainment to transcendence. As the external, law or *li* is of value for humans because it provides a means to the ideal, love in Christianity and *jen* in Confucianism. Confucianism and Christianity further explain the external in the light of the inward, and thus law or *li* becomes part of the inward orientation, the law of faith in Paul's words and the *li* of heart in Confucian terms.

A similarity also lies in Confucian and Christian attitudes towards word and action. *Jen* as virtue justifies the unity between knowledge and practice. Learning is of great significance for Confucians, who take it as their mission to transmit and glorify the tradition. Confucius believed that virtue could be obtained through teaching and learning, and consequently he did not appreciate the innate knowledge very much: 'I am not born with knowledge. Rather, I love the ancient tradition and seek it earnestly' (*Analects*, VII, 20). Confucius was so happily engaged in this seeking that he forgot his food and worries and was not aware that old age was coming (VII, 19). Seeking is not a mere process of learning. It also includes practising according to what one has learnt. What caused concern to Confucius was failure to cultivate virtue, to teach what has been learnt, to be nearer to what is right and to remove defects (VII, 3). Inappropriate training and insufficient practice are both responsible for human degeneration and erosion of human nature. The growth of humanity within a person is like drawing a picture: the inborn nature is like plain silk, while learning and practice are like painting, neither of which can be without (III, 8). For Mencius, it is essential for self-transformation to maintain the unity between learning and practice, and between knowledge and action. However, the two sides of the unity are more concentrated on their moral content than on their epistemological implication. Thus knowledge and practice are taken solely as moral knowledge and moral practice, and to strike their unity is to return to one's innate nature, or to develop one's innate potential, or to search for the lost good heart: 'The Way of learning is none other than to go after this strayed (lost) heart' (*The Book of Mencius*, 6A:11). This unity was developed in later Confucianism, especially in the idealistic school of neo-Confucianism. Wang Yang-ming insists that learning is not book reading or instruction receiving, nor an outward investigation. Rather it is essentially an inward journey to one's own mind, where not only the truth or sagehood but also all principles (*li*) and virtues (*te*) lie. 'The master of the body is the mind. What emanates from the mind is the will. The original substance of the will is knowledge, and wherever the will is directed is a thing [affair] . . . There are neither principles or things outside the mind.'[41] Progress in learning cannot be made until one has explored the fullness and richness of one's own mind. The mind for Wang Yang-ming is not only the source of virtues but also the ability to judge and determine. Its dual function enables Wang Yang-ming to equate it with the 'innate knowledge of the good' (*liang ch'i*), and the progress of learning with realizing this knowledge (*ch'i liang ch'i*). Seeing, hearing, experiencing and dealing with others is only of marginal value compared with extending and realising innate knowledge, and therefore should never be allowed to impede realizing what is innate, actualizing what remains potential and making manifest what is latent. The knowledge innate in the heart is what one has to acquire, to extend and to manifest. Understood in this way, learning is more a practical action than a theoretical deliberation. Since the sense-activities like seeing, hearing, speaking and moving are all taken as functions of the mind, true knowledge, or moral knowledge, is not in the senses but in the mind. Since this knowledge is that by which one acts morally, and since moral action is that by which one obtains enlightenment, to know is to act: when a thought is aroused, it is already action. For Wang Yang-ming, one who claims to know virtue but does not practise it knows nothing. Knowledge is the direction and beginning of action, while action is the effort and completion of knowledge. To learn is not only to refrain from acting wrongly. More importantly it is to have no evil thoughts and intentions at all.

The similarities between Christian *agape* and Confucian *jen* in dealing with these three man-made tensions, namely, the tensions between the internal and the external, between the predetermination and free will, and between knowledge and practice, arise from a fundamental fact that they are providing a means for, or paving a path to, transcendence. As in *jen* as humanity and *agape* as divinity where the divergence between humanistic and theistic transcendence is revealed, so the divergence between humanistic and theistic ways to the transcendence is exposed in *jen* as virtue and *agape* as response. Both pursue the spiritual emancipation of human beings from their limitations and show a deep spirituality. However, in their exploration of this spirituality, they use different, but frequently interchanged, languages so that their pursuits are expressed differently, ethical pursuit in Confucianism and spiritual response in Christianity.

Let us first look at the role of ethics in the Confucian search for transcendence. The overwhelming emphasis on ethics characterizes Confucian spirituality, so that it is frequently called an ethical doctrine. The first principle of Confucian ethics is that humanity achieves its own transcendence by moral self-cultivation, and that to transcend is to be *jen*. To be *jen* is to be ethical, which involves not only following moral rules but also integrating the external with the internal. Thus, to be moral gains a much deeper significance than mere good. It is the way for a Confucian to express his ultimate concern. Every form of life has its end. How can one transcend the limitation of life and gain an eternal meaning for one's limited life? These are certainly of much concern to Confucianism as well as to many other religious traditions. What characterizes Confucian tradition is its search for eternal meaning in present life and activity, while setting aside concern for life after death (*Analects*, XI, 12). In one respect, Confucians find the ultimate meaning of life in the continuity of family, in which filial piety plays a primary role. In another respect, the succession of cultural tradition provides Confucians with an eternal meaning. For this reason, Confucius took the transmission of the ancient culture as his mission endowed by *Tian* (XI, 5). Yet in another respect, endless effort in self-cultivation brings one's virtue to its maturity, which not only manifests one's own value of life, but also leaves behind the great treasure to later generations, by which one has transcended one's limitation and reached the eternal. Confucius once stood by a stream and proclaimed that one's life could be eternal as the river went on and on (XI, 17). What was in his mind at that moment was probably that the temporality of life should not be an obstacle for one's search for eternity, nor should it be allowed to disturb one's mind. Understood in this way, what is really meant by saying 'a person of *jen* has no worries' (IX, 29), is that a person of *jen* has transcended one's limitation by completing his mission in this world and this life.

Christianity uses a different language to explore its spirituality, in which ethics has its role to play, but not the decisive element. Christianity also uses ethical language, but in a very different way. Human morality is of significance for Christian *agape*, but it is not self-explanatory. *Agape* in humanity assumes the form of response rather than of virtue. The source and resource for human moral growth is God, and the fundamental question for Christians is the relationship of humans to God. Human morality and community are meaningful only in the sense that they are identified by the Holy Spirit as the means of reconciliation with God. Human responsibility and effort play their part in the disciplined response to divine *agape*. However, as sinners, humans cannot secure salvation by themselves.

From this fundamental divergence in the common pursuit of transcendence comes a series of similarities and differences between

Confucian virtue and Christian response. Both *agape* and *jen* point to
the ultimate creation of harmony in human life, and are therefore
treated as the source of the virtuous life. Both *agape* and *jen* show
the way to attain to the harmony between humans and the ultimate
meaning of life, and are therefore seen as the virtue of the virtues.
However, *jen* as the source of virtue is obviously different from *agape*
as the response that produces virtues. As the source of a virtuous
life, *jen* is itself harmony. As response to the divine command,
human *agape* is only the means to harmony, which is to be found in
Jesus Christ. Although we may agree that a response so understood
is an active and positive process, nevertheless *agape* as response is
much less humanistic than Confucian *jen*.

Both *jen* as virtue and *agape* as response underlie human responsibility for their own growth, either morally or spiritually. However,
the nature of responsiveness limits *agape* to the area in which the
human search for the ultimate has a moral quality. As response,
agape does not leave much room for human improvement or self-
cultivation. Although the value of human effort in self-improvement
is not totally denied, and in fact becomes an important feature of
the Christian doctrine of *agape*, virtue nevertheless is endowed by
God through human faith, hope and love. Therefore, the growth of
virtue in the human heart may be said to be fundamentally a matter
of instant enlightenment by the Spirit of Jesus Christ. By way of
contrast, *jen* as the root of virtue makes room for human effort
in its cultivation, or, to put it in other words, *jen*'s growth depends
upon human cultivation. *Jen* provides humans with a beginning. Its
flourishing depends on how it is developed, or in the language of
neo-Confucianism, on wiping off all that is dirty. In this sense, *jen*
as virtue is not only a quality of goodness, but also a continuing
progress in human activity in which *jen* comes to full completion.

Both *jen* and *agape* have an overall concern for humanity. However, in humanistic *jen* this concern includes both moral and non-
moral values, while in theistic *agape* it excludes non-moral value.
This contrast is obvious when comparing the *Analects*, in which
concerns about health, administration and skill are taken as essential
parts for attaining to *jen*, and the New Testament, in which neither
Jesus nor his disciples talked much about these **human** matters. It
is natural for a humanistic principle to incorporate every aspect
of human life into an entity and to take the development of this
entity to its utmost as its first and foremost task. For Confucians, it
is necessary to cultivate one's character. However, this cultivation

does not assume only one form, sitting contemplation or performing one's duties – although these are of greatest significance. One may do so in enjoying life, appreciating the natural beauty or in skilfully managing one's work so that it is done efficiently as well as easily. When Confucius was asked about what he expected from life, his answers included both great ambition (V, 26) and personal enjoyment (XI, 26). For Christians, however, the attainment to *agape* is solely a response to God's calling and an appreciation of the sacrifice of Jesus. In this response, the moral implication is subdued in one's subjection to the divine mercy, and the non-moral values are not considered important for reconciliation with the Transcendent. Although we can read passages from the New Testament about enjoyment and health, enjoying life and being healthy are not taken seriously as long as they are by-products of one's faith (Mark 2:17; 3 John: 2), and are seldom mentioned as they may distract one's concentration on the divine calling.

6

Jen as Universal Love and *Agape* as Neighbour-Love

A religious principle implies transcendence and provides people with a path to the transcendent goal. To proceed to this goal, one needs not only the inner qualities which are manifest either as human virtue or as human response to the divine calling, but also a guideline for dealing with inter-human relationships, by which one either extends one's virtue to others or practises the divine discipline in human interaction. Manifested in inner qualities, the principle enables one to establish the ideal in one's own heart and in one's own life; and functioning as a guideline, the principle aims at changing 'deteriorated' human relationships so that the ultimate goal can be revealed in peace and the harmony of humanity.

Confucian *jen* as a humanistic principle takes completely fulfilled humanity both as the required inner quality and as the ultimate goal itself. To fulfil humanity, *jen* devotes itself to the resolution of social problems and difficulties, in which it claims to have found the ultimate meaning of life. Confucians believe that most of these problems arise from the failure to establish an everlasting affirmative relationship between an individual and other people. Therefore, the solution is that one must treat others as one would like to be treated oneself. This is what is called 'love' in the Confucian doctrine of *jen*. This love differs from pure liking or fondness. It is ethical by nature. Since Confucians define transcendence in human moral life, ethical love can be essentially identified with transcendental love. Christian *agape* looks beyond human society to an ultimate transcendental goal, and takes divine love as the source of human love. However, it stresses that this goal cannot be sought and the source will not be available except in and through personal and social relationships. Without a sincere engagement in human life and community, and without a true love for one's fellow-men, one has no way to be in God's grace and to respond to God's calling. Thus, neighbour-love becomes a fundamental element of the Christian understanding of *agape*. Neighbour-love is transcendental by nature, because it is essentially a response to God's calling. When responding to the divine grace, neighbour-love is applied in human relationships and consequently it becomes ethical.

Confucianism and Christianity have both applied their principles to social and communal life and have found in human love for one another the best expression of their ideals. Confucian love is ethical first and then becomes transcendental in application, while neighbour-love is first transcendental and then is applied to ethics. This fact underlies their different conceptions of human love, which is what we call the third contrast between Confucian *jen* and Christian *agape*: for Confucians, love for others is primarily an extension of one's own virtue to other people and to all beings and things, in which one finds the completion of the cultivation of one's character; while for Christians, love, or neighbour-love, is essentially a further response to God's calling, in which one's love for God is completed and one's faith in God is manifested, and by which one will enter the realm of transcendence.

JEN AS LOVE: UNIVERSAL BENEVOLENCE AND BENEFICENCE

Cultivation of one's own character and promotion of one's own virtue are the grounds on which Confucians have established their doctrine of *jen*. When applied to society and community, the aim of this doctrine is to bring benefit to the people, peace to the state and harmony to the world. To achieve this, it is necessary to establish a benevolent government. To establish a benevolent government, it is necessary to learn *Tao* and cultivate virtue. All these depend upon *jen*.[1] First, *jen*, as the principle and substance of self-cultivation, cannot be realized in pure speculation, nor in living an isolated life. Cultivation of one's own character, although a personal matter, must be carried out in a social context and completed in dealing with interpersonal relationships. Virtues have to be acquired and strengthened in social interaction, and the realization of *jen* takes place in human relationships, especially in the process of integration between oneself and others, and between oneself and the universe. In this sense, Confucian *jen* is directly opposed to two other ways of life. One is the way of extreme egoism which claims, according to Yang Chu (440–360 BCE?), that one should always take one's own interests as one's first and only consideration, and should not give up even a single hair to benefit others or the world. The second is the way of withdrawal, which, according to Chuang Tzu, urges people to retreat from the world and concentrate on their own cultivation of *tao* and *te* [virtues]. Confucianism, on the contrary, insists that neither withdrawing from the world nor preserving oneself at the expense of others can lead to *jen*. For Confucians, to cultivate oneself, one must help others, both benevolently and beneficently. That is to say, love for others is the only way for one to attain to *jen*. Secondly, *jen* is not only a state of consciousness, which needs social encouragement, but it also is a socially-oriented commitment, which will naturally flow from one's virtue over to others and which manifests itself in one's attitudes to, and treatment of, others. As human excellence, it enables one to harmonise social relations, and as universal commitment, it aims at integrating all beings and all people. Therefore, *jen* is *a priori*, because it is innate and exists independently of experience. *Jen* is also *a posteriori*, because it is the lively affection that relates 'you' and 'me', 'us' and others, humans and all existing things. Our innate and acquired character is refined in human interaction as universal love. This love is not only good will and kind feeling; it is the whole-hearted and sincere commitment to eternity and universality. That is to say, love for others is the content of Confucian transcendence.

The greatest contribution that Confucius made to the understanding of *jen* is not his explanation of *jen* as virtue, nor his promotion of *jen* as the highest virtue – these had been, either implicitly or explicitly, discussed before him – but his redefinition of *jen* as love and his refinement of such love as ethical commitment and transcendental principle. In this love Confucian secularism and transcendentalism are integrated. As ethical commitment, *jen* is a selfless altruism which, when sincerely practised, leads individuals from the commonplace to the truly worthwhile, and from what one is to what one should be; as a transcendental principle, *jen* underlies all existence and is the power which unifies humanity and the universe, and which, when fulfilled, enables one to take heaven as father, earth as mother, all humans as brothers and sisters, and all things as companions – what one should be has become what one is. These two aspects of love are two interdependent aspects of *jen*: ethical commitment provides the transcendental principle with its concrete contents, so that *jen* as love is both benevolence – the will of good to others, and beneficence – the constant practice of Five Virtues in the world: respectfulness, liberality, truthfulness, diligence and generosity (*Analects*, XVII, 6); while transcendental principle refines and orients the ethical commitment, so that love can be expressed in its widest possible extent, not only in personal relationships – all within the four seas are one's brothers (XII, 5) – but also in active engagement in the process of universal integration (IX, 5).

Some scholars have failed to recognize that love is the fundamental meaning of *jen*; others who have come to recognise this meaning have failed to recognize that *jen* as love is not only a virtue but also an ethical and religious commitment; still others, who have recognized this commitment, have failed to perceive that *jen* as love is universal. In their translations or discussions of *jen*, either love is not mentioned, or it is regarded as only one virtue among many. Alternatively, love is portrayed, not as the strength but as the weakness of *jen*, because it is a so-called 'graded affection'. Even Wing-tsit Chan, who has extensively examined the historical development of *jen* in the Confucian tradition and the misunderstandings of *jen* in the West, comes to the conclusion that *jen* should be translated as 'humanity' in the sense of human excellence, rather than as 'love' in the sense of universal devotion,[2] because he too is disturbed by the idea of 'graded love'. What we must do in this section, therefore, is to clarify these confused notions by focusing attention on the three-fold task: (1) of demonstrating that love is essential for a correct understanding of Confucian *jen*; (2) of arguing that *jen* as love is not a natural feeling, but an ethical commitment which stems from an innate feeling but goes beyond it, a universal commitment which begins with family affection but is not limited to it; (3) of illustrating that *jen* as universal love is unconditional and transcendental, in contrast both to a 'mutuality of love' and to a utilitarian 'love for the sake of its benefits'.

It is a consistent tradition of two and a half thousand years of Confucianism to define *jen* as love or universal love. There is no doubt that Confucius took *jen* as 'love' (*Analects*, XII, 22). Mencius clearly emphasized that '*jen* is to love others' (4B:28), so linking individual human beings with one another, and that '*jen* is to love all' (7A:46),[3] so associating individuals with the whole of humanity, and even with all existing beings. Tung Chung-shu of the Han dynasty confirmed that '*jen* is the name for loving humans' and that '*jen* is to love others'.[4] Yang Hsiung (53 BCE-18 CE) believed that '*jen* is to see and love', and that 'to love universally is called *jen'*.[5] This tradition was continued by later Confucians, and Wing-tsit Chan's assertion that 'from the time of Confucius through the Han dynasty (206 BCE-200 CE) *jen* was understood in the sense of love'[6] is correct if he means thereby that *jen* as love was the dominant view during this period. However, it would be questionable if it was implied that after that period *jen* was no longer assumed to be 'love'. In fact, the interpretation of *jen* as love was not only accepted by the Confucians of the Tang dynasty; it was also propagated by the Confucians from the Sung and Ming dynasties until the present century. What differentiates the neo-Confucian understanding of *jen* from that of the earlier Confucians is that the former tried to search for the deeper meaning of *jen* in the nature, rather than in the form, of love. Chen Chun (1159–1223), one of the most famous disciples of Chu Hsi, summarized this transformation in this way:

> After Confucius, no one correctly comprehended the true meaning of *jen*. Scholars in the Han period used *jen* to mean favour or benefit. *Jen* was deeply entangled with the feeling of love. As a result, it was believed that something loftier and nobler than *jen* existed. In turn, *jen* became an inferior and crude concept. In the Tang Dynasty (618–907), Han Yu upheld *jen* as universal love, yet basically he still followed the traditional understanding of the term. It was starting with Master Cheng [Cheng I] that *jen* came to be understood as nature, while love was interpreted as feeling. *Jen* and love thus became clearly differentiated. Unfortunately, the disciples of Master Cheng went overboard in this differentiation and forgot about love altogether. In their attempt to look for something vast and lofty, they lost sight of the fact that *jen* is the nature of love, and love is the feeling of *jen*. Even though we may not regard love as the correct label for *jen*, the two must never be completely separated from each other.[7]

From this paragraph we can see (1) that *jen* was fully explained in terms of love until the time of Cheng I; (2) that there was a short period after that when Confucian scholars abandoned this interpretation; (3) that Chu Hsi and his disciples believed that this was a mistake and must be corrected; (4) that it was considered wrong to label *Jen* as love because it was not love itself but the nature of love; (5) that it was also considered wrong to separate *jen* from love because *jen* was the principle of love. Therefore, the question facing neo-Confucians was how to relate *jen* and love, rather than whether or not love should be included in the meaning of *jen*. Chu Hsi defined *jen* as the virtue of mind and the principle of love and thereby tried to restore the position of love in the understanding of *jen*: 'What is the mind of *jen*? In Heaven and Earth it is the mind to produce things in abundance. In human beings it is to love others warmly and to provide them with benefits.'[8] For later Confucians, *jen* as love was not only a principle or essence, but also a function or operation (Chen Chun); *jen* was taken to mean not only loving others equally, but also loving all beings and all things universally (Wang Yang-ming); and *jen* was not only the mind of love but also the power of love (Kang Yu-wei 1858–1927).[9]

Within the Confucian tradition and between the Confucian and other traditions, the hotly argued question is not whether love is the meaning of *jen*, but whether this love should be interpreted as universal or as partial. *Jen* expresses itself in an ethical love that is by definition universal. There should be no doubt that Confucius took *jen* as universal love. Confucius and Mencius not only defined *jen* as love but also revealed its procedures of *chung* and *shu*, the practical ways of *jen* as well as the universal application of *jen*: there is nothing partial or graded in these procedures. However, traditionally and still popularly, Confucian *jen* is said to be 'graded', a preferential love that has no universal implication. Although Confucius, Mencius and other Confucians did not place any qualification on love for others, they are presumed to have propagated an ideal of *jen* that is confined to family affection and limited to filial piety and fraternity in its application. Some scholars have recently challenged this view of Confucian *jen*, and have explored the universal nature of *jen* as love through reinterpreting Book I, 2 of the *Analects*. In order to clarify and correct confusing interpretations of this paragraph, Robert Allinson, for example, puts forward three arguments: (1) that filial piety, in this context, 'is considered hypothetical and not categorical in axiological status'; (2) that filial piety 'is not characterised as an exclusive form of love, but rather is designated as an epistemological guide and as an ontological locus for our ethical feelings and values'; (3) that Confucius himself emphasizes 'the Golden Rule as constituting the most basic principle of his teachings'.[10] To take the argument further, I will advance four reasons why *jen* as universal love in the past came to be perceived as graded, or partial, love. In so doing, I will show that graded love is not the essence of *jen* and that it characterizes only the application and practice of *jen*.

The misunderstanding first arises from a misinterpretation of the saying: 'A person of *jen* dedicates himself to the root. When the root is firmly established, the Way will grow. Filial piety and brotherly respect are the root of *jen*' (*Analects*, I, 2). Many people have expressed their doubts as to the authenticity of this paragraph, pointing out that it was spoken by one of Confucius' disciples rather than by Confucius himself, and have argued that this paragraph was possibly added later, and so did not represent the teaching of earlier Confucians. More important and more relevant to our view is how to understand the word 'root'. The term *ben* (root) in this paragraph means the starting point of practising *jen* rather than the essence of *jen*.[11] *Jen* must be *practised* in a graded procession, moving from one's own parents to others' parents, from one's own brothers to others' brothers, and from one's own children to others' children. However, 'starting with one's love for family' does not mean that this love is the whole of *jen*. When interpreting this paragraph, the Cheng brothers of the Sung dynasty distinguished *jen* itself from the practice of *jen*, and believed that filial piety and brotherly respect were only the root (beginning) of the practice of *jen*, but not the root of *jen* itself:

> It means that the practice of humanity [*jen*] begins with filial piety and brotherly respect. Filial piety and brotherly respect are items in the practice of humanity [*jen*]. It is all right to say that they are the root of the practice of humanity [*jen*] but not all right to say that they are the root of humanity [*jen*] itself. For humanity [*jen*] is nature, while filial piety and brotherly respect are its function.[12]

In practice, it is natural for Confucians to carry out *jen* by starting with loving one's parents and brothers. Considering that *jen* must be practised first in the family, Mencius claims that 'to love one's parents is *jen*' and 'it is in serving one's parents that *jen* bears fruit'.[13] However, he never says that *jen*, as love, must stop at serving one's own parents. It is not true to say that Confucian love is not universal because it starts with family love. What Confucianism intends to argue is: if one does not even love one's parents or brothers, how can one love others? and if one does not practise love in one's own family, how can one practise love in the world?

Failure to see the difference between *jen* as ethical love and love as a natural feeling is also responsible for the misunderstanding that deprives *jen* of its universality. As we have said above, *jen* is manifested as love in the ways of *shu* and *chung*. Filial piety and brotherly respect are the first applications of *chung* and *shu*, so providing a concrete analogy from what one likes to what one

should like.[14] By the procedures of *chung* and *shu*, not only has
one found a guide for the whole of life, but one has also refined
one's natural feelings and social emotions. In *chung* and *shu*, one
moves from self-centred desires to the integration of oneself with
others and further with the whole world. Also by *chung* and *shu*,
Confucians differentiate *jen* as ethical love from love as liking.
The latter is a natural and spontaneous feeling, unrefined and
undefined, while the former is a moral commitment and sincere
devotion, refined and defined as an ethical principle. The Chinese
word for ordinary love is '*ai*', which refers to a feeling of fondness
and a preference of choice.[15] Such feelings and preferences are
necessary parts of *jen*. However, *jen* cannot be reduced to them.
Jen is the refinement and development of natural and spontaneous
feeling. *Jen* is essentially an ethical love. When Confucius says (IV,
3) that only a person of *jen* knows how to love [*hao*] others and how
to dislike (*wu*) others, he makes *jen* superior to spontaneous love:
the former is the precondition for loving and the guide for how to
love. For this reason both Confucius and later Confucians identify
jen and love on the one hand, yet carefully differentiate them on
the other. Mencius claims that love (*ai*) applies to things, while *jen*
is essential for relating to humanity; or that love (*ai*) is more general
in its denotation, because it refers only to feeling or emotion, while
jen is more specific, because it directly concerns the human pursuit
of the ideal. Natural love must be refined by sincerity and respect,
and only then can it become part of *jen*. Without a sincere heart and
respect for the loved one, love would even go against true humanity.
Confucius rejects any idea that filial piety is limited to feeding one's
parents and says that, to be filial, one must treat one's parents with
reverence and sincerity (II, 7 and 8). Mencius points out that 'To
feed others without love is to treat them like pigs; while to love
them without respect is to treat them like domestic animals' (7A:
37). *The Great Learning* sees *jen* as adjusting and refining natural
feelings, because few can be naturally impartial when dealing with
others. Human beings 'are partial toward those whom they love,
partial toward those whom they despise and dislike, partial toward
those whom they fear and revere . . . '. Partiality prevents human
beings from seeing what is good in those whom they dislike and
what is bad in those whom they love. The author(s) of the Great
Appendix of the *Book of Changes* explicitly put forward the view
that *jen* is the root while *ai* (love) is the branch and the leaves. Only
when the root is well cultivated, can the ability to love develop.[16]

These quotations from Confucian classics demonstrate that partial love is not the characteristic of *jen* and that *jen* must come from cultivating and directing one's natural feelings. Other Confucians tend to separate *jen* as love and love (*ai*) as feeling by asserting that *jen* relates to human nature while love relates to human emotion. For them, *jen* can be defined in terms of love, while love cannot be equated with *jen*: 'a man of humanity [*jen*] loves [*ai*] universally; but one may not therefore regard universal love [*ai*] as humanity [*jen*]'.[17] It is obvious that they separate *jen* from love, not because they want *jen* to be partial and love to be universal. On the contrary, they take *jen* as the principle of love, and as such as universal and therefore the basis of love. As the principle of love, *jen* is the seed of love, the power to love and the essence of loving. *Jen* defines love because it is the root and source of love; love cannot define *jen* because it is only the expression of *jen*. In the light of these explanations, it is not difficult to see that, while love as the expression of *jen* may be partial or limited, *jen* as the refinement, or principle, of love is universal and unlimited.

All Confucians believe that *jen* as love should first be practised in one's love for one's parents and brothers, but none of them holds that *jen* is only love of parents and brothers. The misinterpretation of *jen* as graded love is the result of failing to understand the relation and difference between *jen* and affection [*chin*]. *Chin* was originally a noun referring to family members or relatives. Later it was used as a verb to refer to affection for one's family, and included various affectionate attitudes, towards parents (*hsiao*), children (*tz'u*) and elder brothers (*ti*). *Jen* and *chin* are subtly related and yet carefully differentiated both in the *Analects* and in the *Book of Mencius*. A frequent quotation from *Mencius*, in which love is graded between parents, people and things, is that 'A person of *jen* is to *chin* [be affectionate to] his parents and to *jen* all people. He *jen* all people and *ai* [loves] all things' (7A:45). However, in this paragraph it is far from clear, as both ancient commentators and modern scholars have assumed, that *jen* means a secondary love, inferior to one's affection for parents and superior to one's care for things, and that therefore the extent and depth of one's love depends on whom one is loving. Rather, it is logically consistent with the whole of Confucian doctrine of *jen* to suggest that, when Mencius asserts that love should admit of distinctions, what he intends to affirm is that, while *jen*, as love, is universally the same, it is applied and practised with distinctions, and that therefore there are different kinds of love. For him, different applications of love need different emphases: *ai* is for things, and is essentially good-will, kindness and a personal concern; *jen* is for unconditional and universal love of humans, and takes *chung* and *shu* as its procedures for treating others as oneself; and *chin* is for parents and relatives, and involves attachment and intimacy. Generally speaking, these three kinds of love, or three practices of love, are together taken to be the *jen* proper. Their difference is significant only in terms of practice or of emphasis. Specifically speaking, these three are arranged in a sequence of practices of *jen*. To *jen* people, one has first to *chin* parents, whereby one comes to appreciate the greatness of humanity; and to *ai* things and creatures, one has first to *jen* people, whereby one comes to understand that human nature is the same as the nature of things. Anyone who ignores his duties or abandons his respect towards his parents can by no means love other people sincerely; and anyone who does not love people can by no means be truly kind to things.[18]

To argue for *jen* as universal rather than graded love, we have to reinterpret the debate between Confucian *jen* and Moist *ch'ian ai*, which, more than anything else, is responsible for the fact that Confucian *jen* has been perceived as a doctrine of graded love. The founder of Moism was Mo Tzu (fl. 479–438 BCE), whose teaching was very popular for a period but died out before the Han dynasty. From then until the recent past, his teaching was known primarily through the attack on it by Mencius. The central concept of Mo Tzu's teaching, '*ch'ian ai*' (simultaneous love, a shortened version of '*ch'ian hsiang ai*' – simultaneously mutual love),[19] has been interpreted as 'universal love', in contrast to so-called Confucian 'graded love' (*jen*). However, according to Wing-tsit Chan, it 'is better translated as "mutual love"'.[20] The Moist motive for practising '*ch'ian ai*' is based on human mutuality: love others if you want to be loved yourself; do not bring harm upon others if you do not want to be harmed yourself. This does not seem very different from the Confucian way of practising *jen*, because both follow the same way from oneself to others in expressing love. Just as Mo Tzu intends that this mutuality of love should extend to all corners of the world, so Confucians intend that *chung* and *shu* should be done universally. It would be ridiculous to think that *shu* and *chung* differ in quantity and quality when applied to parents and to others. Why, then, did Confucians, especially Mencius, attack the Moist concept of '*ch'ian ai*' and contrast Confucian *jen* with Moist *ch'ian ai?* Was it because they did not agree with 'universal love' as interpreted traditionally? If the difference does not lie between the universal and the partial, where does it lie? In order to determine the characteristics of *jen*, it is necessary to investigate how Confucian *jen* differs from Moist love, and to examine carefully the reasons why Mencius rejected Mo Tzu's concept of love.

Mencius attacked Mo Tzu because he believed that *ch'ian ai* was propagating an extreme view of altruism. This can be seen from paragraph 7A:26, where Mencius criticizes Yang Chu for adopting extreme egoism and Mo Tzu for advocating the opposite extreme, namely, absolute altruism. An absolute altruism benefits others at the expense of one's own and one's parents' good. Mencius says that 'the reason for disliking those who hold to one extreme is that they destroy the Way. They take up only one thing but neglect a hundred others'. It is clear that for Confucians to go 'too far' is as bad as not to go far enough, because both violate the middle way. The middle way is essential for practising *jen*. Human beings, though possessing the seeds of a good nature, can very easily go to extremes if they are not regulated by the Way. Without a proper sense of the middle way, without being regulated by *li*, even behaviour which is normally good may appear ridiculous and become inappropriate. Since *jen* and the middle way are closely connected, and the middle way is taken to be an important path towards fulfilling *jen*, anything that violates the middle way opposes, or destroys, *jen*. The 'too far' that Mo Tzu is believed to have gone lies in the fact that, by insisting on extreme altruism, he has neglected one of the basic duties to the family and denied that familial love is the primary procedure of human love. Confucius and Mencius, of course, agree that one should be ready to practise *jen* at the expense of one's own interests, even of one's own life.[21] However, among all those whom one should love, one's parents come first. Since affection for one's parents is the starting point and the first practice of *jen* as love, Moism is held to contravene the natural and moral law of humanity, to destroy the basis of love, and to obstruct the application of Confucian *jen*. Denying that love must be carried out in an ordered sequence and practised with different emphases, by which human love is completed and *jen* is brought to mature, Moist equality between loving parents and loving others is believed to be against human nature and to contradict social reality. In theory, such equality is an empty and abstract concept, because it is detached from the concrete contents of love. In practice, it is harmful to human efforts to bring harmony and peace to the world, because it ignores the concrete human situation in which universal love can be realized. Therefore Mencius attacks Mo Tzu's *'ch'ian ai'* as a denial of the special relationship with one's father, a denial which causes human beings to degenerate into animals.[22]

Mencius attacked Moism because he believed that *'ch'ian ai'* was conditional on mutual love. Mo Tzu holds that lack of mutual love is responsible for all the harm in the world:

> As feudal lords do not love one another, they will fight in the fields. As heads of families do not love one another, they will usurp one another. As individuals do not love one another, they will injure one another . . . Because of want of mutual love, all the calamities, usurpations, hatred, and animosity in the world have risen.[23]

Mo Tzu claims that mutual harm should be replaced by mutual love and mutual benefit, because, when mutual love prevails, virtues and values like kindness and loyalty, parental affection and filial piety, peace and harmony, will come into being. Why should one practise mutual love? Mo Tzu's answer is that:

> Those who love others will be loved by others. Those who benefit others will be benefited by others. Those who hate others will be hated by others. Those who harm others will be harmed by others.[24]

This mutual love does not initially seem to differ from the way of Confucian *jen*. Confucius and Mencius certainly agree that love should be mutual. Father should be kind to son and son should be respectful to father; ruler should treat his subjects with propriety and subjects serve their ruler with loyalty. However, a belief that 'mutuality is the way to practise love' is different from a belief that 'love must be mutual'. Mencius believes that *jen* will evoke mutual love, but it should not be motivated by mutual love, just as a father should not love his son in order to be loved by his son, nor should a son show filial piety to his father in order to be treated kindly by his father. It is intolerable for Mencius even to think of love in such a way that a son might cultivate his filial piety to parents because he believed that his filial piety would be rewarded by kindness, while he could be justified in not loving his parents if he believed there would be no love given in return for his filial piety. Love, in effect, evokes love from the beloved: 'He who loves others is constantly loved by them' (4B:28). However, the motivation of *jen* as love should not be conditional on the return of love. On the contrary, when one is not loved by others, one should examine oneself to see if one has been wanting in *jen*, rather than give up one's love for others. It is in this self-examination that *jen* is manifested, because *jen* is rooted in self-cultivation rather than mutuality. Confucius takes 'making demands on oneself rather than on others' as the way to *jen* and the sign of the nobility of humanity, and believes that 'It depends upon oneself alone rather than anybody else to practise *jen*' (XII, 1). *The Great Learning* regards it as the only method of practising the Way. *The Doctrine of the Mean* takes sincerity as the means by which *jen* is extended. For Mencius, without sincerity, one cannot love other people, nor can one love even one's own parents.[25] He believes that to be *jen* is like being an archer. One has first to compose oneself and then shoot. If one misses the target, instead of murmuring against the target or complaining of others, one should turn and look for the cause of failure in oneself (2A:7). It is always possible for love not to be returned. When this happens, Mo Tzu sees in it the cause of chaos, while Mencius sees in it evidence that one's own *jen* has not yet matured, and believes that, when one cultivates *jen* to the utmost, everyone in the world will come to respond.[26]

Mencius attacked Moism also because he believed that *ch'ian ai* based love on utilitarian considerations and grounded mutual love in mutual benefit. Confucian *jen* is to love without thought of return and to strive consciously for integration between oneself and others. If one is always thinking how to derive benefit from others, or how to be benefited by one's own love, one cannot practise *jen*. If everyone thinks of love as a means by which he himself is benefited, love will no longer exist and *jen* will no longer have any value. In the beginning of the *Book of Mencius* there is a dialogue between Mencius and King Hui of Liang. When the King asked Mencius, who had come from a long way away, how he would benefit his state, Mencius asked in reply what was the point of talking about 'benefit'. If all persons, from king to commoner, asked how they might benefit themselves, they would lose all concern for others and engage in a struggle of everybody against everybody else. So the state would be put in peril. Instead, if all adhered to *jen* and righteousness, they would respect and love others as themselves, and there would soon be prosperity. By attacking Moists for basing love on benefit, Mencius separated *jen* from selfish considerations.

Confucians seldom deny the importance of property and wealth for the good of people and for the triumph of *jen*. Making people rich is an essential condition if the world is to enjoy peace and harmony. Enabling people to have a reasonably prosperous life is one of the important means of *jen's* fulfilment. However, Confucians never think of wealth as private benefit, nor do they think of riches as the ultimate goal. Wealth, property and benefit should be taken into account only when they are conducive to the cultivation of *jen*,[27] and love should in no circumstance be determined by self-interest. For Mencius, all talk about self-benefit and self-profit, and all acting on the principle that benefit is the basis, or companion of, *jen* and righteousness, is the way to disorder and chaos; on the other hand, practising *jen* and righteousness, and taking these as the basis and condition of wealth and benefit, is the way to peace and harmony.

From our investigation into the difference between Confucian *jen* and Moist love we have been convinced that Mencius does not reject *ch'ian ai* because he opposes universal love. The difference between *jen* and *ch'ian ai* is not that *jen* is partial, graded or limited love, while *ch'ian ai* is universal, equal and unlimited love. For Mencius, the difference is that *ch'ian ai* is extreme, conditional and utilitarian love, while *jen* is properly regulated, ethical and universal love, independent of the return of love and the calculation of benefit and profit. That Confucian *jen*, as love, is universal is not only obvious in theory, it is also evidenced in practice when Confucians champion a harmonious world in which the old are well supported, the young properly educated, and people not only love their own children and respect their own parents, but also love other people's children and respect other people's parents. To realize such a society, the only guide for human beings is the practice of *chung* and *shu* universally. Human beings are born with love for some and not for others. In order to be universal, *jen* does not require one to abandon one's love for parents or friends. Rather it requires that through love of one's own parents and children one should come to love other people's parents and children, and through one's own familial love one should come to understand other people's familial love. This is a process of extension from loving those whom one naturally loves to loving those for whom one feels no natural affection. As Mencius puts it, 'a person of *jen* extends his love from those he loves to those he does not love, while a person without *jen* extends his ruthlessness (non-*jen*) from those whom he does not love to those whom he loves' (7B:1).

How can this love, or this procedure of *jen*, be said to be graded love?

This has clearly demonstrated that *jen*, the central theme of Confucianism, is universal rather than partial, ethical rather than spontaneous, and essential rather than superficial. As universal love, *jen* is based on one's own cultivation of virtue, and can then be extended to all others and to the whole world. This cultivation must be carried out in social contexts and start with familial love. One who truly loves his parents will surely come to love others' parents, and will lead others to love their parents. Not only is one's own love the way to fulfil *jen*, but it also sets an example for others, so that love may develop in their hearts and lives too. The extension of one's own *jen* and the exemplariness of practising *jen* are the key to understanding the universality of Confucian *jen*.

On the one hand, everybody has his own love. In extension of this love to what he originally does not love, *jen* is manifested. If everybody can do this, universal love will come into being. On the other hand, one's own affection for parents and love for other people provides an example for others – for all people, if one is the sovereign – so that they may follow this example and cultivate the same affection and love. When all people love their parents and respect their elders, when all people properly appreciate affection between parents and children, between elder and younger brothers, and between one another, and when all people consciously carry out *chung* and *shu* in their lives, *jen* is fulfilled, and order and peace come to the world.[28] In the process of bringing peace and order to the world, Confucian *jen* manifests its ethical and universal characteristics. The natural goodness of human beings provides only the possibility of *jen*. To be *jen*, one has to refine one's innate feelings in the context of family, cultivate one's potential in the context of society, and refine and extend natural love in the context of all human relationships.

Giving up one's natural love is not the way of practising *jen*. Rather, *jen* orientates natural feeling by the procedures of *shu* and *chung*, so that partial love is transformed into ethical and universal love, which in turn becomes one's own nature and enables one to treat others as oneself and to be harmoniously integrated with the whole universe, so that the Confucian transcendental goal can be attained.

AGAPE AS HUMAN RESPONSE – NEIGHBOUR-LOVE

Having discussed Confucian *jen* as love, it is natural for us now to look at Christian *agape* in the light of neighbour-love, which is in every aspect a Christian conception corresponding to Confucian *jen* as love. Further, in order to have a full picture of Christian *agape*, we must also consider neighbour-love, which is the other half of human *agape*, after examining its transcendental significance and its way to transcendence.

Human *agape* is not only a value or norm, but fundamentally, as we have shown in the last chapter, a command and the human response to it. As a command, *agape* expresses itself as the divine law, which orders everybody to obey. As a response, *agape* comes to be a human quality related to the divine grace. Although this response is primarily directed to the Law-giver himself and is therefore religious, it is also directed to other humans who are one's fellow-men and under the same law as oneself, and thereby it becomes ethical. God is imminent in humans and the love of Christ is the love of humanity. Therefore, God's love and love for God must be expressed in human love for one another. Or, more precisely, love for neighbour is taken as a necessary part, or procedure, of God's love and as an efficient way of loving God. The three dimensions of *agape*, transcendence, the way to transcendence and the manifestation of the way, are distinguishable, so that we can study them respectively, but are also inseparable, so that lack of any of them will lead to a mispresentation or misunderstanding of Christian *agape*.

The close relationship of human response as neighbour-love and as love for the divine can be seen in the fact that both are commanded and that love for one's neighbour is deliberately associated with love for God. It is probable that Jesus, when answering the question which of the commandments was the most important, listed two commandments as the greatest among all commandments.[29] From the formula of the Great Commandment, many Christian theologians have inferred that love, or *agape*, is first of all directed to God and only secondary to one's fellow-men, on the ground that there is a hierarchical order between these two commandments, since Jesus said that the *first* commandment is to love God and the *second* is to love one's neighbour. It is indeed true that God is always the focus of religious and ethical devotion in the Judeo-Christian tradition. However, as far as what is ascribed to Jesus in the Synoptic Gospels is concerned, we may well argue differently that love for God and love for one's neighbour are two sides of one commandment.

Along these lines, there have been many scholars who have seen it as one of their most important tasks to stress both the identification and the inseparability of these two commands. For example, Nygren argues that 'It is not true to say that to love God is a religious thing, while to love one's neighbour is a universal precept of ethics. The love of one's neighbour ceases to be Christian love if it is separated from its religious context.' Both, according to him, are a unity of love originating in divinity, although he believes that 'it is equally fatal to merge them into one'.[30] Furnish stresses that

> it is significant that this so-called 'double commandment' joins closely together love of God and love of neighbour. Each of the Synoptic evangelists in his own way stresses the equal importance and interrelation of these two. Loving the neighbour is no less an act of obedience than loving God and is part of the total response to the sovereign claim of God under which man stands.[31]

Both Nygren and Furnish perceive the inseparability of these two commandments, although in a different light. Further to their arguments, we shall explore three aspects in which these two commands are in fact taken as one. First we can see that in Mark, Jesus was asked what was the greatest commandment (singular) of all commandments and he replied with two commandments (plural). This means that in Jesus' mind the combination of these two commandments, distinguished as the first and the second, composes the most important *single* commandment. It would be incorrect if one of them, for example, love for God, were singled out as the chief commandment, because it would be only half of it. Secondly, there is indeed an order between these two commandments, since they are marked as the first and the second. However, the affirmation of these two commandments is followed by a claim that 'There is no other commandment greater than these' (Mark 12:31) or by a statement that 'All the Law and the prophets depend upon these' (Matthew 22:40). This means that, as regards importance, there is a difference between these two commandments and the others, and between them and other teaching, but no difference between these two commandments themselves. 'The union of the singular "no other commandment" and the plural "[than] these" maintains the distinction between the two precepts, but puts both of them into a special category.'[32] Thirdly, in the Lucan version (10:25–28), this idea is more clearly expressed: these two commandments are simply combined to refer to the most important thing one should do to inherit eternal life. In this version, the order of 'first' and 'second', common to the Marcan and Matthean versions, is deleted, so impressing on us that they are in fact one. Although this version is in response to a different question and is uttered by the expert on law, nevertheless it is still taken as the same sum of the law and the prophets, because the answer is approved by Jesus.[33] This again is evidence that human *agape* in Christian doctrine is one coin with two sides, the one love for God and the other love for humans.

Like any other quality of humanity, human *agape* in relation to other humans is firmly based on a theistic foundation and religious faith. Both the commandments of love for God and love for one's neighbour are preceded by the statement, 'The Lord our God . . . '. Not only the love for God but also the love for one's neighbour is commanded by God, so giving this love divine authority.[34] The question remains, how to respond to God's command. There is a clue in the greatest commandment in the Marcan version. When the teacher of the law who had asked the question extended the most important commandment by adding that it was 'more important than all burnt offerings and sacrifices', Jesus gave his approval and said that the teacher was 'not far from the kingdom of God' (Mark 12:33–34). The human response to God's command, according to Jesus, could be expressed, not by offering sacrifices nor by religious ceremonies, but only by one's love for God and love for one's neighbour. In this way, Jesus again put love in the centre of his teaching.

The love commanded is itself modeled on the love shown by the one who gives the command: 'Be merciful, just as your Father is merciful' (Luke 6:36). In this sense, Nygren believes that 'Christian love has its pattern in the love manifested by God, therefore, it too must be spontaneous, uncaused, uncalculating, unlimited, and unconditional'.[35] This love was manifested especially in the new way of life which was initiated by Jesus himself. In a sinful world, what is most urgently needed is divine forgiveness. This has been brought by Jesus on the cross: 'Father, forgive them, for they do not know what they are doing' (Luke 23:34). Such ignorance is the reason for God's command and the urgency for human love. On this background, Jesus was believed to have come to bring knowledge to the people, first by preaching the good news, so that the people would know what was commanded by God; and secondly by his own sacrifice, so that the people would know what the love commanded by God was. For Paul, the compelling motive for human love is the realization that, although humans are sinners, they are still loved by God. Thus, redemption, sacrifice and forgiveness become the most significant features of Christian love. Because of the identification between love for God and love for humans, the focus of love is shifted from differentiation to unification: the difference between 'a Jew' and 'a Greek', 'a slave' and 'a free man', 'a male' and 'a female' has disappeared, because all of them are one in Christ Jesus (Galatians 3:27–28). Although this idea is explored in the context of the Christian community, it also contains an element of a universal Christian love.

As commanded, Christians should respond with love to all who hear and obey this command. The love which comes from God is given to the Son, who in turn gives it to all who follow him. This chain of love can, in theory, extend without limits, from Jesus to his disciples and from his disciples to all others. 'As the Father has loved me, so have I loved you . . . My command is this: Love each other as I have loved you' (John 15:9, 12). In giving this love, Jesus endured much hardship and suffering. Therefore, when passing this love on to others, Jesus' disciples will also endure hardship and suffering. However, as beginning and end of this circle of love, it is God's love that supports and motivates it. Those who are hated, excluded, insulted and rejected because of their Christian ministry are promised recognition and reward by God (Luke 6:22). In this sense, human *agape* is not a humanistic love but a theistic love, although it appears in the form of neighbour-love.

The value of this love lies in its altruistic motive and its benevolent action. In a radical formula, one is required to give up not only one's material, but also one's spiritual benefits: 'For I could wish that I myself were cursed and cut off from Christ for the sake of my brothers, those of my own race, the people of Israel' (Romans 9:3). Altruistic love in its absolute form, or love for the sake of love, is recognized as the ideal pattern for Christian neighbour-love, and is best expressed by Søren Kierkegaard in his contrasting neighbour-love with erotic love and friendship: both erotic love and friendship are determined by their object, only love for one's neighbour is determined by love itself. One's neighbour may be anybody, unconditionally anybody. Love for one's neighbour makes no distinction in its object, because 'it [neighbour-love] is a characteristic by which or in virtue of which you exist for others'.[36] Neighbour-love is given to others who are regarded for their own sake, whether or not this love brings benefits to oneself. H. Richard Niebuhr explores other-orientated love in a much wider context and gives a detailed description of the Christian ideal of neighbour-love: 'Love is rejoicing over the existence of the beloved one . . . it is the commitment of the self by self-binding will to make the other great'.[37]

The Gospel according to John explores the divine foundation of Christian love. On the one hand, love for others is a response to the divine command, which enables one to abide in love; on the other, love for others is the application of the divine love, which enables one to bear the fruits of love (15:7–8). These two aspects of love are unified in friendship (15:15) between Jesus and his followers in his promise that 'You are my friends if you do what I command' (15:14). In this formula, the reciprocity of being loved by Jesus and obedient response to Jesus' command is obvious. This reciprocity troubles some modern theologians, who find it unacceptable that John should promote a love that is given only to those who have loved Jesus. They insist that this concept of love is a step backward from the 'ethical universalism' of the Synoptic writers.[38] It is true that John modifies unconditional love and makes it conditional on one's response to God's calling. However, it is not a transformation from the universalism of love to a relativism of love. Unconditional love and conditional love are used to refer to two kinds of relationships: that between humans and God, and that between humans and other humans. God and humans do not belong to the same order of being, and therefore there is no competition between God's love and human love. Since a true human love is rooted in a love of God, love between humans is always taken as conditional upon the establishment of a right relationship between God's calling and human response. Under the love of God, 'all men' enjoy an equality with one another. Their love for others is also conditional upon the love they receive from Jesus. Understood in this way, the difference between John and the other Gospel writers is very small. What John has done is simply to have made the implicitly theological claim explicit, and to have applied it to a closely-knit Christian community.

How is one to love others? This, in early Christian teaching, is the question of how to carry out the law and the commandments. In answer to this question, Jesus offered a summary of the law and the prophets: in everything, do to others what you would have them do to you (Matthew 7:12). This summary has been called the

Golden Rule. As a rule, it has two functions. One is to tell people what love is and the other is to show people how to love. There is a difference between these two functions, and they can be easily confused, thus causing misunderstandings. As a way for loving, the Golden Rule relates desires to behaviour, so that one should do only those things that one would like done to oneself. As the content of love, it stresses the need to do good to others. This requirement becomes more explicit in the parable of the Good Samaritan: 'Go and do likewise [help those in need of help]'. Of these two functions, the emphasis on how to love is more important than the emphasis on what love is. A rule is a guide for behaviour. Just as a line cannot be drawn straight without a ruler, so love cannot be properly exercised without a recognizable way. This practical requirement also finds support from the fact that Jesus states the Golden Rule in the context of a comparison with family relationships, and in particular with the relationship between the Father in heaven and the seeker on earth. All parents, good and bad alike, know how to give good gifts to their children. Following their own instincts, then, they should also know how much more will God give to those who ask him. And following upon that, they should also know how to treat others.

By extending one's natural instincts to a universal love and extending divine love to human love, Christian theologians engage in an argument similar to that extension from family love to universal love made by Mencius. As in the case of Confucian *jen,* this extension by analogy must not be understood to be based on self-love, but simply as a way to the understanding of universal love. Understood as the content of love, the Golden Rule would appear to be an ethic based on self-interest, whether, as Bultmann says, a 'morality of naïve egoism',[39] or, as in Tillich's words, a 'calculating justice' waiting to be transformed into 'creative justice'.[40] Even Nygren, for whom this is not a serious problem, is led to resolve the disharmony between self-love and neighbour-love by saying that 'Self-love is man's natural condition; it is also the basis of the perversion of his will to evil. Everyone knows how by nature he loves himself. So, runs the commandment . . . When love gains its new direction, when it is turned away from the self and directed to one's neighbour, then the natural perversion of the will is overcome.'[41] However, all these difficulties and problems would be dispersed if we saw the commandment as an expression of the way to love rather than the content of love. The conscientious self provides the starting point for reflection on one's relation with others and one's search for the ultimate meaning of life. The Golden Rule does not imply that one should do good to others in order to do good to oneself, or because one wants to be repaid by others. Both implications are absent from any of the commandments of which the Golden Rule is a summary. They also contradict the texts themselves. Jesus rejected any reciprocal intention in love and demanded that one love those from whom nothing good could be expected in return, and even those who one knew were ungrateful (Luke 6:35).

Human *agape* for others originates from the divine love, is commanded by God and is altruistic by nature. However, who are the 'others'? Many phrases are used in the Bible to express what is meant by 'others', phrases such as 'friends', 'people of Israel', and 'brothers'. But the most common word used by Christians is 'neighbour', and the human response to the divine charity in human relationships is customarily called 'neighbour-love'. Therefore, to understand the nature and scope of Christian love, we have to ask to whom the term 'neighbour' refers.

Ethically speaking, 'neighbour' refers to an open relationship between individuals and between communities. Although the term 'neighbour' is used in the O.T. of those to be loved (Leviticus 19:18), there it has only the narrow meaning of friends, associates or kinsmen, 'and in principle the Judaism of Jesus' day never overthrew the particularity of the concept of neighbour-love. Nor was the situation in any way different in Greco-Roman society'.[42] Its reference to an open human relationship appears, but only implicitly, in the Jewish conception of a covenant which creates an 'artificial brotherhood' between individuals or between groups. However, the covenant-neighbour is first of all a fellow-member of the Covenant people, and this membership implies certain reciprocal obligations and rights. Two of these obligations are expressed, negatively, in the eighth and ninth of the Ten Commandments, and another is expressed, both negatively and positively, in the command to love one's neighbour: 'do not seek revenge or bear a grudge against one of your people. Love your neighbour as yourself' (Leviticus 19:18).

It is clear that the term 'neighbour' in the O.T. has a restricted sense: only the members of the Covenant-people are one's fellowmen, in contradistinction to aliens and strangers. It is in the N.T. that the term is extended to include a much wider and more varied usage. One such usage follows the O.T. tradition and refers to the brotherhood of Christian faith. 'The NT demands love for the brother and love for the neighbour equally. This means that the two terms are considered synonymous as far as their claim upon us is concerned.'[43] Anyone who follows Christ is a brother or a sister. Brothers and sisters are obviously not confined to one's family members or one's blood relatives. They are symbolic terms for the family of God. Anyone who has faith in Jesus Christ is recognized and treated as a brother or a sister in this big family. Loving one another is the first command for this family. The family members should manifest the same care for one another: if one suffers, all others share their suffering; if one rejoices, all others rejoice with him (I Corinthians 12:25–6). In this family, Jesus is said to be the first-born and beloved Son of God and therefore the first brother of the family of believers (Hebrews 2:11), even when he is also served as Lord by his disciples (Colossians 1:7). Since the first 'brother-Lord' loved his 'brother-followers' and died for them all, love must prevail in the community of believers.

The term 'neighbour' is further used in the wider sense that anybody who is brought near to us is our neighbour. By this extension of the term neighbour, Jesus and the early Christian teachers established a universality of love and a universal community of all human beings. This is revealed in the parable of the Good Samaritan. Asked 'who is *my* neighbour?', Jesus replied with the story of a Samaritan, whose behaviour differed from that of a priest and a Levite when they came upon an injured traveller, possibly a Jew. Samaritans were treated as Gentiles by Jews of that time. There are many interpretations of this parable. However, as far as the extension of the term 'neighbour' is concerned, three points should be made. The first is that to the question 'who is my neighbour? Jesus replied with the question 'who was the neighbour to the man in need of help?' By this change, 'Jesus destroyed the old centripetal grading system, in which the centre was "I", but retained the idea of the neighbour as organising principle and founded a new system, in which the centre was "Thou".'[44] According to this interpretation, when someone is considering who is his or her neighbour, he or she should not search for the one who can help him or her, but should look for, and be ready to help, whoever is in need of help. We act as neighbours towards those who, no matter to what class or rank or nation they belong, need help, just as the Samaritan acted towards the injured Jew. The universalism expressed in this parable must have greatly impressed the early Christians, because this conception is applied to various situations and in various ways.

For example, although Paul does not use the word 'neighbour' to refer to the universalism of Christian love, he nevertheless expresses the same idea in his 'doing good to one another and to all' (I Thessalonians 5:15). Doing good to all is elsewhere equated with doing evil to nobody. In this way, Paul tacitly extends the love between members of the church or the body of Christ to including all men and women, wherever and whoever they may be. In the concept of 'neighbour', the distinction between this nation and that nation, between friend and stranger, between native and foreigner, has been eliminated. Distinction and separation have given way to a universal compassion that binds together all humans. In this way the concept of neighbour is extended so widely that the traditional restriction of the Jewish concept is removed.

The second point we must learn from this parable is that in the 'neighbour', Christians see a picture of Christ himself: compassionate, merciful and loving. Jesus did not say whether this Samaritan believed his teaching or not (he might never have heard Jesus' preaching). He simply insisted that this Samaritan was the neighbour of the traveller because he 'had compassion' on him. Since 'compassion' (or 'mercy') is, outside the parables, applied elsewhere in the gospels only to Jesus, what the Samaritan did was simply to act in the way that Jesus acts. Furthermore, since neighbour-love is to do others good, and therefore whoever does one good is one's neighbour, doing good to others not only brings them benefit, but also brings near to them the humanity which is revealed in Jesus Christ. Anyone who does good to others is their neighbour, partly because his or her love reminds them of the love of Jesus Christ, and partly because doing good to others is an expression of love. In this way, the figure of Jesus becomes universally available, and the neighbours who should love one another need not necessarily belong to the same faith, so long as it upholds a tradition of compassion and mercy. Although their forms of humanity may differ, the essence of Buddhist mercy or Confucian *jen* is not remote from the essence of Jesus' neighbour-love. As far as their conceptions of universal love are concerned, the gap between the different traditions is narrow.

The third point to be noted about this parable is that 'neighbour' is a reciprocal term, and that two people are neighbours to each other, each helping the other in one and the same act. In one sense, this is determined by the fact of human community, whereby one person needs another in order to survive. In another sense, it means that in helping others one is also helping oneself. Normally, those who help others act as neighbours to these others. However, the latter also, because their suffering and need of help, provide an opportunity for the former to express their humanity are neighbours to the former. Human compassion has to be motivated not only by Jesus Christ, but also by other humans who are in need. A self-absorbed or indifferent person is a neighbour to nobody, nor can he or she have neighbours.

Understood on the basis of these three points, the term 'neighbour' can be a truly universal term, and its application can exceed the limitations of nation, faith, tradition and class. Admittedly, such an application remains a matter of theoretical argument, and in practice it has seldom been applied by Christians either in the past or in the present. However, even its theoretical development has brought a better understanding of human nature and the human future. Especially striking is the fact that what Jesus taught in the parable of the Good Samaritan is similar to what Mencius taught in his parable of the child about to fall into a well. In both these parables, love is directed to a person whom one has never met or heard, and is to do good to a stranger without thinking of one's own interests or calculating one's own benefits. To achieve the same purpose, however, that is, to extend the range of love, Jesus and Mencius gave different examples. Jesus chose a Samaritan, a Gentile-like foreigner for the Jews of that time, to prove that even a Samaritan could be one's neighbour and have compassion on the suffering, and tried thereby to destroy the boundaries between different peoples and different faiths. Mencius used a child falling into a well to evoke the powerful instinct of human love, because for him the urgent need was to apply family affection to all people under heaven. Their difference can also be seen in their concepts of human nature. For Jesus, universal love is possible because everyone, whether a Jew or a Samaritan, is motivated by the Spirit of God, while for Mencius, it is possible because everybody has a good heart, which comes from the *jen* and righteousness of Heaven.

The universality of human *agape* is especially expressed in Jesus' command of loving one's enemy. In Christianity, to love one's enemies is a natural extension of loving one's neighbour, when this is understood universally. In this universal love, love should be given not only to one's friends, fellow-men, or even strangers whom one does not know and who will therefore involve a risk, but also to one's enemies, who are to be regarded as a threat to one's life as well as one's welfare. In one sense, love for enemies is especially characteristic of Christian love, and serves to differentiate Christian love from Jewish love and, indeed, from love as interpreted by most human traditions. Jesus, it is recorded, dismissed the old tradition of loving one's neighbours and hating one's enemies:

> If you love them that love you, what credit is that to you? Even 'sinners' love those who love them. And if you do good to those who are good to you, what credit is that to you? Even 'sinners' do that . . . But love your enemies, do good to them, and lend to them without expecting to get anything back. Then your reward will be great, and you will be sons of the Most High, because he is kind to the ungrateful and wicked. (Luke 6:32–35)

By analysing the term 'enemy', we may grasp the universality of Christian *agape.* In the N.T., the term 'enemy' is used mainly in four senses: the enemies of God (Luke 19:27), contrasted with God's chosen people; the Gentiles, contrasted with Jews; those who persecute (Matthew 5:44), hate (Luke 6:27), curse and abuse (Luke 6:28) you, or even those who do not love you, contrasted with your neighbours who show mercy and do good to you; and those who are immoral, unrighteous and unjust, contrasted with those who are good and righteous. Above all, to love your enemies means to love those who persecute and curse you, which is much more difficult than loving one's friends and neighbours. Because it is more difficult, it is more valuable. Even Gentiles love their brothers and neighbours: what difference, then, is there between a disciple of Jesus and a non-believer, if the disciple loves only those who love him or her? Perfection cannot be attained by loving only one's friends: much more important is one's love for one's enemies. To love one's enemy, one should do several things which contrast with the old tradition: doing good to those who hate you, blessing those who curse you and praying for those who ill-treat you. We may also add non-resistance to an enemy who is beating, robbing and abusing you; and giving a would-be borrower more than you are asked to lend. Through this love, enemies are no longer enemies, but are treated as neighbours and loved as neighbours. By the command to love one's enemies, the category of 'neighbour' is extended to its fullest universal sense.

The universality of human *agape* in Christian doctrine is possible only on the divine foundation: whether neighbour-love or enemy-love, it is sanctioned by God's command. In the case of loving one's neighbour, this love is firmly established in God's love. As Nygren points out, 'There is no need to look for some valuable quality in the neighbour, concealed behind his actual state, to find an explanation why he should be loved. God's own love is explanation and sanction enough: "so shall ye be children of your Father which is in heaven".'[45] Love of one's enemy is also established in God's love, because God's love and mercy are universal, causing the sun to rise on the evil as well as on the good, sending rain on the righteous and the unrighteous alike, and being kind both to the grateful and to the ungrateful. The ultimate sanction of this love also lies with God: if you love your enemies, you will be called the son of God, you will be rewarded [with eternal life] and you will become perfect like God in heaven. Only in this transcendental background can we fully understand the universality of Christian love with regard to one's neighbour and enemies.

LOVE AND RELIGION

In most religious traditions in the world, either love is an indispensable element of faith or love is itself taken as faith. In these traditions love is a unifying force and plays an essential role in their development. Love and faith become one reality with two names or two features. This promotion of love to the level of faith creates a doctrine in which religion and ethics are unified into one: faith is ethically love, while love is religiously faith.

As we have seen above, both Christian *agape* and Confucian *jen* are interpreted as love in general, especially as the love of others. Love, the love of others rather than the love of self, is understood as the content of their doctrine of transcendence and the core of their ethical theory and practice. However, the differences in their transcendental orientations and in their approaches to transcendence bring out two distinct ways in their ethical thinking, the humanistic way and the theistic way. In Confucianism, cultivation of one's virtue is the way to transcendence. However, to cultivate one's virtue, one must practise it in human relationships, that is, in loving others both benevolently and beneficently. Only by loving others can one's virtue be manifested and one's limitations be overcome. In this sense, love for others is not only a social value and norm but also a transcendental approach. In Christianity, love for God is the way to transcendence. However, to love God one must also love one's neighbour, that is, love any person who is in need. Only in neighbour-love can one's love for God be fulfilled and one's being be unified with the being of Christ.

In the humanistic system of Confucianism, *jen* is the cosmic centre as well as a human entity. When it is cultivated in the human heart, it makes humanity great and fulfilled. When it is fulfilled, it flows over one's self to human community, presented as sincere love for others. In love, humanity is further developed and flourishes, so it is manifested both within one's own self and in one's relationship with others. In the theistic doctrine of Christianity, *agape* is essentially a divine quality and manifests in the human relationship with divinity. When God's grace descends to the human heart, humans respond both with love for God and love for neighbours. Love for one's neighbour is the other half of human response to God's love and is a manifestation of one's faith in God and one's hope for transcendence.

Thus, in *jen* as love and *agape* as neighbour-love, we have found an exemplary illustration of how Christianity and Confucianism are related and how they are differentiated. As human love, both call for universal benevolence and beneficence, to treat others as oneself. As different ways of loving, they present different orientations with different emphases, one on the theological dimension of love, the other on the ethical value of love. These often lead to misunderstandings between these two traditions. In the eyes of Christian *agape*, the ethics of Confucian *jen* is a science which helps individuals find satisfaction for their own needs, and leads to their own personal goodness, and is therefore characteristically an individualist ethics, while the ethics of Christian *agape* is a universalistic science that originates from God's grace and seeks the satisfaction of the needs of all humans. In the eye of Confucian *jen*, however, although Christian *agape* is Goodness itself rather than a means to some other goal, it is conditional on much else and therefore is only of secondary importance. Confucians would say that, over against the 'inferior quality' of *agape*, *jen* is the essence not only of humans but also of the universe, and is the fundamental force which actively pursues unity between humans and the cosmos.

These differences and misunderstandings between Christianity and Confucianism, like many others we have discussed in previous chapters, come mainly from the divergences in their conception of transcendence, their way to transcendence and their idea of what is love. Although both stress that love for others is essential for transcendence, they part on whom to love, why to love and how to love. To carry forward our comparison between Confucian *jen* and Christian *agape*, therefore, we must appreciate properly the different position and value of love in Confucianism and Christianity, and examine carefully how they are related, transcendentally and ethically, with other elements of religion, such as hatred and fear.

The love that is not applicable universally is seldom of sufficient value to qualify it as the principle of a religion. Both Confucians and Christians have realized this and have extended their conception of love as widely as possible. Generally speaking, not only are family, friends and acquaintances included among the objects of love, but all humans are to be cared for as oneself. To love others is to take them into one's own sphere of concern and make them an integral part of one's own person. In this sense, their doctrines express a kind of universalism of love. Taking care of, being concerned for, and doing good to, others is the basic requirement of universal love. In this way, loving becomes an ethical relationship as well as a transcendental pursuit, in which love for others finds its full value.

In the form of love for others, universal and fundamental *jen* and *agape* underlie various kinds of human love. One of these is sexual love. Like any other kind of love, the Christian conception of sexual love is firmly based on its transcendental goal and therefore has three characteristics: first, that sexual love should be bound by commitment and marriage, sexual immorality being a sin (Matthew 15:19); secondly, that marriage symbolizes the relation of Jesus and the Church (Ephesians 5:25) and therefore should be strengthened by fidelity and love rather than undermined by casual sex; and thirdly, that married love is an expression of reverence for Christ (Ephesians 5:21). Married love is important, because it gives order and direction to sexual desire and helps the married couple to pursue perfection in Christ. However, married love is only part of Christian love and must not be identified with the Christian principle, partly because its universal concern is limited by its association with sex. Like Christianity, Confucianism discusses sexual love between men and women, and warns against sexual love outside of marriage. In a similar way to that in which Christianity makes sexual love a means towards love for Christ, Confucianism subjects sexual love to the cultivation of character:

the moral value of sexual love is more important than its biological function. Influenced by the Taoist world-view, some Confucians have explored married love in its symbolizing of the interaction between two cosmic and creative forces: heaven and earth, or *yang* and *yin*. Thus married love is endowed with a sort of metaphysical meaning. However, this does not change its basic idea that sexual love is not an essential element in their doctrine of *jen*. Both in Christianity and in Confucianism, indulgence in sexual love is frequently said to be a threat to the attainment of one's ultimate goal. In some strands of Christian thinking virginity is proclaimed to be the ideal, and only the duty of procreation can render sexual intercourse licit, even in marriage. Confucius, too, condemned indulgence in sex and called for humans to guard against it. This attitude was taken to its extreme in later Confucianism, when it became part and parcel of state ideology that sex was immoral in all its forms. Compared with Christianity, however, Confucianism did not develop in marriage reverence for the divine. It therefore lacks the Christian conception of the divine blessing of marriage and the shared obedience to God and to each other of husband and wife. As a result, for Confucianism sexual love is even less universally applicable than it is for Christianity, and in Confucianism sexual love has a less important role to play in the application of *jen* than it has in the Christian doctrine of *agape*.

Another form of love is that between friends. Friendship is of great significance both in the Christian tradition and in Confucian doctrine. In both traditions friendship is praised more than many other kinds of love: love finds its elegant form in friendship. For some people, friendship is a covering term for all good relationships, as M. C. D'Arcy points out: 'The perfection of love . . . is to be found in personal friendship, whether between a man and a woman, between man and man, or between man and God.'[46] The emphasis on friendship in ancient Greek culture left a deep impression on early Christian thinking, and friendship was regarded as almost the core of Christian virtues. Friends were people bound together through faith in Christ, and therefore, in the context of Christian fellowship friendship was sometimes said to be brotherly love. Within the household of faith, everyone was a friend of everyone else, and all were friends of Jesus Christ. In this sense, friendship was not very different from *agape*. However, since then the situation has changed. 'To the ancients, friendship seemed the happiest and most fully human of all loves; the crown of life and the school of virtue. The modern world, in comparison, ignores it.' The reason why love of friends is thought in the modern Christian world to be inferior to other forms of love is a utilitarian consideration: 'Without *eros* none of us would have been begotten and without affection [family love] none of us would have been reared; but we can live and breed without Friendship.'[47] From this, we can see the modern conception of friendship differs from the ancient conception. In the modern world friendship is no longer taken to be a universal relationship, as people become more and more used to living their lives within their homes or on their own. It has lost its function in the family as well as in most relationships between men and women. It has shed its role of encouraging people to pursue their faith and ideal, and so has become of little value for promoting the Christian principle.

Much of the process that Christian friendship has undergone applies also to Confucianism. The *Analects* starts with a paragraph in which the coming of a friend is said to be one of the three greatest joys of life. Friends are able to encourage, stimulate and develop one's conscience, and can help one to learn the Confucian classics and cultivate one's character. The most important virtue in friendship is 'faithfulness' or 'trustworthiness'. It is required that one should examine oneself three times a day, and one of the tasks is to examine whether or not one has been faithful to one's friends (*Analects* I, 4). Friendship is valued because it is an effective means to attain the virtue of *jen* (XII, 24). Therefore, Confucius taught his disciples to make friends with those whose virtue is superior to their own, but not with those whose character is inferior (I, 8). These considerations give friendship a much lower position in Confucianism, a means to the end of *jen*. Although friendship may in theory be understood as holding between all human beings, its objects in fact are very limited. In Confucian texts friends are not those whom we like or love, but those who share with us the same values and who undertake the same *Tao*.

Underlaid by *jen* and *agape*, love in Confucianism and Christianity is not love only for one's family, relatives and friends. Either as Christian value or as Confucian virtue, it is deeper than the sexual relationship and wider than friendship. It is to love others as oneself. 'Others' here may refer to strangers, with whom one has no biological nor social connection. Thus, 'why love?' becomes a crucial question for establishing a universal relation between the loving and the loved. To answer this question, Christians appeal to their transcendental understanding of love, and satisfy their inquiry in relating human love to divine love: divine love is the root, basis and source, while human love, in all its variety, is a response to God's love. There is a similar – similar but not identical – relation between Confucian *Tian* and human beings in the early classics, in which *Tian* is said to be the root of human *jen*, and humans love because *Tian* loves. However, human response to the love of *Tian* is not strongly emphasized. What is stressed is that humans should imitate the pattern of *Tian* and follow *Tian's jen*. To follow *Tian's jen*, one must practise virtues in human society. In this way, the transcendental pursuit of early Confucianism is transformed as an ethical approach, and the focus of love is shifted from one of transcendental calling to one of human cultivation.

For a Christian, loving God and loving one's neighbour are ordained by God and a response to the calling of Jesus Christ. Therefore, the reasons for loving one's neighbour lie essentially in the binding force of the covenant between God and humans. God's love is expressed in Christ and in his sacrifice on the cross. First, then, humans should imitate God in his love: 'Be imitators of God, therefore, as dearly loved children and live a life of love, just as Christ loved us and gave himself up for us as a fragrant offering and sacrifice to God'; secondly, love is a consequence of God's forgiveness: 'Be kind and compassionate to one another, forgiving each other, just as in Christ God forgave you' (Ephesians 5:1–2; and 4:32); thirdly, God's love overwhelms us: 'Christ's love compels us' (II Corinthians 5:14); fourthly, love offered to strangers and service given to one's neighbour are themselves love and service offered to Christ, since in many parables God himself appears as a stranger, or prisoner, or shepherd.

The Confucian way of answering the question 'why love?' exhibits differences when compared with that of Christianity. The fundamental root of love lies in human nature, which comes from *Tian*. Human nature compels us to love, first of all, our parents, then others' parents, and then human beings in general.[48] However, more attention is given in Confucianism than in Christianity to human effort in expressing love. The innate nature of love needs human activity if it is to be actualised, and when one has cultivated one's virtue, one will naturally love others, do good to people and bring peace to the world. This is why Confucius called for continually learning and practising (*Analects* I, 1), Mencius stressed that one must cultivate *jen* and *yi* as farmers cultivated five grains

(*The Book of Mencius*, 6A:19) and Tung Chung-shu emphasized that to manifest one's nature, one must pursue learning and practice as an egg must be hatched to become a chicken and a silk cocoon must be unravelled to make silk.[49] From the creation of *Tian* to the expression of the various forms of human love there is no simple relationship of command and response, but a humanistic progress made by humans themselves.

As love, both Confucian *jen* and Christian *agape* are universal. However, they adopt different approaches to the universality of love. Confucians call for one's affection for family as a practice of being *jen* to the world and oneness with the universe. Although family love is the first step to universal love, these two kinds of love are the same in nature and complementary in function. Christian love is practised first in the Christian community or the church, which is taken as a first step to loving one's neighbour. According to Christian doctrine, the way to love is reflected in one's faith in God whose light shining in the human heart shows how one must love both God and humans: you are to love others as God has loved you. However, what is the love for God? Some theologians argue that this love is completely different from one's love for other humans. For example, Nygren insists that it is necessary to distinguish sharply between human love for God, which is called faith, and human love for one's neighbour, which is called *agape*. He explains *agape* as a spontaneous and uncaused love, and therefore denies that it can be a proper name for human love for God.

> In relation to God, man is never fully spontaneous. Man's self-giving to God is no more than a response, at its best and highest, it is but a reflection of God's own love.[50]

Is it possible for a love that originated in God to appear in two completely different forms, one which can never be 'spontaneous', and one that must always be 'spontaneous'? C. S. Lewis rejects the view that there is an impassable gulf between human love and the divine love, because

> Our loves do not make their claim to divinity until the claim becomes plausible. It does not become plausible until there is in them a real resemblance to God, to Love Himself.[51]

Human love contains as many elements as the divine love: need-love; gift-love; and appreciative love. These mix and interact with one another, moment by moment. In this way, Lewis adds a human factor to theistic doctrine and maintains that human love can be exercised in a variety of ways, sacrificing neither its divine nor its moral status.

Without being troubled by the question whether there is a difference between human love for the transcendent and human love for other human beings, Confucianism proclaims that human love is both ethical and transcendental, or else that because human love is ethical in nature, it functions as the way to the Transcendent. In principle, love for others is an extension of one's virtue and so the more one cultivates one's nature, the more one loves others. In practice, love for others is a natural extension of one's love for one's parents, and so the more one loves one's parents and brothers, the more one loves others: 'A person of *jen* extends his love from those whom he loves to those whom he has not yet loved' (*The Book of Mencius,* 7A:1). Understood in this way, Confucians do not value highly a love which is caused by things outside of that love itself. *Tian* indeed has a commanding power and imposes the principle of *jen* upon human behaviour. However, whether to love or not to love, whether to love wholeheartedly or only half-heartedly, whether to love for the sake of others or to love for one's own gain, these are matters for one's own choice and depend upon one's own moral achievement. The progress of humanity and the love for others are moved by developing one's innate quality of *jen*. When one possesses *jen* to its utmost, one's love is as universal and spontaneous as the love of *Tian*. This is what is said about sincerity [*cheng*] in *The Doctrine of the Mean*: 'Only those who have possessed the fullest sincerity [*cheng*] can order and adjust the great relationships of mankind, establish the great foundations of humanity, and know the transforming and nourishing operations of heaven and earth' (chapter 32).

Human love is basically an affirmative feeling, attitude or action. Loving something or some person means that we care for that thing or person, and will do that thing or person good. In this sense, love is contrasted with hatred. To love is to affirm, embrace and support, while to hate is to reject, set one's face against and destroy. Hatred is a negative rejection of and moving away from what is hated, while love is an appreciation of and an approach to what is loved. However, love and hatred are interwoven in religious traditions. On the one hand, both Confucian doctrine of *jen* as love and Christian teaching of *agape* are engaged in getting rid of hatred from the human heart. On the other hand, they define love and hatred in two different ways so that the relationship between love and hatred is presented, respectively, along the lines of humanism and of theism.

In Christianity as a theocentric religion, love is primarily friendship with God and obedience to his commands, and hatred is enmity with God and rejection of his law. In Confucianism as an anthropocentric tradition, love originates in human nature, while hatred is regarded as a deviation from human nature. The theistic element in the Judeo-Christian tradition carries with it a transcendental absoluteness which then flows over into the *negative* responses to love, so that hatred is directed to evil which rejects God. However, the conception of hatred which occurs in the O.T. is greatly changed in the teaching of Jesus and his disciples. Since God has accepted his enemies as his sons, hatred itself is contrary to God's love. The old saying that 'You should love your neighbour and hate your enemy' (Matthew 5:43) is consequently transformed into a new teaching 'loving neighbours as well as enemies and doing good to those who hate you' (Luke 6:27). Compared with the Jewish tradition, Christianity places more emphasis on the value of dispersing hatred. One way is to realize that Jesus draws this hatred upon himself, as he told his disciples: 'the world cannot hate you, but it hates me because I testify that what it does is evil'; 'if the world hates you, keep in mind that it hated me first' (John 7:7; 15:8). Another way to disperse hatred is to emphasize God's command of love against hatred. Hatred is said to be an insuperable obstacle to one's salvation and to being loved by God: 'Anyone who claims to be in the light but hates his brother is still in the darkness'; 'anyone who hates his brother is a murderer, and you know that no murderer has eternal life in him' (I John 2:9; 3:15; 4:20). In this sense, St. Augustine speaks of love as life itself, while hatred is death. To love means to have eternal life in Christ, while to hate means to separate from Christ and death.[52]

The humanistic nature of *jen* also precludes hatred as rejection or resentment. However, since love is an extension of one's virtue and hatred is the result of failure to cultivate one's character, to turn from hatred to love is to cultivate one's virtue. Hatred (*wu* or *tseng*) is also used to refer to one's dislike of what is contradictory to *jen*. A *chun tzu* prefers the presence of *jen* to the absence of *jen*, love being given to the former while hatred is given to the latter (*Analects*, IV, 6). Paragraph 24 in the Book XVII of the *Analects* can be taken as

a footnote for what Confucius means by hating the absence of *jen*:
a *chun tzu* dislikes those who spread slanderous rumours about
others; who, as inferiors, slander their superiors; who dare to do
anything but with no sense of *li*; and who are stubborn in carrying
out their own ideas. In this paragraph, it is clear that what one
should shun is not the person, but his or her shortcomings or bad
habits. With a humanistic spirit, most Confucians dislike the idea
of hating others, whoever they may be. For them, hatred spoils the
human heart. Only those who do 'not harbour the feeling of hate
or desire to hurt' can attain to *jen*.[53]

Human love is also interwoven with fear. In one sense, fear is
the response to mystery surrounding the core of religious practice
and ritual, while love is the key to unlock this mystery; fear leads
one to shun the frightening, while love directs one's admiration
and attachment to what is loved and even to what is feared.
Therefore, both *jen* and *agape* are taken as a way to disperse fear.
Although a difference has been detected between the O.T. and the
N.T. concerning the relationship of love and fear,[54] it is difficult
to draw a similar line between love and fear in the Christian
doctrine of *agape*. Primarily, Christian fear is due to the possibility
of disobeying, failing or losing God. On the one hand, Christians
believe that God's love has embraced or will embrace them so that
there is no fear at all in their heart. Those who fear are those who
have no faith in God. 'Fear not' becomes one of the central themes
of Christian preaching. To drive out fears from people, the preacher
proclaims obedience to God, peace of mind in obeying God's will,
and eternal life in God's love. 'God is love. Whoever lives in love
lives in God, and God in him . . . There is no fear in love. Perfect
love drives out fear, because fear has to do with punishment. The
one who fears is not made perfect in love' (I John 4:16, 18). On the
other hand, Christian doctrine retains fear as a way to love: God
as the Creator is both terrifying and attractive, and his love for
his creation is an 'awe-ful' love, beyond human comprehension.
So although 'perfect love casts out fear' as terror, it retains 'fear'
as 'wonder in the face of mystery'. In this way, as the transcendence
of God the Creator is taken as the source of a truly human love,
it introduces an element of absoluteness into the human response
and a fear into human love for God. Fear of God is believed in the
O.T. to be a characteristic of the chosen people,[55] while in the N.T.
it is put forward as a powerful motive for Christian conduct: 'it is
a fearful thing to fall into the hands of the living God' (Hebrews

10:31). One must work out one's 'own salvation with fear and trembling' (Philippians 2:12). The more one fears the judgement of God, the more one is moved to love and obey God.

In Confucian doctrine, there are two kinds of fear, different in their nature: fear (*ju*) without courage, and fear (*wei*) with respect. A person who fears because of a lack of courage is a coward, resulting from not cultivating his character. The weapon for fighting this kind of fear is the cultivation of one's character. This cultivation will lead one to be a person of courage, who knows nothing of fear (*Analects* IX, 29). However, a person who fears with respect is a *chun tzu*. In the second sense, fear is taken as one of the qualities which a virtuous person must possess. 'There are three things of which a *chun tzu* stands in awe: of the Mandate of Heaven, of great men and of the words of sages. A base person [*hsiao* JEN] does not know the Mandate of Heaven and consequently does not stand in awe of it, is disrespectful to great men, and makes sport of the words of sages' (*Analects*, XVI, 8). The Mandate of Heaven is absolute and mystical, and must be obeyed and followed with fear and respect. Just because the person of *jen* knows the sovereignty of *Tian*, he constantly stands in awe of its Mandate. A person who does not know the Mandate does not fear it, and thus has nothing to do with *jen*. As far as great men and the words of sages are concerned, it is essential for a person who is cultivating his or her character to hold them in awe, because without great men or/and the words of sages society would be in chaos, and humans would be like animals.

If we compare Confucian '*Tian*'s Mandate' with Christian 'will of God', Confucian 'great men' with Christian 'saints', and Confucian 'words of the sages' with Christian 'words of Jesus Christ', there are indeed many similarities between these two traditions in their dealing with human love and fear. Like Christians who overcome fear by having faith and hope in Christ, Confucians find the way to turn fear into love in having faith in the power of virtue: '*Tian* begot the virtue that is in me. What have I to fear from such a one called Huan Tui?'[56] However, the difference between Confucian *jen* and Christian *agape* in doctrine has also found its way into their understanding of fear in practice. The Christian doctrine of hell as abandonment by God is a corollary of its belief in God's salvation, and in the medieval Church at least, the pains of hell were painted in lurid colours arousing great fear among those who neither believe in nor obey God. For a Confucian, however, the deep source of the negative fear is not the mystery of God's creation and judgement, but human ignorance, immaturity and inadequate cultivation. When one cultivates one's character, one's virtue will grow. Growth of one's virtue enables one to take the universe as one's own body, in which one needs neither fear nor anxiety (*Analects*, XII, 4) and to consider life and death one's destiny, in which there is nothing fearful (XII, 5). From this comparison, we may infer that fear remains a mirror image of love in a theistic faith, while it is only an incidental accompaniment of a humanistic ideal.

7

Jen and *Agape*:
an Open Horizon

In the last three chapters we explored Confucian *jen* and Christian *agape* in their three contrasts, which demonstrate the divergence between a humanistic and a theistic tradition. As we have repeatedly argued, the divergence between a humanistic and a theistic tradition is that they characterize two different types of spirituality and manifest two different ways of attaining to its transcendence. As the central theme of Christian spirituality, *agape* underpins the Christian transcendence in divine grace, so that human love is not self-explanatory and must be defined by God's love. To attain to the transcendental ideal, a spiritual responsiveness is needed. As the fundamental principle of Confucian spirituality, *jen* identifies the Confucian transcendence with the fulfilment of humanity, so that human beings are responsible for their own growth and progress, both moral and spiritual. To attain to the transcendental ideal, a moral cultivation of one's own *jen* and an extension of one's own virtue to the world are necessary. In demonstrating the characteristics of their spirituality, Christianity and Confucianism have used two kinds of language, the language of theology and the language of ethics. In Christian spirituality, ethical matters are expressed in theological terms and in a creational context. The source and resource of moral growth is therefore God and the fundamental question is the relationship of humans to God. In Confucian spirituality, however, transcendental ideal is described by an ethical terminology and in a moral context. To be transcendental is to be moral and to cultivate one's virtue. Thus, although the transcendental Being or Power (*Tian*) plays a role in human attainment to the transcendental goal, the source and resource of human transcending is essentially humanity and therefore the fundamental question is the relationship of humans to humans.

Being aware of these contrasts, we have also argued that Christian *agape* as the underlying idea of a theistic tradition displays a greater similarity than had been anticipated to Confucian *jen* as the principle of a humanistic tradition. In the sense of similarity, their divergences are mainly a matter of contrasts between the different languages they use to describe their spirituality rather than their spiritual contents, or contrasts between different emphases they put on the way to transcendence rather than their underlying pursuits. Although the Confucian ideal is different from the Christian ideal, the one ethical and the other spiritual, both are concerned with human transcending the limitation of life to attain to eternal life. Although the Confucian approach to transcendence differs from the Christian way to transcendence, both stress that transcendence cannot be attained except by being one with the ultimate. Although the motive of Confucian love differs from the motive of Christian neighbour-love, taking care of others, doing them good and treating them as oneself are common to their conception of human love. Furthermore, the similarities between Confucian spirituality and Christian spirituality are enlarged by the fact that neither of them exists in isolation, especially in the modern world. One is in constant interaction with the other, and in this process of interaction one changes itself as it changes the other.[1] Consequently, the line of demarcation between these two types of traditions has become so blurred in the process of exchange that it can be rigidly maintained only as a matter of theoretical abstraction.

Since Confucianism as a humanistic tradition and Christianity as a theistic tradition are clearly distinct from, and yet closely related to, each other, the similarities between *jen* and *agape* for which we have been arguing should not be taken to imply total identity, nor should their differences, to which we have also been attending, be taken to imply total polarity. Similarities and differences are embedded in cultural co-existence, develop in religious interchange, and manifest themselves in social and communal attitudes and behaviour. In searching for the similarities and differences between *jen* and *agape* in respect of their conceptions of transcendence, their theory and practice, and their way of relating the secular and the sacred, we have applied the general principle of a comparative study of religions, namely, that their similarities must be examined in their differences and their differences examined in their similarities.

A comparative study of *jen* and *agape* is characterized by the fact that both are fundamental principles in their respective traditions, underlying all other principles and doctrines. We have seen that *jen* is treated as the central thread running through the whole of Confucian teaching, and that it is *jen* that gives meaning to the Confucian virtues. *Jen* has been discussed in the interrelationship between Confucian Transcendent and human beings, and has been taken to be both the movement between them and the foundation of their unity and harmony. We have also seen how *agape* is taken to be the summary of the law and the bond that binds all the Christian virtues together. *Agape* embraces both divine calling and human response, and contains within itself the reason and possibility for humans to be reconciled with God, which is the Christian's primary concern and ultimate goal.

In any developed religious system there is more than one principle. However, the significance and value of these principles vary. Normally, one is predominant, while the others are subsidiary. *Jen* and *agape* are such predominant principles in Confucianism and Christianity respectively. As fundamental principles, *jen* and *agape* shape and order the other principles. A principle that does not shape and order other principles cannot be fundamental. However, this does not mean that in order to be fundamental, a principle must replace, devalue or deny the other principles. *Jen* or *agape* is fundamental because it informs all other principles, yet leaves them room to function in their own ways, and because it governs all other concepts, yet co-exists and co-operates with them. Its power and strength come from its interaction and coordination with them, rather than from its conflict and contradiction with them.

Confucian *jen* is the spirit and value of the whole Confucian system, but it often appears only indirectly in the other virtues, so that each of them both represents *jen* and at the same time has its own function and value for the realization of *jen*. Confucius believed that *jen* was the foundation on which one could build one's moral character, because it was the source of the good life and the power of goodness. However, he also called people to set their heart on *tao*, to practise the virtues and to take recreation in the arts of rituals, music, archery and the like (*Analects*, VII, 6). To become an eminent human is Mencius' ideal. In his opinion, to become eminent one has to base oneself on *jen* and follow the path of righteousness.[2] *Jen* is thus taken as the starting point for a virtuous life and the basis for universal harmony. All virtues have their own value, while *jen* underlies them all. For example, to perform one's duties either as a subject or as a son or as a young brother is important, because in these performances the realization of *jen* takes place. On the other hand, performing one's duties cannot be independent or detached from the spirit of *jen*. It must be preceded by the heart–mind of *jen*. 'Ministers must cherish *jen* and righteousness to serve their sovereign; sons must cherish *jen* and righteousness to serve their fathers; younger brothers must cherish *jen* and righteousness to serve their elder brothers' (*The Book of Mencius* 6B:4). The cherishing of *jen* in one's heart is a precondition for any moral action and is what makes an action valuable. Yet to cherish *jen* in one's heart, one must perform one's duties.

It is evident that, in the main stream of Christian writings, love is taken to be the basis for the proper functioning of other concepts, while room is left for, and significance attached to, other principles such as faith and hope. Some modern Christian theologians, however, press this tradition to imply that love is not only an inclusive principle but also a superseding principle. For example, Joseph Fletcher sets out his 'situation ethics' in six propositions, of which the first two are that 'Only one "thing" is intrinsically good; namely, love: nothing else at all'; and that 'The ruling norm of Christian decision is love: nothing else.'[3] This theory has certain advantages. By making love the superseding principle, it is easy to reveal the central thread running through the various teachings of Jesus Christ and his disciples, and the highest good that binds all Christian virtues into one system. However, it also raises serious problems in its failure to balance the binding principle and the other Christian values and to leave room for the other concepts and values to function. In fact, like *jen*, *agape* is the underlying idea only in the sense that all other principles must be based on it for their meaning and related to it for their application. Love includes these principles and concepts but does not dissolve them. It informs their fulfilment, in which it finds its own completion.

The primary reason why *jen* and *agape* are fundamental principles and underlying ideas is that they are equated with the source and path of transcendence. In Christianity *agape* is essentially identified with the Spirit of God in Jesus Christ. Christ is the embodiment of love and promotes love in the human heart by his own self-offering and sacrifice. Human love is the sign and symbol of faith in Christ and is the proper response to God's calling. In Confucianism it is argued that *jen* comes from, and is the essence of, *Tian*. 'Heaven

[*Tian*] loves the people, and the sovereign should reverently carry out (this mind) of Heaven [*Tian*].'⁴ This transcendental love is taken as the motive and reason for human love, although in this quotation human love refers primarily to the sovereign's care for his subjects.

Because of the difference between Christian God and Confucian *Tian*, 'to *jen*' is not the same as 'to love'. Transcendence in Christianity signifies, in one sense, reunion with the Creator and Lord. For Christians, love is essentially divine love. Human love is made possible by the sacrifice of Jesus and flourishes only by subjecting oneself to God's sovereignty, confessing one's sin, and relying wholeheartedly on God's mercy. Therefore, Christian love is first of all a downward vertical movement from God to believers, and the ultimate aim of the latter is to transcend themselves in unity with God. Only as a consequence of this downward movement can a horizontal interchange of love between humans be meaningful and desirable. In Confucianism *Tian* is taken both as transcendence and as the totality of natural and human existence. *Tian* is the source of humanity and the ultimate power to function and manifest itself in humans. Thus, by identifying *jen* with *Tian*, the Confucian ideal is firmly associated with the human pursuit of transcendence and with the perfect, which cannot be attained except in human cultivation of their own character and extension of their own virtue to others and to the whole universe. On the one hand, *jen* is a two-way vertical movement between humans and the Ultimate: the love of *Tian* manifests itself in the good nature of humans, while human love fulfils the benevolence of *Tian*, the law of its production and reproduction and the harmony of its creation. On the other hand, *jen* is a two-way horizontal movement between humans, and between humans and nature. Transcendence is not a departure from humanity, nor an opposition to the natural world, but a fulfilment of humanity in the whole universe and in being one body with all beings and things. The ultimate aim of *jen* is to achieve a unity with the universe through manifesting one's own virtue. Therefore, 'to *jen*' is to fulfil one's own potentiality, the potentiality of others, and the potentiality of all things. As far as the relationship between humanity and nature is concerned, the traditional concept of Confucian *jen*, when interpreted as love, has a wider range than the traditional understanding of Christian love. In traditional teaching about *agape*, there was no room for nature or things, since these were believed to have been created only for the benefit of humans who alone can have faith in God. By contrast, in Confucian, or at least in neo-Confucian, *jen*, nature and things are as important objects of love as humans are. The person who has embraced *jen* is to take the whole universe as his or her own family. In the classical words of Chang Tsai, 'Heaven is my father and Earth is my mother, and even such a small creature as I find an intimate place in their midst. Therefore that which fills the universe I regard as my body and that which directs the universe I consider as my nature. All people are my brothers and sisters, and all things are my companions.'[5]

A theistic spirituality is often characterized by the exclusiveness of its principle, while a humanistic spirituality is characteristically inclusive in application of its central principle. The exclusiveness of Christian *agape* is bound up with the exclusiveness of faith in God. *Agape* is first of all taken as God's care for his people and then as a path through which humankind may be reconciled to God. Christianity begins with the good news of the gospel, and the centre of the gospel is about the love of God. The concept of a fallen world logically leads to a belief in the need for its restoration and salvation. Since salvation is in the name of Jesus Christ, who alone is the Saviour, the Way, the Truth and the Life, all other claims to salvation are false. Only in him is the true love of God to be known and shared.

Since Confucianism takes as transcendence the perfection of humanity, in attaining to this ideal exclusiveness is needed much less than in Christianity. Consequently, Confucian *jen* must be inclusive, so that it can be in agreement with the Confucian conception of transcendence. *Jen* as love is a human compassion for other beings and things, and a human intention to be at one with the universe. The inclusiveness of *jen* has a direct impact on the Confucian understanding of good and evil. Goodness, which in Christian thinking is ascribed ultimately and exclusively to God, is the character of the Confucian universe, and evil, which in Christian teaching is taken as a force opposed to God's will, is only the non-development, or deprivation of original goodness. The ontological opposition between the Christian and non-Christian principles is seldom reflected in the understanding of Confucian *jen*. Although most Confucians fully realize that heretical or unorthodox theories can block human efforts to bring harmony to the world, it is their constant endeavour to search for unity between different traditions. The majority of Confucians optimistically believe that the reconciling elements in different traditions, which have certainly existed although they have not yet been fully appreciated, will in time become dominant and will thus bring harmony between all traditions, religious or philosophical. All humans and all human traditions share the same fundamentals, just as all beings and things share the same basic elements. In search for the truth, some Confucians even come to the conviction that traditions and religions differ only as offering different paths to the same ultimate goal.

However, exclusiveness itself can become inclusive, while inclusiveness is never completely and absolutely open. The two-way orientation of *agape* is clear. It is exclusive, because it is conditional upon the recognition of the authority and mercy of God and upon the appreciation of the sacrifice of Jesus. It is inclusive, not only in the sense that it is open to anybody with faith and, as the fundamental principle, shapes and orders the other Christian principles, but also in the sense that it can be, and has been, interpreted in such a way that it extends beyond the boundaries of faith so as to become universal, as in the case of the Good Samaritan. In modern times, exclusiveness and inclusiveness are also interwoven. On the one hand, we may observe that in various forms of modern theology the universalism of *agape* is being emphasized, and that in many Christian churches the claims of exclusiveness for Christian faith have been greatly moderated. On the other hand, since Christian churches are experiencing difficulties in a multi-cultural society, the exclusive interpretation of Christian faith and consequently its concept of *agape* is gaining new strength. The debate is not yet finished, and its positive and negative impact on the concept of Christian *agape* is still to be seen.[6] Interaction between exclusiveness and inclusiveness in Christian theory and practice will remain a main feature in Christian countries.

On the other hand, the inclusiveness manifested in Confucian *jen* is not so open that it can be taken as a model for our attitude to other traditions. The contrast between inclusiveness and exclusiveness, rejection of the latter and insistence on the former, is not always explicitly stated either in traditional Confucian doctrine or in its modern adaptations. The inclusiveness of Confucian *jen* in the classical period remained in most cases potential or theoretical, while its appearance in neo-Confucianism was more of a reluctant response to the fact that Buddhism and Taoism had at that time penetrated every aspect of life, than a positive declaration or projection. Besides, it was constantly claimed that Confucianism was a 'civilized' tradition, in contrast to other religions which were 'barbarian'. When Confucius or Mencius taught love for others, it is misleading to interpret this love as a love for all races and ranks, without considering the difference between the cultured and the uncultured, rulers and those ruled, the morally mature and the morally immature. Although the 'uncultured' were not openly barred from access to the ultimate and *jen*, their situation was thought to be much more difficult, and to depend for enlightenment largely upon the 'cultured'. Applied like this, the inclusiveness of *jen* is not far from the exclusiveness of *agape*, as far as this concerns the division between the faithful and the unfaithful.

Whether inclusive or exclusive, a fundamental principle must have its own way of penetrating into the whole of its own system, motivating human enthusiasm, and helping to relieve human suffering. That is to say, it must be dynamic rather than static. It is a mistake to contrast *agape* and *jen* in the sense that the one is static and the other is dynamic. It is also incorrect to say that *jen* and *agape* operate dynamically in exactly the same way. The difference between *jen* and *agape* is not a matter of whether they are dynamic or not, but of why and how they are dynamic. For the former, the dynamic comes from humanity and expresses itself in an upward movement from the human heart to transcendence, while in the latter, it comes essentially from divinity and manifests itself in a downward movement from transcendence which then penetrates the human heart, human behaviour and human attitudes.

God is the source of the dynamic of Christian *agape*, or, in Nygren's words, the love of God is the source of all that can be called *agape*.[7] In God, *agape* is both will and action. God's action is prevenient, both in creation and in subsequent acts of grace, creating not only humans in his own image, but also human willingness to be reconciled to God. God's *agape* also sets an example for humans to be reconciled among themselves. God's *agape* is poured into the human heart and into the human community in which human nature is nurtured and fulfilled. Human community, when established according to God's will, prescribes right relationships in which *agape* applies to individuals as well as to humankind as a whole. On the surface, *agape* in human beings appears to be a passive response. However, the creative permeation of God's love into humanity transforms this passivity into activity: the human response to God is also a response to one another, and thus *agape* and righteousness become one. The righteousness that is sought among humans is essentially from God and the love of God. This righteousness is retrospective in so far as it is based on truth and judgement, but it is also prospective as directed towards reconciliation and harmony. A characteristic of the Christian concept of righteousness is that it is specially directed towards those who claim no righteousness of their own. In righteousness, God's *agape* claims precedence over secular institutions such as family, state, status, property, and purity, although the claims of these are not totally denied, and in righteousness, God's *agape* creates the category of the neighbour, by which is meant anybody in need who comes one's way. In this way, *agape*, originally the divine power, becomes human consciousness, conscience and behaviour. Human love is no longer a merely passive and external obedience to a superhuman command. It becomes the active motive of human beings themselves to do everything that is commanded, so that divine command and human will become one.

The dynamic of Confucian *jen* is rooted in the humanity inherent in human nature and takes a path towards its transcendence different from that of Christian *agape*. The Way (*tao*) underlies human efforts in attaining to transcendence. However, it is humankind who can make the Way eminent and great, not the Way that makes humanity eminent and great (*Analects*, XV, 29). The Way is in, or itself is, the humanity exhibited in human existence and activity, and therefore is the Way of *jen*: 'The Way is not far from humanity. To pursue the Way and yet stay away from humanity cannot be in the Way' (*The Doctrine of the Mean*, 13). In humanity the Way and *jen* are identified, acquired not only through intellectual endeavour, but also through moral practice. These two activities combine into a single effort to realize humanity in one's being and action. Therefore, to follow the Way and fulfil *jen* is by no means contrary to one's nature. It is within one's will and power. To be *jen* is to be a true and complete human. *Jen* is thus the beginning and end of human growth, both spiritual and moral. Transcendence is the same as the perfection of humanity. Humans can transcend because the seed of *jen* is originally in their nature. However, human perfectibility is only the potential for the fulfilment of *jen*, or the stimulus for human effort in transforming the limited and imperfect, and one cannot attain to transcendence until one has fully explored one's own heart and extended one's virtue to others. In this process, human institutions such as the family, community and state, prove to be necessary for the fulfilment of *jen*, which is, in turn, guided, adjusted, mediated and inspired by one's *jen*-nature. The dynamic of *jen* attains its full capacity in moving a person to return to his own self, or more accurately, to explore what is hidden in his own nature, to realize the potential in his heart, and to fulfil the destiny of his being. When one has successfully achieved this, one will be consciously aware that one's being is also the being of others, one's nature also the nature of the universe, and that whatever one does, one is assisting Heaven and Earth in their work of production and reproduction.

Jen and *agape* manifest themselves in human consciousness and become the decisive element of human conscience. However, neither should be interpreted only in terms of psychology or morality. They not only participate in human activity but also underlie the whole process of the universe. In this way, they are both within humanity and outside of human existence. However, in respect of humanity's own responsibility the focus of Confucian *jen* differs from that of Christian *agape*. The different foci lead to two ways to human transcendence. In Christianity, God is the 'author' of *agape* and hence, either directly or indirectly, the author of all forms of human love. The authorship of God, however, does not imply that humans are exempt from responsibility for their own actions. Instead, it means that God, or Jesus Christ, rather than human nature or determination, is the initiator and constant resource of human fulfilment. To search for the power of love outside divinity is like searching for a tiny object in the darkness. Only by the light of God's revelation is it possible to find it. In Confucianism, on the other hand, the 'author' of *jen* and, directly or indirectly, of all its applications is humanity. Although it is stated in the Confucian classics that humans have a divine origin in *Tian*, it is insisted that humans are responsible for their own transcendence. Only by their own words, merits and virtue can they transcend the limitations of their life and become immortal. The harmony and peace of the world will come only through the growth of humanity, both in individuals and in community. The process of human growth is in a social context. However, without the awakening of self-consciousness, individuals cannot have a proper role in human community, nor can they carry out their social duties. In this sense, *The Great Learning* calls all people, from the Son of Heaven (literally the Sovereign) to commoners, to root themselves in self-cultivation. It is necessary for a person to cultivate his own character, because self-cultivation is the precondition for human fulfilment. It is possible for him to cultivate his own character, because he has been endowed within himself with the resources to be developed and the ability to develop them.

It would be too simplistic to conclude from the different 'authorship' of *jen* and *agape* that Christian *agape* appeals to a passive subject who blindly follows a God-ordained path to his destiny, while Confucian *jen* calls for a creative agent who participates in the onto-cosmological process for the completion of his destiny. Except in respect of origin and source, Christian *agape* emphasizes, as strongly as Confucian *jen*, human participation in the life of the world, human responsibility for their own lives, and freedom to act and to love. It defines human nature and fulfilment in terms of community, grounds righteousness in right relationships, and considers neighbour-love the fulfilment of God's love. It also seeks for the unity of various forms of love, or, as John Burnaby put it: 'Charity . . . is the measure of an active conviction that unity in love is the greatest of all good things, expressing itself in the effort to overcome all hindrance to that unity.'[8]

As summarized above, we have in depth and breadth discussed *jen* and *agape*, especially in their similarities and differences. However, our work does not yet cover all those aspects which are relevant to a comparative study between Confucian *jen* and Christian *agape*. There are still many more questions of practical significance to be answered. It is necessary to extend our attention to these themes, however impossible that would be if we were to expect a full discussion of them within the present structure of our study. As an alternative, we will raise these themes as questions for further study.

First, the difference between *jen* and *agape* leads to different understandings of natural law, which contributes, at least partly, to different political ways between governing by law in Europe and ruling by virtue in Confucian China. Natural law in Christianity draws upon Greek philosophy, in which the divine law is above human law and makes it possible. When Thomas Aquinas elaborated Christian doctrine in the light of Greek metaphysics, he took God's Law as the final criterion and foundation for human action. According to him, natural law is the participation of created things in God's eternal law, from which they derive their inclinations to their proper acts and ends. Natural law is in accordance with reason, which is the guide for human behaviour. Reason is the ability to inform, judge, transform and complete, which not only leads to the fulfilment of human needs and aspirations but is also based

on the dynamic of God's *agape*. Therefore, to follow God's law is
to follow one's reason and not to be misled by one's emotions.
The correspondence between God's law and human reason makes
it possible that human law based on human reason is obeyed, so
that human *agape* flourishes, not only in human consciousness but
also in human endeavour, thus creating a harmonious and peaceful
world. In Confucianism, the idea of natural law is expressed in
the concept of *Tao* (the Way), although the similarity between
them, like any other two Confucian and Christian ideas, such as
yi and righteousness or justice (which will be discussed later), is
of meaning only in a specific context and any equation of them
without criticism will surely distort both and mislead readers. As
defined above, in Confucian contexts *tao* is primarily taken as the
summary of Heavenly and human principles, rather than as the
mystical being or origin of the cosmos, as in Taoism. In the *Analects*,
tao seems to be used in various ways, all of which are developed
from the pictographic meaning of a road, path or way. The usage
of this character in this book falls into two general categories: the
universal Way, and specific ways. Specific ways in which things are
done refer to methods, principles or doctrines. Thus Confucius and
his disciples frequently talk about the 'ways of the former kings'
(*Analects*, I, 12), the 'way of the Master' (IV, 15), or the 'way of
the good people' (XII, 20). Although on many occasions Confucius
uses *tao* in this sense, in his thinking the greatness and nobility of
tao can be seen only in the other sense, that is, the Way of the
universe and the Principle of Heaven and Earth, which governs the
world and to which he is himself committed. However, the heavenly
principle does not exist in isolation. It is identified with humanity
and is in humanity. The function of *tao* is to govern the evolution
of the universe as well as to guide human behaviour in society and
the family. Since the evolution and movement of the universe is
essentially moralized and humanized as the manifestation of *jen*,
tao is the Way to lead to a virtuous life. To know the *tao* of Heaven
is to know human nature. As universal principle, *tao* predetermines
the course of human development, that is, towards goodness rather
than evil, love rather than hatred, and participation in community
life rather than escape from the world.[9] It becomes human nature
as soon as an individual comes into being and provides humanity
with the ability to become perfect as soon as an individual begins
to learn and act.[10] Humanity is thus 'designed' but freely 'creates'
itself according to its 'designation'. Understood in this way, the

most important thing in the main stream of Confucian politics is not a system of law, but the cultivation of virtues, and ruling by virtue is like the Pole Star which remains in its place while all other stars pay their homage to it (*Analects*, II, 1).

Secondly, the difference between *jen* and *agape* leads to different appreciations of social justice. Confucian *jen* and Christian *agape* express themselves in an altruistic concern for others and in taking the claims of others as a priority. In Christian spirituality love and justice go hand in hand, and both are included in *agape*, which is the supreme power for creating harmony not only between human beings and their Creator, but also in human community. To create harmony, human love must be embodied in action that aims at establishing justice in society. In justice, love makes its contribution to human flourishing, not for the individual alone but also for the common human enterprise. In Confucianism, *yi* (righteousness) plays a similar role in actualizing and realizing *jen* as justice for *agape*.[11] It is true that *jen* develops primarily through self-cultivation, for which contemplation and meditation are important. However, what distinguishes Confucian self-cultivation from Taoist and Buddhist meditation is its emphasis on the fact that interior meditation and external participation in social reconstruction must not be separated from each other. Although *jen* is considered of first importance for the peace and harmony of the world, it must be assisted by *yi* which, in some cases, implies the embodiment of *jen* in social relationships, or, as Mencius puts it: '*jen* is the peaceful residence of humanity, while *yi* is the proper way to its fulfilment' (*The Book of Mencius*, 4A:10). Without taking the proper path, one cannot attain to the peace of the world and the perfection of humanity. The potential significance of discussing *jen* and *agape* in their relation to justice or righteousness is due to the fact that justice or righteousness may raise a serious problem for them in situations in which they are in conflict or when both cannot be realized at the same time. In such situations, should social justice be done at the expense of *jen* or *agape*, or should it give way to *jen* or *agape*? Whether in Confucianism or in Christianity, harmony between the transcendental ideal (*jen* or *agape*) and the social ideal (justice or righteousness) is always sought. In some circumstances, however, conflict occurs between the requirement of the former and the responsibilities for the latter. In such cases one is compelled to choose. In making this choice, Confucianism and Christianity both tend towards a de-ontological rather than a utilitarian judgement, insisting that *jen* or *agape* should not be compromised, however desirable the consequences may appear to be if one chooses otherwise.

Thirdly, it would be of practical significance if a comparison between the Confucian discussion of *jen* and material benefit and the Christian discourse on *agape* in relation to social reform was carried out. In a Confucian context, it is of great value for the realization of *jen* that economic development is promoted, public welfare protected and social justice achieved.[12] However, it is also constantly stressed: (1) that such utilitarian targets cannot be reached except by moral cultivation; (2) that compared with utilitarian success, it is more important to have a heart of *jen*, and (3) that a departure from *jen* would spoil the attempt to rebuild peace and harmony in the world, and therefore a sage-king, for example, would never gain the world by perpetrating one single wrongful deed or killing one single innocent man (*The Book of Mencius*, 2A:2). To resolve the tension between the pursuit of *jen* and material considerations, Confucius takes moral principles as the criterion of material benefit: wealth and rank that go against righteousness are like floating clouds and should never be allowed to destroy one's integrity. He then separates public interest from private benefit and takes only the former into his account of *jen*. Private and selfish interests lead one to becoming non-*jen* and immoral. Mainly because of this emphasis in the Confucian tradition, individualism had no chance to develop in traditional Chinese politics and ethics.[13] In a Christian context, there can be another kind of tension, not between material considerations and religious salvation, a tension which was resolved in Jesus' contrast between wealth and realization of the kingdom of God (Mark 10:23), but between love for Christ and concern for social reform. Human *agape* is understood primarily as love for Jesus Christ, who is alone the author of human love for others. Jesus is taken as the symbol and hope of salvation, because he came to save sinners, the poor and the outcast. Thus in some cases a tension may possibly arise between love for Christ and love for the poor. When Jesus praised the woman who had poured over him a whole jar of perfume, which could otherwise have been sold and the money used to help the poor (Mark 14:3–9), he replied to those who objected to this extravagance with the words, 'The poor you will always have with you, and you can help them any time you want. But you will not always have me.' This may seem to intensify the tension rather than resolve it. Although in the parable

Jen *and* Agape: *an Open Horizon*   227

of the sheep and the goats (Matthew 25) Jesus identifies himself with the poor, it seems to be that Christian theology has paid insufficient attention to the questions of why the poor will always be there and how to change the social system that polarizes the rich and the poor. This leads to an ambiguity in the conception of *agape* between love as personal concern and love as social reformation, or between having a loving disposition towards others and a determination to reform the institutions that obstruct such love. The effect of this ambiguity on the Christian Church has been twofold: on the one hand, it has promoted religious faith to what may be its highest level, so that love for God becomes supreme over any other kind of love; on the other hand, it has provided an excuse for the Christian Church's association with the reactionary forces in society, especially during the transitional period between the medieval age and modern times.

Lastly, a discussion of Confucian *jen* and Christian *agape* in their similarities and differences is not only of theoretical interest but also of practical and ethical importance. On the one hand, *jen* and *agape* are of primary significance for Confucian and Christian doctrine, while on the other hand, it is said that it is difficult for most people to put them into practice and that even the great figures in these traditions still fall short of them. We are impressed by the fact that Confucius was disappointed because so many people did not practise *jen* with the same sense of urgency as they pursued their pleasure in sex and recreation (*Analects*, IX, 18). To practise Christian love is even more difficult, if not totally impossible. Reinhold Niebuhr expressed it in this way:

> The perfect disinterestedness of the divine love can have a counter-part in history only in a life which ends tragically, because it refuses to participate in the claims and counter-claims of historical existence. It portrays a love 'which seeketh not its own'. But a love which seeketh not its own is not able to maintain itself in historical society. Not only may it fall victim to excessive forms of the self assertion of others; but even the most perfectly balanced system of justice in history is a balance of competing wills and interests, and must therefore worst anyone who does not participate in the balance.[14]

However, the clouds that darken the possibility of carrying out *jen* and *agape* would disperse if we came to appreciate the fact that *jen* and *agape* refer primarily to the ultimate ideals of a whole tradition although they are indeed of practical use in encouraging people to pursue the ultimate. The sublimity of *jen* and *agape* can be most clearly seen in the extreme difficulty of attaining to them. Just as the sun and moon give warmth and light to all people everywhere, and anyone can be inspired and encouraged by them without being able to grasp and embrace them, so *jen* and *agape* are the constant power in Confucianism and Christianity which leads their believers from the actual to the ideal, and from estrangement to reconciliation, even though very few can actually become one with them.

The difficulty of becoming one with *jen* or *agape* is not in any case taken to be a total impossibility. Confucians distinguish between what is internal to humans and what is external to them. In the former, humans can do everything, while the latter is the province of natural or divine causation. Confucius is aware that whether or not the Way prevails in the world depends upon Destiny (*Analects*, XIV, 36), which is beyond and prior to human effort. On the other hand, humans are believed to be able to carry out *jen* as soon as they desire it (VII, 30). *Jen* is to be found nowhere if not in the process of wide and determined learning, earnest inquiry and reflection on what is at hand (XIX, 6), although such learning and inquiry refer not only to book-reading, but to all kinds of learning and practice, whereby one can understand the essence of human relationships and of universal principles. Anybody who complains that he is unable to carry out *jen* is scorned as having no will to do so (VI, 12), because *jen* is in the human heart and in the process of pursuing it. Similarly, Christians are also aware that they may not achieve all that they desire and cannot decide their course of destiny. They are advised to leave these matters to God, who alone is omnipotent and omniscient. However, no matter how weak a man is, he will become upright and have *agape* in his mind if he has faith in God, just as a mustard seed, the smallest among all seeds, will, when planted, grow and become the largest of all garden plants (Mark 4:31–32). In this sense, Confucianism and Christianity maintain that neither *jen* nor *agape* is beyond the range of human ability. To love and to *jen*, one must begin now and act with one's whole. Whatever the result of one's efforts, and however frustrated one may be in the pursuit of *jen* and *agape*, the one who tries his best will be a person of *agape* and *jen*, namely, a person who is in unity with *agape* and *jen*. To illustrate this, we may quote a paragraph from *The Book of Mencius*:

If you say to others that you cannot stride over the North Sea carrying Mount Tai under your arm, you are true to your words because you indeed have no ability to do so. However, if you say that you are unable to do a little service like breaking off a branch of a tree for an elder, you merely do not want rather than have no ability to do so. (1A:7)

To be a person of *jen* and *agape* begins with concern for and sincere service of others, however small this service may be. It is within everyone's ability to carry out *jen* and *agape:* what one needs is only the will and the enthusiasm.

Notes

Chapter 1 Introduction

1. Hans Küng in his book *Global Responsibility* calls for a 'Global Ethic'. He insists that the world's problems demand that we take responsibility for the problems and look together for solutions to them. However, the final solution must come from the reconciliation between different religions: 'No survival without a world ethic. No world peace without peace between the religions. No peace between the religions without dialogue between the religions.' *Global Responsibility* (SCM Press, London, 1991), p. xv.
2. David Little and Sumner B. Twiss, *Comparative Religious Ethics* (Harper & Row, San Francisco, 1978), pp. 17–18.
3. Hendrik Kraemer provides a classical example of this attitude towards comparative studies when he says that 'All ethics in the world, except the Christian ethic, are some form of eudaemonism'. *Christian Message in a Non-Christian World* (Kregel Publications, Grand Rapids, 1956), p. 88.
4. Max Weber, *The Sociology of Religion*, 4th edn, trans. Ephraim Fischoff (Beacon Press, 1963), p. 1.
5. David Little and Sumner B. Twiss, *Comparative Religious Ethics* (Harper & Row, San Francisco, 1978), p. 58.
6. 'In true faith, the ultimate concern is a concern about the truly ultimate; while in idolatrous faith preliminary, finite realities are elevated to the rank of ultimacy.' Paul Tillich, *Dynamics of Faith* (Harper & Row, New York, 1957), p. 12.
7. Unfortunately, environmental ethics is often neglected in many religious traditions, where human beings are given superiority over nature and nature is regarded as the instrument of the human search for the ultimate meaning of life.
8. Hans Küng and Julia Ching, *Christianity and Chinese Religions* (Doubleday and Collins, 1989), p. xii.
9. Ibid., xii–xv.
10. The discussion of Confucianism as a religion will be carried out in detail in the first section of chapter 2.

11. The first person who clearly contrasted Confucianism as a humanistic religion (*jen tao chiao*) and Christianity as a theocentric religion (*shen tao chiao*) was Kang Yuwei. See *Confucianism*, edited by Ch'u Chai and Winburg Chai (SUNY Press, Worbury, New York, 1973), p. 162.

12. *The Doctrine of the Mean* (*Chung Yung*), 20:19. The author is responsible for the translation and interpretation of most quotations from the Confucian classics, although frequent references are made, wherever available, to popular English versions, especially those by James Legge, Arthur Waley, D. C. Lau and Wing-tsit Chan. The Chinese texts of the Four Books are based on *Sishu Zhangju Jizhu* (*Collected Commentaries on the Four Books*), by Chu Hsi (Zhonghua Shuju, Beijing, 1983), and of Confucius' *Analects* on *Lunyu Yizhu* (*The Analects with Translation and Annotations*), by Yang Bojun (Zhonghua Shuju, Beijing, 1980).

13. For example, Tony Lambert gives detailed statistics about Chinese Protestants. In 1979, the number was 700,000, or about the same as that in 1949 when the People's Republic of China was set up. However, in 1989, registered Protestant Christians in China were as many as 4,551,981. See his book *The Resurrection of the Chinese Church* (Hodder and Stoughton, Sevenoaks, 1991), p. 144.

14. Hans Küng and Julia Ching, *Christianity and Chinese Religion*, pp. 95–6.

15. Tu Wei-ming, 'Toward a Third Epoch of Confucian Humanism: A Background Understanding', in *Confucianism: The Dynamics of Tradition*, ed. Irene Eber (Macmillan, New York, 1986), pp. 3–21. Rodney Taylor responds positively to Tu's point of view and actually pushes it forward by saying that 'the third epoch is already underway, that it is open ended and its possibility for growth virtually limitless.' *The Religious Dimensions of Confucianism* (State University of New York, 1991), p. 147.

16. Marshall Hodgson, *The Venture of Islam*, vol. I (University of Chicago Press, 1974), p. 24.

17. Two systems of spelling Chinese characters in Western languages are currently used in publications. One is the Wade-Giles' romanization, which is still popular in Western countries, Taiwan and Hong Kong, the other is pin-yin, which prevails on the mainland of China. For example, the Way will be *tao* in the first and *dao* in the second. For readers' convenience, we will not follow a fixed rule. Rather, most characters will be spelled in the form as they are recognized and used in Europe, and only those which are new to European readers are rendered according to the pin-yin system.

18. Anders Nygren, *Agape and Eros – A Study of the Christian Idea of Love*, part I, trans. A. G. Herbert (Society for Promoting Christian Knowledge, London, 1932), p. 25.

Chapter 2   Confucianism and Christianity

1. Paul Rule takes this Latinization as a Jesuit invention and argues that while the Jesuits' 'Confucius' introduced a Chinese tradition to Europe, this tradition was greatly changed by their own ideas and ideals. See his book, *K'ung-tzu or Confucius? – The Jesuit Interpretation of Confucianism* (Allen & Unwin, 1986).
2. He was believed to be a descendant of the royal house of the Shang dynasty (1776–1122 BCE) and his ancestors had been living in the state of Sung until his grandfather was forced to move to the state of Lu. In the *Analects*, IX, 6, we read his description of his young life: 'I was of humble station when young, so that I was able to do many menial things.'
3. For example, G. A. Kennedy in his 'Interpretation of the *Ch'un Ch'iu*' (*Journal of the American Oriental Society*, LXII, 1942) strongly argues that Confucius did edit the *Spring and Autumn Annals*. Lifu Chen believes that 'Confucius edited the *Book of Songs*, and the *Book of History*, compiled the *Book of Rites*, and the *Book of Music*, annotated the *Book of Changes*, and wrote the *Spring and Autumn Annals*. These were called the "Six Classics" . . . ' in *The Confucian Way – A New and Systematic Study of the "Four Books"* (The Commercial Press Ltd, Taipei, 1972), p. 2.
4. For example, H. G. Creel came to an overall negative conclusion: 'Our examination of the various books Confucius is supposed to have written . . . leaves us with the conclusion that we have no convincing evidence that he wrote or even edited anything at all. This is not an original verdict; an increasing number of scholars have reached this same conclusion in recent years.' H. G. Creel, *Confucius and the Chinese Way* (Harper & Bros, New York, 1960), p. 106.
5. Yang Bojun, *Lunyu Yizhu* (Zhonghua Shuju, Beijing, 1980), p. 31.
6. Some scholars have argued that this was a fiction concocted by later Confucians. For a critical examination of this and other events that are believed to have happened to Confucius, see John K. Shryock, *The Origin and Development of the State Cult of Confucius* (Paragon, New York, 1966).
7. *Tian* in Chinese has non-religious usages and religious usages. The religious *Tian* has four implications: a unity of cosmic existences which is taken as the totality of human circumstances; a place where gods, spirits or human immortals live; a divine order which governs the universe, and a personal Lord who is in charge of the worlds of gods, human beings and spirits (ghosts). It is not easy to separate these four implications, even within the same context. *Tian* is normally translated as Heaven, and thus misunderstanding, caused by its confusion with the Christian concept of heaven, often occurs. In order to avoid such confusion, this author will translate *Tian* as Heaven only in its first

and second meanings, and use *Tian* itself for the third and fourth usages, when it is applicable.

8. There was an explanation for this relationship, which, though it appeared in a much later age, was said to have been the idea of the Shang people. It is said that 'wang' (king) (王) is composed of three horizontal lines which represent heaven, earth and humans, and a vertical line which refers to the king. Only by the king can the three realities be connected and form a unity.

9. *Shi King* (*The Book of Poetry*), trans. James Legge, in *The Sacred Books of China* part I, in *The Sacred Books of the East*, ed. F. Max Müller, vol. III (Motilal Banarsidass, Delhi, 1970), p. 184.

10. *Shu King* (*The Book of History*), trans. James Legge, in *The Sacred Books of China* part I, in *The Sacred Books of the East*, ed. F. Max Müller, vol. III (Motilal Banarsidass, Delhi, 1970), p. 127.

11. Arthur Waley notices that in the *Book of Poetry*, *hsiao* refers almost exclusively to piety towards the dead, while in the *Analects*, it is used for both piety to the dead and love of the living parents. Arthur Waley, *The Analects of Confucius* (George Allen & Unwin, London, 1938), p. 38.

12. A. C. Graham, in *The Concise Encyclopedia of Living Faiths*, ed. R. C. Zaehner (Hutchinson, 1988), p. 370.

13. Gilbert Rozman, in *The Confucianism World Observed – A Contemporary Discussion of Confucian Humanism in East Asia*, ed. Tu Weiming et al. (The East-West Centre, Honolulu, 1992), p. 40.

14. H. A. Giles, *Confucianism and its Rivals* (Williams & Norgate, London, 1915), p. 67.

15. Ninian Smart, *The World's Religion: Old Traditions and Modern Transformations* (Cambridge University Press, 1989), pp. 103–4.

16. This view comes from his comments on the introduction to this thesis.

17. *The Confucian World Observed – A Contemporary Discussion of Confucian Humanism in East Asia*, ed. Tu Weiming et al. (The East-West Centre, Honolulu, 1992), p. 10, p. 12 and p. 5.

18. There was no Chinese term which had the same denotation as 'religion' in English. The modern Chinese use a term coined by combination of two characters, *tsung* and *chiao*, which originally meant the ancestral or traditional and the teaching. In the mind of the ancient Confucians, the noble or orthodox teaching was concerned with the exploration of the proper relationship between *Tian* and Humans; while the bad or devalued teaching was concerned with superstitious practices. Popular Taoism, popular Buddhism and folklore were taken as the latter, while Taoist, Buddhist and Confucian teachings proper were thought of as belonging to the first category.

19. *The Oxford English Dictionary*, second edition, vol. XIII, p. 569.

20. Fung Yulan, *A Short History of Chinese Philosophy* (Macmillan, 1961), p. 3.

21. Jacques Gernet, *China and the Christian Impact – A Conflict of Cultures*, trans. Janet Lloyd (Cambridge University Press, 1985), p. 16.
22. *The Oxford English Dictionary*, prepared by J. A. Simpson and E. S. C. Weiner (Clarendon Press, Oxford, second edition, 1989), pp. 568–9.
23. Ninian Smart, *The World Views* (Macmillan, 1983), pp. 7–9.
24. In *The Confucian World Observed – A Contemporary Discussion of Confucian Humanism in East Asia*, ed. Tu Weiming et al., p. 12.
25. *The Analects*, VI, 20. Arthur Waley seems to be more enthusiastic about Confucius' attitude to spirits. He translates this paragraph as 'The master said, he who devotes himself to securing for his subjects what it is right they should have, who by respect for the spirits keeps them at a distance, may be termed wise.' He further explains: 'When the Spirits of hills and streams do not receive their proper share of ritual and sacrifice, they do not "keep their distance" but "possess" human beings, causing madness, sickness, pestilence etc.' (*Analects of Confucius*, p. 120, footnote 2.)
26. When he was in danger, Confucius showed little fear because he was confident that 'Tian produced virtues that are born with me' (VII, 23).
27. V. Ferm, *An Encyclopedia of Religion* (Greenwood Press, 1976), p. 150.
28. Matteo Ricci first noticed that these Confucian schools or academies (*shu yuan*) were equivalent to Christian preaching houses and that Confucians too were 'impressed by the resemblances between the [Jesuit] preaching houses and their own traditional academies'. E. Zürcher observed that 'the atmosphere of *shu yuan* did have something solemn and almost holy': each meeting began with a ceremony in honour of the founder and Confucius; the rules of conduct were codified according to a convention, which often included pious hymns sung by choirs of young boys. See Jacques Gernet, pp. 17–18.
29. *The Confucianism World Observed – A Contemporary Discussion of Confucian Humanism in East Asia*, ed. Weiming Tu et al. (The East-West Centre, Honolulu, 1992), p. 10.
30. John Bowker, *The Sense of God – Sociological, Anthropological and Psychological Approaches to the Origin of the Sense of God* (Clarendon Press, Oxford, 1973), p. viii.
31. *Analects*, VII, 34. This paragraph is translated variously. According to Legge, Confucius is here expressing his belief in the spiritual world. But for Creel, in contrast to the anxiety of his disciples, it expresses Confucius' self-control and independence of thought.
32. Chung-ying Cheng, *New Dimensions of Confucian and Neo-Confucian Philosophy* (State University of New York Press, Albany, 1991), p. 454.
33. 'In the absence of all metaphysics and almost all residues of religious anchorage, Confucianism is rationalist to such a far-going extent that it stands at the extreme boundary of what one might possibly call a religious ethic.' Cited in H. G. Creel, *Confucius and the Chinese Way*

(Harper & Bros. New York, 1960), p. 120. Creel's comment is that 'it would be pleasant to be able to say that Weber's comments on Confucius and Confucianism were all equally penetrating, but unfortunately this is not the case' [note 8, p. 310].

34. *The Religious Dimensions of Confucianism* (State University of New York Press, Albany, 1990), pp. 2–3.
35. C. K. Yang, *Religion in Chinese Society* (Cambridge University Press, 1961), p. 26.
36. Paul Badham, 'The Meaning of the Resurrection of Jesus', in *The Resurrection of Jesus Christ*, ed. Paul Avis (Longman and Todd, London, Darton, 1993), p. 24.
37. For example, in Genesis (18–19), when the Lord could not find ten righteous people in Sodom and Gomorrah, he destroyed the city. Again in Exodus, we read that the Lord, in order to force the Egyptian Pharaoh to allow the Israelites to leave, turned the water into blood so that Egyptians could not drink; plagued the whole country with frogs, gnats, flies, boils and hailstones; and at last 'struck down all the firstborn in Egypt, from the firstborn of Pharaoh who sit on the throne, to the firstborn of the prisoner, who was in the dungeon, and the firstborn of all livestock as well' (Exodus 12:29).
38. Ninian Smart, *The World's Religions*, p. 212.
39. Ibid., p. 209.
40. Justin Martyr (c. 100–165) was probably the first Christian thinker to do so. In his *Apology*, he argued that the divine Logos was equal to the personification of divine wisdom: Jesus, the Word of God.
41. An often quoted question of Tertullian (160?–225) was 'What has Athens to do with Jerusalem?' See *The World's Religion*, p. 248.
42. Ninian Smart, in explaining the Christian victory in the Roman world, suggests that this victory came from its eight 'inherited advantages': monotheism which could be easily universalized; God–human in Jesus which was familiar to the Greco-Roman world; the connection with the Platonic tradition which had been embraced by the educated class; the nature of its mysticism; the periodic persecution which reinforced the solidarity within the groups; the lack of a coherent ideology of the Roman Empire; and the consistent organization and positive attitudes to the world (*The World's Religions*, pp. 241–2).
43. The *Analects* can in some respects be compared with the Synoptic Gospels of the Bible, not only in terms of their contents, form and style of recording the Master's sayings, activities and historical background, but also in terms of their being the source from which later Confucians developed various philosophical, religious and ethical interpretations.
44. In his book *Confucius – The Secular as Sacred* (Harper Torchbooks, 1972), Herbert Fingarette demonstrates the significance of the fact Confucius obtained his sacredness through secular ways.

45. Tu Wei-ming, 'The Confucian Sage: Exemplar of Personal Knowledge', in *Saints and Virtues*, ed. J. S. Hawley (University of California Press, Berkeley, 1987), pp. 75–86.

46. Mark 11:23. The sick were healed, not simply by Jesus, but through their own faith: 'Your faith has healed you' (Mark 5:34). Even in the most dangerous situation, one could overcome fear through faith: 'Don't be afraid, just believe' (Mark 5:36). Faith is in the heart. Therefore Jesus also said that a sincere heart is taken as the precondition for the kingdom: 'The Kingdom of God is within you' (Luke 17:21).

47. The *Analects*, VII, 21: 'The Master never talked about prodigies, miraculous powers, disorders and spirits'.

48. Matthew 5:21–22; 5:27–28. These paragraphs have been regarded as especially significant because they demonstrate a radicalization, if not extremalization, of the Mosaic law.

Chapter 3   *Jen* in Confucianism and *Agape* in Christianity

1. *Tao Te Ching*, chaps xviii and xxxviii. In these contexts, *Jen* is translated by Arthur Waley as 'human kindness', by James Legge and D. C. Lau as 'benevolence'.

2. *The Complete Works of Chuang Tzu*, trans. Burton Watson (Columbia University Press, New York, 1968), pp. 44, 155, 171, 259.

3. *Sources of Chinese Tradition*, edited and compiled by Wm. Theodore de Bary, Wing-tsit Chan and Burton Watson, vol. I (Columbia University Press, New York, 1960), p. 262.

4. *Fo Xue Da Ci Dian* (*Dictionary of Buddhism*) ed. Ding Fu Bao, (Wen Wu Chu Ban She, Beijing, 1984), pp. 366–7.

5. Where and how the concept of *jen* is used in these two books and a general treatment of the origin and evolution of Confucian *jen* have been examined by Wing-tsit Chan in his article 'The Evolution of the Confucian Concept of Jen', *Philosophy East and West*, vol. 4, no. 4 (University of Hawaii Press, Honolulu, 1955).

6. While statistics alone cannot decide how important a concept is in a book, they do reveal something. Thus, *jen* with its 157 appearances in *the Book of Mencius* gives it some priority over *yi* (righteousness) which appears only 108 times.

7. Commentators' explanations of why Confucius was said to have talked seldom about *jen* vary: either because it was a difficult subject; or because Confucius did not want to talk about such an important subject in an ordinary way; or because *jen* was an ideal which was not easy to realize; or because Confucius did not want to associate *jen* with profit . . . Among western translators, Arthur Waley adopted the suggestion that, in seldom speaking of matters from the point of view of what would pay best, but only from the point of view of what

was right, Confucius 'refused to define Goodness [*jen*] or accord the title Goodness to any of his contemporaries'. *The Analects of Confucius* (George Allen & Unwin, London, 1938), p. 138. James Legge simply left it alone: 'about not speaking of *jen*, there is a difficulty which I know not how to solve' *The Life and Teachings of Confucius* (Trübnere, London, 1887), p. 167.

8. When asked for a single word that could guide one's whole life, Confucius replied, 'Is it not *shu*? What you do not like yourself do not extend to others' (XV, 24). Concerning this reply, we can make two points to challenge the traditional opinion that Confucius took *shu* as the central theme of his doctrine, and to argue that *shu* is a way of practising *jen* but not *jen* itself. The first is the degree of uncertainty in his reply, revealed by '*chi shu hu*' ('Is it not *shu*?' or 'Is it *perhaps* shu?'); the second is that Confucius was speaking here about how to guide one's life, not about the central concept of his teaching, the former being the practical presentation of the latter.

9. Robert E. Allinson, 'The Golden Rule as the Core Value in Confucianism & Christianity: Ethical Similarities and Differences', in *Asian Philosophy*, vol. 2, no. 2 (1992), pp. 176, 184, note 10.

10. 'Not complaining' is regarded as a necessary condition for the realisation of *jen*. 'A *chun tzu* [equal to a person of *jen*] is always examining himself, while a *hsiao jen* (a mean person) is always complaining of others' (VII, 37). If a person pursues *jen* and then acquires it, he will have no complaint at all (VII, 15). Among the qualities Confucius ascribed to himself, the first was that he would never complain of heaven and others (XIV, 35), but always examine himself.

11. That these three are practices of *jen* is also supported in another paragraph (XIII, 19) where Confucius, when asked about *jen*, replied with three descriptions of the ways to be *jen*: Be respectful in private life, serious in handling affairs, and sincere in treating others.

12. In a similar sense, Mencius takes *chung* as teaching or leading others to be good (*Mencius*, 3A:4).

13. '*Shu* here seems to be a form of the Golden Rule, though formulated in a negative way. But elsewhere (6:28) Confucius formulates what seems plainly to be another version of *shu*, a positive formulation that in effect enjoins us to treat others as we would be treated.' Herbert Fingarette: 'Following the "One Thread" of *The Analects*', *Journal of the American Academy of Religion*, vol. XLVII (September 1979), pp. 375–6.

14. Wing-tsit Chan, in *A Source Book in Chinese Philosophy* (Princeton University Press, Princeton, 1963), pp. 785–6.

15. Wing-tsit Chan, 'The Evolution of the Confucian Concept of *Jen*' (1955), p. 314. In another article 'Chinese and Western Interpretations of *Jen* (Humanity)', *Journal of Chinese Philosophy* 2 (1975), pp. 107–29, he discusses the Chinese understanding of *jen* under seven headings:

(1) *jen* as the general virtue; (2) *jen* as love; (3) *jen* as universal Love; (4) the identification of *jen* with nature and principle and the doctrine of 'principle is one but its manifestations are many'; (5) the man of humanity regards Heaven and Earth and the ten thousand things as one body; (6) *jen* and the process of production and reproduction (recreation and re-creation); and (7) *jen* as 'the character of the mind and the principle of love'.

16. In English translations, *jen* has been represented by a variety of terms. However, their logical connections enable us to classify them into three groups: (1) humaneness, human-heartedness, manhood at its best, humanity, true manhood . . . (2) benevolence, altruism, kindness, compassion, morality, virtue, perfect virtue, goodness . . . (3) charity, love, universal love . . . Of these three groups, the first, through identifying *jen* with human beings, reveals the character of Confucianism as humanism; the second, by referring *jen* to a specific or general virtue, shows the quality of a virtuous life which has been championed by Confucianism as a human ideal; and the third is a reflection of Confucian universalism and religiosity. In this way, these three groups reflect the three aspects of the Confucian doctrine of *jen*.

17. Tung Chungshu, quoted in Fung, vol. II, p. 38.

18. Quoted in Fung, vol. II, p. 32.

19. Tung Chung-shu, *Chun Chiu Fan Lu* or *Luxuriant Dew of the Spring and Autumn Annals*, 2.11, quoted in Fung, vol. II, p. 38.

20. Wing-tsit Chan (ed.), *A Source Book in Chinese Philosophy*, p. 286.

21. Wing-tsit Chan, *Chu Hsi – New Studies* (University of Hawaii Press, Honolulu, 1989), p. 152.

22. Chu Hsi, 'Treatise on Jen'. See Wing-tsit Chan 'Chu Hsi's "Jen-shuo (Treatise on Humanity)"', in *Chu Hsi – New Studies* (University of Hawaii Press, Honolulu, 1989), pp. 151–83. Wing-tsit Chan translates '*hsin chi te*' as 'the character of mind'. 'Character' here is obviously not strong enough for '*te*', which is the moral quality of the character. Therefore, I translate it as 'virtue'.

23. As one of his students, Chen Chun, explained it: '*Jen* is the totality of the mind's principle of production. It is always producing and reproducing without cease. Its clue becomes active in the mind. When it sets forth, naturally there is the feeling of commiseration. As the feeling of commiseration grows in abundance to reach a thing, it becomes love. Therefore, *jen* is the root of love, commiseration the sprout from the root, and love the sprout reaching its maturity and completion. Looking at it this way, we can easily see the vital connection between *jen* as the principle of love and love as the function of *jen*' (Chen Chun, *Pei-hsi Tzu-i*, section 50, part 1, p. 24b). Quoted in Wing-tsit Chan, *Chu Hsi – New Studies*, p. 163.

24. *I Shu (The Inherited Works of the Cheng Brothers)*, 2A, 3a; 2A, 2a.

25. Wang Yang-ming, *An Inquiry to the Great Learning*, see Wing-tsit Chan, *A Source Book in Chinese Philosophy*, pp. 659–60.
26. Carsun Chang, *The Development of Neo-Confucian Thought*, vol. II (Bookman Associates, New York, 1962), p. 48.
27. John Macquarrie, *In Search of Humanity – A Theological and Philosophical Approach* (Crossroad, New York, 1982), p. 172.
28. There have been many arguments over the nature and function of *agape*, and some of them deny the connection between *agape* and human love for God. The most powerful of these arguments comes from Anders Nygren, who reserves *agape* for God's love alone, while he names the human love for God 'faith': 'Faith includes in itself the whole devotion of love, while emphasizing that it has the character of response, that it is reciprocated love. Faith is love towards God, but a love of which the keynote is receptivity, not spontaneity' (*Agape and Eros*, p. 127). To counteract this argument, Peter Baelz comments that it falls short of the truth because it ignores the fact that a fully personal love is essentially 'both *relational* and *reciprocal*'. 'A Review of *The Model of Love – A Study in Philosophical Theology*', by Vincent Brummel (Cambridge University Press, 1993), *The Journal of Theological Studies*, vol. 45, part 2, October 1994, p. 790.
29. W. Gunther and H.-G. Link, 'Love', in *The New International Dictionary of New Testament Theology*, ed. Colin Brown, vol. II (The Paternoster Press, Exeter, 1976), pp. 538–9.
30. In the Hebrew Scriptures *'ahebh* and its derivatives are used in relation to both persons and things or action; *chesed* is conditional upon the covenant and thus is differentiated from *'ahabah* that is unconditional; *rhm* indicates sympathy with those who need help, and *rahum* means to be merciful. In the LXX, *agape* together with its derivatives becomes a common translation of *'ahebh* and its derivatives, and occasionally of other Hebrew words for love. Gottfried Quell and Ethelbert Stauffer, *Love*, trans. J. R. Coates, Adam and Charles Black (1933), p. 1.
31. Here again we have an exception. Cyrus, king of the Persians, was praised and anointed because he subdued nations before the Lord and opened the door before him so that the gates would not be shut (Isaiah 45:1). From this fact we may infer that the chosen people might include those who helped the Israelites and therefore carried out God's will.
32. *Love*, p. 18.
33. The tradition of the O.T. and hence the N.T. has much less concern with nature than many other traditions in the world. One reason for the exclusion of environmental concern from Judaic and Christian morality lies in its theology: God's creation of nature is primarily for humans. Therefore, in the sake of the three dimensions of religion between God, humans and nature which we have discussed in chapter 1, the aspect of ecological ethics is consciously missing. It becomes the three dimensions between God, humans and humans. This had

a direct influence on European ways of life and the deficiency was not made up until St. Francis of Assisi came to link the Gospel love with a love for nature and a communion with animals and the whole of creation. However, this understanding was only a by-product of monastic life and was not strong enough to change the basic orientation of Christian morality.

34. *Love*, p. 12.
35. 'If you come across your enemy's ox or donkey wandering off, be sure to take it back to him. If you see the donkey of someone who hates you fallen down under its load, do not leave it there; be sure you help him with it' (Exodus 23:4, 5).
36. For example, the Golden Rule, 'do to others what you would have them do to you' (Matthew 7:12) 'only differs from Hillel's famous rule by being couched in positive terms'. *Love*, p. 45.
37. It has been claimed that there is already a movement of love from the collective to the individual displayed in Ezekiel (chapter 18). Nevertheless, God's love is not characteristic of the latter in the overall teaching of the O.T.
38. *Love*, p. 48.
39. 'We continually remember before our God and father your work produced by faith, your labour prompted by love, and your endurance inspired by hope in our Lord Jesus Christ'. I Thessalonians 1:3.
40. 'We loved you so much that we were delighted to share with you not only the gospel of God but our lives as well, because you had become so dear to us.' I Thessalonians 2:8.
41. Daniel Day Williams, *The Spirit and Forms of Love* (Harper & Row, 1968, New York and Evanston), p. 53.
42. Williams, p. 56. Also see Anders Nygren, *Agape and Eros*, p. 650.
43. Augustine, *On the morals of Catholic Church*, XV.
44. Williams, pp. 67, 68.
45. Quoted in Johannes Jorgensen, *St. Francis of Assisi* (Longman Green, 1954), p. 78.
46. While the opposition between knowledge and love propagated by St. Francis is in contrast to Confucian understanding, we have found in it an extremely similar idea to the idea advocated by Taoist masters. It says in *Tao Te Ching* that ordinary learning is to increase one's knowledge every day; while the learning of *Tao* is to decrease one's knowledge every day. Decrease and decrease until there is nothing left in one's heart, one will be in the most natural situation in which one can easily be unified with *Tao*.
47. Williams, p. 76.
48. There is frequent use of *eros* in the Christian tradition to refer to love. However, as we will see, this usage of *eros* is taken over from Platonic philosophy, in which it is endowed with a much wider meaning than sex, although it is rooted in sexual relationship.
49. Among numerous scholars who have criticized Nygren's argument,

John Burnaby stands in the front. In his *Amor Dei – A Study of the Religion of St. Augustine* (Hodder & Stoughton, London, 1938) he demonstrates that there is not such a sharp division between divine love and human love as insisted by Nygren.

50. Anders Nygren, *Agape and Eros – A Study of the Christian Idea of Love*, part I, trans by A. G. Herbert (Society for Promoting Christian Knowledge, London, 1932), p. 23.
51. Ibid., p. 25.
52. Ibid., p. 33.
53. Ibid., p. 162.
54. Ibid., p. 163.
55. Ibid., p. 164.

Chapter 4 *Jen* as Humanity and *Agape* as Divinity

1. In this chapter, in order to make a distinction between these two characters with the same sound, I use the capital JEN to refer to human beings, the italic *jen* to refer to the Confucian principle.
2. Some scholars suggest instead that the character *jen* symbolizes a person carrying a heavy burden and walking bent-backed under the road. They conclude that *jen* is originally a word that signifies 'bearing and enduring', thus valuable human qualities. See Sato Hitoshi, 'Chu Hsi's Treatise on *Jen*', in *Chu Hsi and Neo-Confucianism*, ed. Wing-tsit Chan (University of Hawaii Press, Honolulu, 1986), p. 213.
3. C. P. Fitzgerald points out that 'The true meaning of *chun tzu* in the feudal age was simply an aristocrat . . . The nobility of feudal China owed their position to descent and not to education . . . they were sharply separated from the *hsiao jen*, the mass of the people, who had no political rights . . . and could not rise by wealth or ability.' Fitzgerald goes on to describe something of the way of life, education and moral code of the Chinese aristocrat. 'The *chun tzu* were not unlettered nobles like the feudal barons of medieval Europe. They were polished aristocrats who served as counsellors, officers and governors in time of peace and as generals and warriors in war. The nobles fought in war-chariots . . . the mass of the people on foot around them. Archery was a noble sport, strictly organized in ceremonial contests. The education of the nobles also included music, arithmetic and poetry, and most important of all, the strict fulfilment of the rites and ceremonies which governed all social relations.' (*China – A Short Cultural History*, Cresset Press, pp. 58, 59.
4. Tu Wei-ming, 'The Creative Tension between Jen and Li', *Philosophy East and West*, vol. 18 (1968), no. 1–2, p. 31. His argument that Confucius 'almost never gave anyone the title of *jen*–JEN (a person who has embodied *jen*)' cannot justify his distinguishing a *chun-tzu* from a person of *jen* while identifying a person of *jen* with a sage.

Nor did Confucius often give the title of *chun-tzu* to a particular person, because both *chun-tzu* and a person of *jen* were regarded as titles for an ideal personality. They are composed of many good qualities, and different people can show different aspects of these qualities, but few of them can be said to have completely embodied all of them. The only exception in the *Analects*, in which Confucius praises one of his disciples as a *chun-tzu*, is found in V, 3. However, what is meant there by a *chun-tzu* is only that this disciple has had many qualities belonging to the ideal personality, not that he *is* the ideal.

5. The *Analects*, IV, 5. One exception perhaps is in XIV, 6, when Confucius said that it is possible for a *chun-tzu* not to be with *jen* while none of the base persons [*hsiao JEN*] is with *jen*. While this saying can be used to support the view that there is a difference between a *chun-tzu* and a person of *jen*, we may also use it to prove that to be a person of *jen* involves a constant effort, and is not an achieved state, during which one has to make constant effort. There is no doubt that Yan Hui was the most prestigious disciple of Confucius'. But the praise from the master was only that 'Yan Hui can be in line with *jen* for three months' (VI, 7).

6. There are many other titles which Confucius uses at the same level as a *chun-tzu*. *Jen-JEN* (a person who has embodied *jen*) is used in XV, 9 and XX, 1; *jen-che* is used widely to mean a person who has the virtues of *jen* (for example, IV, 2, 3; VI, 22, 23, 26; IX, 29; XIV, 4); and *shan-JEN* is used for a good person (VII, 26). All these titles are the same, in the sense that they are an embodiment of *jen* and have reached a certain level in self-cultivation, so that they can be differentiated from a base person or a common person, but they do not signify its peak, so there still is a long way for them to go to be perfect.

7. David L. Hall and Roger T. Ames, *Thinking Through Confucius* (State University of New York Press, Albany, 1987), p. 84.

8. Arthur Waley, *The Analects of Confucius*, VII, 26, p. 128. Confucius also talked about the difficulty of becoming a *chun-tzu*: 'I have never yet seen one who really cared for *jen*.' However, there is a difference between 'cannot hope ever to meet a sage' and 'have never yet seen a person of *jen*'. He believed that 'if anyone ever manages to be in *jen* with his whole might for a single day, I cannot see why he can not do it'. From the sentence that Confucius had not yet seen a person of *jen* we can infer that there were such persons around, only he had not come across them (IV, 6).

9. 'The man of *jen* is identical with the sage or the superior man (*chun-tzu*) . . . ' (Timothy Tian-min Lin, 'The Confucian Concept of Jen and the Christian Concept of Love', *Ching Feng*, vol. 15, 1973, pp. 162–72).

10. The *Analects*, VI, 30. See also Arthur Waley, *The Analects of Confucius*, 28, 122. Mencius remarked upon the gap between a person of *jen* and a

sage in another way: 'The desirable is called 'good'. To have the good in oneself is called 'true'. To possess the true fully in oneself is called 'beautiful'. But to shine forth with the full possession of the beautiful is called 'great'. To be great and to be transformed by this greatness is called 'sage'. To be sage and to transcend understanding is called 'divine' (VII B, 25). The first three qualities may be understood as those of a person of *jen*, while the last three are in the range of being a sage.

11. The *Analects*, VII, 34. In *The Book of Mencius* (3A:2), when the paragraph quoted above was commented on, 'unwearying effort to learn' was said to be 'wisdom', while 'unflagging patience in teaching others' was '*jen*'. Since Confucius possessed both qualities, he was certainly a true sage.

12. *The Book of Mencius*, 7B:16. See also *The Doctrine of Mean*, chap. 20.

13. *The Book of Mencius*, 6A:11; 4A:10. The popular translation of *jen* and *yi* is 'benevolence and righteousness'. However, although *jen* is used in the sense of benevolence and *yi* in that of righteousness in many paragraphs of *The Book of Mencius*, 'benevolence and righteousness' cannot reveal the real meaning of these two concepts, and therefore should not be used indiscriminately.

14. Chang Tsai, *Western Inscription*, see Wing-tsit Chan, *A Source Book in Chinese Philosophy* (Princeton University Press, 1963), p. 497.

15. *The Book of Mencius*, 2A:2. *Chi* is a special word in Chinese culture and its implications may vary from the basic material to the spiritual power. Any existence is composed of *chi* and the quality of *chi* decides the quality of beings. Mencius used this term to explain how a great human can reach his identification with the cosmos and bring about the harmony by his own cultivation.

16. The *Doctrine of the Mean*, chap. 23, see James Legge, *The Life and Teachings of Confucius* (Trübnere, London, 1887), pp. 306–7. This last stage of the development of the person of *jen*, as related in *The Book of Mencius* and in the *Doctrine of the Mean*, is no longer a mere person of *jen*. Having cultivated one's sincerity and *jen* to the utmost, one has completed the integrity of human beings and the universe, and therefore is taken as a transcendental sage.

17. Quoted in Fung Yu-lan, *A History of Chinese Philosophy*, vol. II, pp. 491, 493.

18. All quoted in Fung Yu-lan, vol. II, pp. 520–1.

19. J. Percy Bruce (trans.), *The Philosophy of Human Nature, by Chu Hsi* (Arthur Probsthain, London, 1922), p. 353.

20. Many theologians have argued against any attempt to identify God's love and the love of his creatures. However, they have overlooked a fundamental fact that God's love must be embodied in his creation. Without the love of human beings, God's love cannot be appreciated, although it may exist ontologically. In this sense, God and human beings are epistemologically related in their love.

21. Quoted in *Amor Dei – A Study of the Religion of St. Augustine*, by John Burnaby (Hodder & Stoughton, London, 1938), p. 220.
22. Although the covenant is primarily used for the relationship between God and Israel, it applies to any kind of 'artificial brotherhood' in the O.T. A covenant may be made between individuals: Abraham is said to make a covenant with Abimelech by giving him some sheep and cattle as gifts (Genesis 21:27); or Jonathan is said to make a covenant with David because he loves David as himself (I Samuel 18:3). A marriage is said to be a form of covenant of which God is the witness, and a husband who has broken faith with his wife will be disfavoured or rejected by God (Malachi 2:13, 14). A king can make a covenant with his people so that he puts them under an oath to carry out his orders (II Kings 11:4). In all these forms of covenant, we see three features of brotherhood: first, a covenant creates certain duties and rights, to which the partners have committed themselves. Breaking the covenant means to despise the oath one has sworn and will certainly be punished. Secondly, a covenant does not mean that the parties are equal. More frequently, the covenant is made between two unequal parties, such as a husband and his wife, a king and his subjects, or a conqueror and his conquered. Thirdly, there is no fixed manner for making a covenant. A gift, handshake, a kiss (I Samuel 10:1) or a meal may be taken as a proper way to make a covenant. These usages obviously affected the Israelite concept of their covenant with God.
23. *Love*, p. 11.
24. The entry on Covenant by J. O. Cobham, in *A Theological Word Book of the Bible*, ed. Alan Richardson DD (SCM Press, London, 1957), p. 55.
25. Norman H. Snaith, *The Distinctive Ideas of the Old Testament* (The Epworth Press, London, 1944), pp. 94–5, 98.
26. Snaith, p. 113.
27. Snaith renders the geographical-political reason for different emphases by the prophets on God's mercy or on God's punishment as that 'Almost everything depends on whether the prophet is dealing with his own or the other section of the Hebrew people. Every prophet finds it easier to speak about the ultimate punishment of rebellion against God, when he is discussing the crimes of the rival people. Every prophet finds it easy to emphasise the wideness of God's mercy when he is speaking of his own folk' (p. 118).
28. Snaith, p. 84.
29. Snaith, p. 88.
30. The conception of Jesus as the atonement of sins also came from the similar idea in the O.T. Snaith retranslated the paragraph of Isaiah 53:11 as that 'The righteous one, my servant, will make prosperous (hiphil of tsadaq), for it was their iniquities (i.e. punishments) he was bearing. Therefore will I give him a share with the many (i.e. with the

many whom he has made to prosper)', so that God seems to more directly reveal the coming of Jesus Christ (*Distinctive Ideas of The Old Testament*, p. 92).

31. When Confucius was asked about the fulfilled (or complete) human, he replied that a fulfilled human was one who was wise, free from selfish desires, courageous, versatile, and refined by rites and music. If these were too difficult to be accomplished, Confucius added that one, who could remember righteousness at the sight of profit, who would be ready to lay down one's life in a dangerous situation and would never forget one's mission, might also be regarded as a fulfilled human (*Analects*, XIV, 12). On the one hand, there seems to be nothing within these qualities that can be considered to be transcendental. On the other hand, as is shown below, when these qualities are developed to their utmost, they enable one to be identical with Heaven and Earth and to be eternal, which is indeed the transcendental ideal for Confucians.

32. *Zhouyi Dazhuan Jinzhu (Today's Annotations on the Chou's Book of Changes)*, by Gao Heng (Qilu Shushe, Jinan, 1979), pp. 72–3. See *The I Ching or Book of Changes*, The Richard Wilhelm Translation rendered into English by Cary F. Baynes (Routledge & Kegan Paul, London, 1968), p. 382.

33. 'A *chun-tzu* is able to govern the people (or to nurture the people) because he has embodied *jen*. He is able to accord to *li* because he has harmonised all that is beautiful into his character. He is able to bring all beings and things into harmony through righteousness because he has surpassed them. He is able to carry out all actions because he has been persevering and firm.' (*Zhouyi Dazhuan Jinzhu*, p. 61, see *The I Ching or Book of Changes*, 'Wen Yan (Commentary on the Words of the Texts)', p. 376.

34. John Calvin, *Institutes of the Christian Religion*, (Philadelphia: Presbyterian Board of Christian Education, 1936), Book III, chap. 2, section 29.

35. There are a number of ways to translate these three parts of one sentence. Two translations for each are presented here so that its full meaning may be better brought forth. The problem is in the second. Chu Hsi interpreted 'to love' as 'to renew' as these two characters in ancient Chinese were interchangeable, while others, for example, Wang Yang-ming of the Ming Dynasty, did not agree because 'to love' was essentially an inner nature, while 'to renew' was more a projection than a cultivation. Having demonstrated that Confucian transcendence consists in both the internal integrity of all virtues and the external unity with the universe, the author believes that 'to love' and 'to renew' are two sides of the functions of *jen*, or two practical ways to Confucian transcendence.

36. Quotations of these five appearances below are in the *Great Learning*, chaps 2, pp. 1–3.

37. *The Book of History*, 'Announcement of Kang', see *The Shoo King*, translated by James Legge, *The Chinese Classics*, vol. 3 (Clarendon Press, Oxford, 1865), p. 388.
38. Wing-tsit Chan, *A Source Book in Chinese Philosophy*, p. 87.
39. The gradual process of one's renewal was especially valued by the rationalistic school of Cheng Yi and Chu Hsi, but disliked and rejected by the idealistic school of Lu Hsiangshan and Wang Yangming. The latter, influenced by the Chan Buddhist idea of contemplation, proclaimed that one could renew oneself and obtain sagehood by a sudden enlightenment.
40. *Zhouyi Dazhuan Jinzhu*, p. 515. See *The I Ching or Book of Changes*, p. 299.
41. Paul puts it paradoxically when he says that 'I love; yet not I but Christ in me'. As far as the Christian conception of renewal is concerned, this sentence may be interpreted either that there is nothing for one to do in renewal, or that one can love only when one opens oneself to Christ and is to be one with Christ. According to the latter, there is room for individuals to participate in their renewal.
42. Bernard Haring, *The Law of Christ*, vol. I, p. 206.
43. More similarities and differences between Mencius and Wang Yang-ming in their conception of sagehood can be found in a discussion by Philip J. Ivanhoe in his book *Ethics in the Confucian Tradition – The Thought of Mencius and Wang Yang-ming* (Scholars Press, Atlanta, Georgia, 1990).
44. Rodney L. Taylor, *The Religious Dimensions of Confucianism* (State University of New York Press, Albany, 1990), p. 40. In chapter three (pp. 39–52), Taylor discusses the meaning of saint in Christianity, sage in Confucianism, and in what sense we can say that the Confucian sage functions in a way similar to the Christian saint. He then concludes that 'the sage and the saint remain within a common mode of expression: the foci for both is found in the balance of imitability and inimitability' (p. 52).
45. 'Since presumably a genuine knowledge of the self entails a transforming act upon the self, to know in this sense is not only to reflect and comprehend, but also to shape and create. For to know oneself is simultaneously to perfect oneself'. Tu Wei-ming, 'The "Moral Universal" from the Perspectives of East Asian Thought', in *Philosophy East and West*, vol. 31, no. 2 (1981), pp. 259–67.
46. See *A Source Book in Chinese Philosophy*, p. 548.

Chapter 5 *Jen* as Virtue and *Agape* as the Human Response of Love for God

1. The *Analects*, XII, 1. Arthur Waley's translation is: 'Yen Hui asked about Goodness [*jen*]. The Master said, "He who can himself submit to ritual [*li*] is Good [*jen*]. If (a ruler) could for one day 'himself submit to ritual, everyone under Heaven would respond to his Goodness" . . . Yen Hui said, I beg to ask for the more detailed items of this (submission to ritual). The Master said, To look at nothing in defiance of ritual, to listen to nothing in defiance of ritual, to speak of nothing in defiance of ritual, never to stir hand or foot in defiance of ritual (p. 162). Compare it with James Legge's translation: 'Yen Yuan asked about perfect virtue [*jen*]. The Master said, 'To subdue one's self and return to propriety [*li*] is perfect virtue. If a man can for one day subdue himself and return to propriety, all under heaven will ascribe perfect virtue to him . . . '. *The Chinese Classics*, vol. I (Trubner, London, 1861), p. 114.
2. This remark of Confucius was recorded in *Tso Chuan*, Chao Kung, Year 12. *The Tso Chuan – Selections from China's Oldest Narrative History*, tr. by Burton Watson (Columbia University Press, New York, 1989), p. 167.
3. Tu Wei-ming, 'The Creative Tension between *Jen* and *Li' Philosophy East and West*, vol. 18 (1968), no. 1–2, p. 34.
4. W. K. C. Guthrie, *The Greek Philosophers from Thales to Aristotle* (Harper Torchbook, 1950), p. 8.
5. *The Encyclopedia of Philosophy*, ed. Paul Edwards, vol. I (Macmillan, 1967), pp. 147–8.
6. 'Shu is away in the hunting-fields; There is no one living in our lane. Of course there are people living in our lane; But they are not like Shu, so beautiful, so good [*jen*].' 'Here come the hounds, ting-a-ling; And their master so handsome and good [*jen*]; . . . so handsome and brave; . . . so handsome and strong'. See *The Book of Songs*, trans. Arthur Waley (George Allen & Unwin, London, 1937), pp. 39, 285.
7. *Nicomachean Ethics*, 1107 a 8, trans. W. D. Ross.
8. The *Analects*, III, 20. Waley's note about this poem is that the poem 'begins by describing a lover's grief at being separated from his lady and ends by describing their joyful union. Confucius sees in it a general guide to conduct, whether in joy or affliction.'
9. Confucius once contrasted the ancient learning with the contemporary learning as 'learning for one's self-improvement' and learning for 'impressing others' (*Analects*, XIV, 24). The former is 'to study out of one's own needs', while the latter is 'to study for the purpose of being praised by others'. This demonstrates again that Confucian ethics is based on human autonomy and Confucian transcendence is human self-transformation in the form of moral effort.
10. '*Jen* is sometimes regarded as very easy (IV, 6; VI, 28; VII, 29)

but sometimes very difficult to achieve (XIV, 2). In some cases, the sacrifice of one's life is considered *jen* (VII, 14; XV, 8); in others, not sacrificing one's life is so considered (XIV, 17–18). Not to remonstrate with one's superior is *jen*, but to remonstrate even unto death is also *jen* (XVIII, 1). To one pupil jen is cultivation of the inner life, but to another its value consists in proper external conduct (XII, 1–2)'. To explain these contradictions, Chan suggests that it is because Confucius was not interested in abstract concepts; or because Confucius was not concerned with the reality or nature of *jen*; or because he was interested primarily in its application, and so on. Wing-tsit Chan, in *Philosophy East and West*, 1/1955, pp. 302–3.

11. We can find a similar attitude in the Christian discussion of the concept of wisdom. According to Søren Kierkegaard, wisdom is inferior to love because it is a characteristic of one's self-love; while *agape* is a characteristic of other-love. In this contrast, wisdom may be a virtue only when it is guided by neighbour-love. *Works of Love – Some Christian Reflections in the Form of Discourses*, trans. Howard and Edna Hong (Collins, London, 1962), p. 211.

12. Cheng Hao: *On Understanding the Nature of Jen*, in Wing-tsit Chan, *A Source Book in Chinese Philosophy*, pp. 531, 523 and 524.

13. Cheng Hao, *Commentary on the Book of Change*, 1:2b, quoted in Chan's *Chu Hsi – New Studies* (University of Hawaii Press, Honolulu, 1989), p. 48.

14. *The Philosophy of Human Nature by Chu Hsi*, trans. J. Percy Bruce (Probsthain, London, 1922), p. 311.

15. H. H. Esser, 'Command', in *The New International Dictionary of New Testament Theology*, ed. Colin Brown, vol. I (The Paternoster Press, Exeter, 1975), p. 335.

16. W. A. Whitehouse, 'Command', in *A Theological Word Book of the Bible*, ed. Alan Richardson DD (SCM Press, London, 1950), p. 49.

17. W. A. Whitehouse, 'Law', in *A Theological Word Book of the Bible*, p. 122.

18. Victor Paul Furnish, *The Love Command in the New Testament* (SCM Press, London, 1973), p. 94.

19. Romans 8:39. See John Burnaby, *Amor Dei – A Study of the Religion of St. Augustine* (Hodder & Stoughton, London, 1938), pp. 85–6.

20. Victor Paul Furnish, *The Love Command in the New Testament* (SCM Press, London), p. 94.

21. C. S. Lewis, *The Four Loves* (Geoffrey Bles, London, 1960), p. 9.

22. Ibid., p. 145.

23. Anders Nygren, *Agape and Eros*, p. 127.

24. W. Gunther and H.-G. Link, 'Love', in *The New International Dictionary of New Testament Theology*, vol. II, p. 545. This is further evidence that Nygren is wrong when he insists that human *agape* is not a proper name for human relations *to* God.

25. H.-G. Link and A. Ringwald, 'Virtue', in *A New International Dictionary of New Testament Theology*, vol. III, p. 927.
26. H.-G. Link and A. Ringwald, 'Love', in *The New International Dictionary of New Testament Theology*, vol. III, pp. 927–8.
27. *Amor Dei*, p. 230.
28. *Amor Dei*, pp. 86–7.
29. Quoted in *Amor Dei*, p. 268.
30. *The Summa Theologica of St. Thomas Aquinas*, trans. Fathers of the English Dominican Province, part I, QQ. L–LXXIV (Burns Oats & Washbourne, London, 1922), p. 117.
31. *Amor Dei*, p. 271.
32. *Agape and Eros*, p. 56.
33. Gene Outka, *Agape – An Ethical Analysis* (Yale University Press, 1972), p. 35.
34. Dietrich von Hildebrand, *Christian Ethics* (David Mckay Company, New York, 1953), p. 413.
35. *City of God*, 15.22.
36. *On Morals of Catholic Church*, 33.73.
37. M. C. D'Arcy, *Mind and Heart of Love*, p. 92.
38. Ninian Smart, *The World's Religions: Old Traditions and Modern Transformations* (1989), pp. 209–10.
39. Confucius emphasized the necessity of obeying rules, in which he saw the way to virtue and harmony. However, he opposed the dogmatism of rules, believing that the real virtue consisted in a flexibility in dealing with the application of *li* (IX, 3). However, the dogmatism and authoritarianism of *li* overwhelmed the harmony between *li* and *jen* revealed in the teaching of Confucius and Mencius when Confucianism was promoted as the state cult, and characterized the later Confucian tradition.
40. Herbert Fingarette, *Confucius – The Secular as Sacred* (Harper Torchbook, 1972), p. 37. This accusation perhaps does not do justice to Fingarette, because by using 'seems' he suggests here that 'a psychological state' is only the surface of *jen*, and because he is going to say that 'The thing we must *not* do is to psychologize Confucius's terminology in *The Analects*' (p. 43).
41. *Instruction for Practical Living and Other Neo-Confucian Writings by Wang Yang-ming*, trans. Wing-tsit Chan (Columbia University Press, New York, 1963), p. 14.

Chapter 6   *Jen* as Universal Love and *Agape* as Neighbour-Love

1. 'How to establish a benevolent government depends upon how to obtain the right people [to govern]; how to obtain the right people depends upon how to cultivate one's character; how to cultivate one's character depends upon how to become identified with *tao*; how to

cultivate *tao* depends upon how to establish *jen* [in oneself as well as in all people]. *The Doctrine of the Mean*, 20:5.

2. For his examination and his opinion, see Wing-tsit Chan, 'Chinese and Western Interpretations of Jen (Humanity)'.

3. Or it can be translated as 'none is not loved by the person of *jen*'. This saying can also be found in various forms in the *Great Learning* and in the *Doctrine of the Mean*.

4. Tung Chung-shu, *Chun Chiu Fan Lu* (*Luxuriant Germs of the Annals of Spring and Autumn*), chaps 29 and 30, see Fung Yu-lan, *A History of Chinese Philosophy*, vol. II, pp. 38–9.

5. Yang Hsiung, *Tai Hsuan Ching*, see Wing-tsit Chan, *A Source Book of Chinese Philosophy*, p. 291.

6. Wing-tsit Chan, 'Chinese and Western Interpretations of Jen (Humanity)', p. 109.

7. *Pei-hsi Tzu-i* (*Meaning of Words*), quoted in Sato Hitoshi, 'Chu Hsi's "Treatise on Jen"', in *Chu Hsi and Neo-Confucianism*, ed. Wing-tsit Chan (University of Hawaii Press, Honolulu, 1987), p. 216. Although his remarks on the early history of Confucian *jen* are not fair, Chen Chun well illustrates in this paragraph how *jen* and love are related and separated in neo-Confucianism.

8. Chu Hsi, 'Treatise on Jen', quoted by Sato Hitoshi, in *Chu Hsi and Neo-Confucianism*, ed. Wing-tsit Chan, p. 220.

9. See Wing-tsit Chan, *A Source Book in Chinese Philosophy*, pp. 660, 499 and 735.

10. Robert Allinson, 'The Golden Rule as the Core Value in Confucianism & Christianity: Ethical Similarities and Differences', pp. 174–5.

11. In the *Great Learning*, the root (*ben*) is also used in the sense of the beginning of a practice. 'Things have their roots and branches. Affairs have their beginnings and ends. Having known what is first and what is last, one is near the Way' (The Text).

12. *A Source Book in Chinese Philosophy*, p. 559.

13. *Mencius*, 7A:17 and 4A:27. The underlying meaning of the fruit or content (*shi*) of *jen* is revealed in the next chapter, when Mencius illustrates how serving one's parents to the utmost will lead to the transformation of the whole world.

14. 'To serve my father as I would expect my son to serve me'. *The Doctrine of the Mean*, chap. 13.

15. Another term [*hao*] is used in a sense similar to *ai* in Confucius' *Analects*. For example, '*hao* JEN' means to love others (IV, 3); '*hao jen*' means to love or be fond of *jen* (IV, 6); '*hao te*' means to be fond of virtue (IX, 18); and '*hao hsue*' means to love learning (XVII, 8).

16. 'He (sage) rests in his own (present) position and cherishes (the spirit of) generous benevolence [*jen*]; and hence he can love'. *The I Ching – The Book of Changes*, trans. James Legge (Dover Publications, New York, 1963), p. 354.

17. Cheng I, *I Shu*, 18:1a, in *A Source Book in Chinese Philosophy*, p. 559.

Understood in this way, the relation between love and *jen* is similar to that between God and love in Christianity. In Christian doctrine, God is love; however, it cannot be reversed to say that love is God.

18. Therefore, this paragraph may be re-translated thus: 'Only those who have cultivated an earnest affection for parents can love (*jen*) people, and only those who have known how to love people can truly love (*ai*) things' (7A:45). The sequence of practising *jen* is made obvious here by the conjunction *erh*, suggesting a conditional, or even a causal, relation between these three. (Compared with other translations of this paragraph, in which *erh* is translated 'but', so that these three kinds of love are contrasted and opposed.) The sequence of starting from loving parents and then extending to loving others and then to loving things is essential for a proper understanding, not only of Mencius' intention in differentiating *chin*, *jen*, and *ai*, but also of his emphasis on cultivating one's affection for the virtuous: 'A person of *jen* embraces all in his love, but what he considers of the greatest importance is to cultivate an earnest affection for the virtuous' (*Mencius* 7A:46).

19. Etymologically, the character *ch'ian* shows us a hand holding two stalks of grain, implying doing two things simultaneously. Therefore, *ch'ian ai* may be meant either that one loves both one's family and others simultaneously – love without discrimination – or that love must be carried out from both sides – loving mutually. However, *ch'ian hsiang ai* can be interpreted only as 'mutual love'.

20. Wing-Tsit Chan, 'The Evolution of the Confucian Concept of Jen', *Philosophy East and West*, vol. 4, no. 4 (January, 1955), p. 302.

21. 'A determined scholar or a person of *jen* never seeks to live at the expense of injuring *jen*. He would rather sacrifice his life to fulfil *jen*' (*Analects*, XV, 9); a person of *jen* 'will give up his life to adhere to *yi* (righteousness, the presentation of *jen*). (*Mencius*, 6A:10.)

22. 'This perverse doctrine would delude people and obstruct the path of *jen* and *yi*, and in the end will lead to savagery among human beings: beasts will be led to devour humans and humans will devour one another' (3B:9).

23. *The Book of Mo Tzu*, 'Ch'ian Ai', part 2. See *A Source Book in Chinese Philosophy*, p. 213.

24. *A Source Book in Chinese Philosophy*, pp. 213–14.

25. 'If one examines oneself and finds a lack of sincerity, one cannot bring pleasure to one's parents' (*Mencius*, 4A:12).

26. 'If one loves others but receives no love in return, one should look inward and examine one's own *jen* . . . When someone is upright [in all aspects], people in the whole world will come to him' (4A:4).

27. 'A person of *jen* develops his personality by means of his wealth, while a person of non-*jen* enlarges his wealth at the expense of his personality.' *The Great Learning*, p. 10.

28. 'If everybody loves his parents and shows due respect to his elders, the world will be at peace' (*Mencius*, 4A:11).

29. Concerning whether or not the most important commandment was formulated by Jesus, we may cite Furnish as expressing a generally held view: 'while we cannot with certainty ascribe the formulation of the Great Commandment to Jesus himself, there is no compelling reason for doubting that some such summary was formulated by Jesus, although it then receives varied interpretations and adaptations in the tradition, both oral and written.' In *The Love Command in the New Testament* (SCM Press, London, 1973), p. 62. These interpretations and adaptations are different in each of the gospel-writers. For example, the love command, with its related themes, plays no great role in Mark, while it is seen by Matthew as a cardinal and formative item in Jesus' teaching and the essence of the law and the prophets.
30. Anders Nygren, *Agape and Eros*, vol. I, pp. 68–9.
31. Furnish, pp. 62–3.
32. Spicq, *Agape in the New Testament*, I:64. Quoted in Victor Paul Furnish, *The Love Command in the New Testament* (SCM Press, London, 1973), p. 27.
33. The argument for this is made by Furnish; see his *The Love Command in The New Testament*, pp. 34–8.
34. Furnish makes this comment on this important issue: 'the Marcan version of the great Commandment has been formulated for apologetic purposes . . . [it] focuses neither upon the meaning of love nor upon the meaning of who the neighbour is who is to be loved. Nor do we have here any special concern for emphasizing or defining the relationship between love for God and love for the neighbour. What is emphasised, doubtless for apologetic-missionary purposes, is the necessary connection between belief in the one God and obedience to the moral (as contrasted with the cultic) law.' *The Love Command in the New Testament*, p. 30.
35. Anders Nygren, *Agape and Eros*, vol. I, p. 65.
36. Søren Kierkegaard, *Works of Love*, trans. Howard and Edna Hong (Collins, London, 1962),p. 211.
37. H. Richard Niebuhr, *The Purpose of the Church and its Ministry* (Harper, New York, 1956), p. 35.
38. A full discussion of these arguments is presented in Furnish, pp. 143–8.
39. Rudolf Bultmann, *The History of the Synoptic Tradition* (Blackwell, 1963), p. 103.
40. Paul Tillich, 'The Golden Rule', in *The New Being* (Charles Scribner's Sons, New York, 1955), p. 32.
41. Nygren, *Agape and Eros*, vol. I, p. 72.
42. Furnish, p. 65.
43. W. Gunther, 'Brother', in *The New International Dictionary of New Testament Theology*, ed. Colin Brown, vol. I (The Paternoster Press, Exeter, 1976), p. 257.
44. Quell and Stauffer, *Love*, p. 47.

45. Nygren, *Agape and Eros*, vol. I, p. 71.
46. M. C. D'Arcy, SJ *The Mind and Heart of Love*, (Meridian Books, New York, 1959), p. 31.
47. Lewis, *The Four Loves*, pp. 69, 70.
48. According to Hsun Tzu, who believes human nature is composed of natural desires and is therefore selfish, this compulsion comes from education as well as propriety. Training cultivates one's second nature and thus also has a binding power on human behaviour.
49. *A Source Book in Chinese Philosophy*, p. 276.
50. Nygren, *Agape and Eros*, vol. I, p. 92.
51. Lewis, p. 16.
52. *On Psalm*, 54.7.
53. Tung Chung-shu, in Wing-tsit Chan's *A Source Book in Chinese Philosophy*, p. 286.
54. St Augustine remarked that 'the Old Testament must inculcate the fear of God, the New Testament will lead on to the love of Him'. Quoted by John Burnaby in his *Amor Dei – A Study of the Religion of St. Augustine*, p. 87.
55. 'Fear the Lord, you his saints, for those who fear him lack nothing' (Psalm 34:9).
56. The *Analects*, VII, 22. Confucius uttered these words when he and his disciples faced a great danger from the attack by Huan Tui who, hating Confucius, sent his men to kill him.

Chapter 7   *Jen* and *Agape*: an Open Horizon

1. P. Van der Veer argues that all religions are in effect syncretistic. See his 'Syncretism, Multiculturalism and the Discourse of Tolerance', in *Syncretism / Anti-Syncretism*, ed. C. Stewat and R. Shaw (Routledge, London, 1994), pp. 197–210.
2. 'When living in *jen* and following the path of righteousness, one will complete the business of a great man' (*Mencius*, 7A:33).
3. Joseph Fletcher, *Situation Ethics – The New Morality* (SCM Press, London), pp. 57, 69.
4. *Shu King (The Book of History)*, translated by James Legge, in *The Sacred Books of China* part I, in *The Sacred Books of the East*, ed. F. Max Müller, vol. III (Motilal Banarsidass, Delhi, 1970), p. 127.
5. Chang Tsai, 'Hsi-ming', in Chan, *Source Book in Chinese Philosophy*, p. 497.
6. According to Paul Badham, the significance of this debate is in its implication that Christian faith is moving towards inclusivism. He takes as an example an open letter 'An Invitation to the Clergy of the Church of England' (20 September 1991). 'This open letter was originally signed by 87 leading Churchpeople, Theological College

Principals, Archdeacons, and Members of the General Synod urging all clergy to resist all involvement with inter-faith worship. Since then they have succeeded in persuading over two thousand clergy, one fifth of the total number of Anglican Clergypersons to sign up . . . They state uncompromisingly their view that "Salvation is offered *only* through Jesus Christ", who is "the only saviour" and "the only way to God"' (Paul Badham, *An Inaugural Lecture: The Case for Religious Pluralism*).

7. Nygren, *Agape and Eros*, p. 736.
8. John Burnaby, *Amor Dei* (Hodder and Stoughton, London, 1947), p. 310.
9. As throughout this thesis, the Confucian theory of human nature is discussed in the contexts of Tzu Ssu-Mencius and the neo-Confucians in the Sung-Ming dynasties, while other Confucians, like Hsun Tzu, with their similarities to and differences from Mencius, are set aside.
10. This view is embraced by modern Confucians, such as Okada Takehiko (see Rodney L. Taylor, *The Confucian Way of Contemplation: Okada Takehiko and the Tradition of Quiet-Sitting*, University of South Carolina Press, Columbia, S.C., 1988, p. 200). According to Rodney L. Taylor, Okata Takehiko believes that 'As the laws of Nature apply to human nature, so in turn do the laws of human nature apply to nature itself. This suggests the extension of the ethical nature of humanity to the nature of all things and thus the degree to which a human articulation of ethics is a part not simply of the human community, but of nature itself.' (*The Religious Dimensions of Confucianism*, State University of New York Press, Albany, 1990, p. 142.)
11. *Yi* is both internalization of *tao* and the externalisation of *jen*. As the former, it is the counterpart of *li* (the moral codes), the essence of human nature (*Analects*, XV, 18). As the latter, it is the same as *li*, the imperative guarding line for behaviour (XVIII, 7), namely: do whatever is proper to the Way and avoid doing anything that is against the Way or does not help the prevalence of the Way.
12. For example, Confucius takes 'increasing population', 'enriching people' and 'educating them' to be three steps of managing a state (*Analects*, XIII, 9). Mencius bases the constant heart of *jen* on the constant means of production (*The Book of Mencius*, 1A:7).
13. The effect of putting public interest above individual interest and emphasizing *jen* and righteousness at the expense of personal rights is twofold: human responsibility for others and for the nation was promoted, and at the same time the structure of authority was strengthened. This often meant tragedy for individuals.
14. Reinhold Niebuhr, *The Nature and Destiny of Man*, vol. 2 (Charles Scribner's Sons, New York, 1949), p. 72.

Bibliography

I. CONFUCIANISM

1. Source Books

Lunyu Yizhu (*The Analects with Translation and Annotations*), by Yang Bojun, Zhonghua Shuju, Beijing, 1980.

Sishu Zhangju Jizhu (*Collected Commentaries on the Four Books*), by Chu Hsi, Zhonghua Shuju, Beijing, 1983.

The Four Books, with Chinese texts and English translations by James Legge, Taiwan, 1980.

The Shu King, The Religious Portions of the Shi King, and *The Hsiao King* (vol. 3); *The Yi King* (vol. 16); *The Li Ki* (vols 27, 28), trans. by James Legge, in *The Sacred Books of China* of *The Sacred Books of the East*, ed. by F. Max Muller, Motilal Bunarsidass, 1968.

The Book of Songs, trans. by Arthur Waley, George Allen & Unwin, London, 1937.

The Analects of Confucius, trans. by Arthur Waley, George Allen & Unwin, London, 1938.

Confucius: The Analects, translated by D. C. Lau, Penguin, 1979.

Mencius, translated by D. C. Lau, Penguin, 1970.

Zhouyi Dazhuan Jinzhu (*Today's Annotations on the Chou's Book of Changes*), by Gao Heng, Qilu Shushe, Jinan, 1979.

The I Ching or Book of Changes, The Richard Wilhelm Translation rendered into English by Cary F. Baynes, Routledge & Kegan Paul, London, 1968.

The Works of Hsün Tzu, trans. by Homer H. Dubs, London, 1977.

The Tso Chuan – Selections from China's Oldest Narrative History, trans. by Burton Watson, Columbia University Press, New York, 1989.

Philosophy of Human Nature, by Chu Hsi, trans. by J. Percy Bruce, Probsthain & Co, London, 1922.

Instruction for Practical Living and Other Neo-Confucian Writings by Wang

Yang-ming, trans. by Wing-tsit Chan, Columbia University Press, New York, 1963.

Sources of Chinese Tradition, ed. by Wm. Theodore de Bary et al., Columbia University Press, New York, 1960.

A Source Book in Chinese Philosophy, ed. by Wing-tsit Chan, Princeton University Press, 1973.

2. Others

Allinson, Robert 'The Golden Rule as the Core Value in Confucianism & Christianity: Ethical Similarities and Differences', *Asian Philosophy*, vol. 2, no. 2, 1992, pp. 173–85.

Andrew, Chih *Chinese Humanism: a Religion beyond Religion*, Fu Jen Catholic University Press, Taipei, 1981.

Chan, Wing-tsit 'The Evolution of the Confucian Concept of Jen', *Philosophy East and West*, 1955, vol. 4, no. 4, pp. 295–319.

—— 'Chinese and Western Interpretations of Jen (Humanity)', *Journal of Chinese Philosophy* 2 (1975), pp. 107–29.

—— (ed.) *Chu Hsi and Neo-Confucianism*, University of Hawaii Press, Honolulu, 1986.

Chang, Carsun *The Development of Neo-Confucian Thought*, volume I and II, Bookman Associates, New York, 1962.

Chen, Lifu *The Chinese Way – A New and Systematic Study of the "Four Books"*, The Commercial Press, Taiwan, 1972.

Cheng, Chung-ying *New Dimensions of Confucian and Neo-Confucian Philosophy*, State University of New York Press, Albany, 1991.

Creel, H. G. *Confucius and the Chinese Way*, Harper & Bros, New York, 1960.

de Barry, Wm. Theodore *The Message of the Mind in Neo-Confucianism*, Columbia University Press, New York, 1989.

Eber, Irene (ed.) *Confucianism: The Dynamics of Tradition*, Macmillan, London and New York, 1986.

Fingarette, Herbert *Confucius – The Secular as Sacred*, Harper Torchbook, 1972.

—— 'Following the "One Thread" of the *Analects*', *Journal of the American Academy of Religion*, vols XL VII, September 1979, pp. 375–6.

Fung, Yu-lan *A History of Chinese Philosophy* (2 volumes) trans. by Derk Bodde, Princeton University Press, Princeton, 1952, 1953.

Hall, David L. and Ames, Roger T. *Thinking Through Confucius*, State University of New York Press, Albany, 1987.

Ivanhoe, Philip J. *Ethics in the Confucian Tradition – The Thought of Mencius and Wang Yang-ming*, The American Academy of Religion, Scholars Press, Atlanta, 1990.

Lin, Timothy Tian-min 'The Confucian Concept of *Jen* and the Christian Concept of Love', *Ching Feng*, vol. 15, 1973, pp 162–72.

Liu, Kwang-Ching (ed.) *Orthodoxy in Late Imperial China*, University of California Press, 1990.

Maspero, Henri *Taoism and Chinese Religion*, trans. by Frank A. Kierman, Jr., the University of Massachusetts Press, 1981.

Munro, Donald J. *The Concept of Man in Early China*, Stanford University Press, 1991.

Needham, Joseph *Science and Civilization in China*, Cambridge University Press, 1956.

Shryock, John K. *The Origin and Development of the State Cult of Confucius*, Paragon Book Reprint Corp, New York, 1966.

Taylor, Rodney L. *The Religious Dimensions of Confucianism*, State University of New York Press, 1986.

Tu, Wei-ming 'The Creative Tension between Jen and Li', *Philosophy East and West*, vol. 18, nos 1–2, 1968, pp. 29–39.

—— 'The "Moral Universal" from the Perspectives of East Asian Thought', *Philosophy East and West*, vol. 31, no. 2, 1981, pp. 259–67.

—— *The Confucian World Observed – A Contemporary Discussion of Confucian Humanism in East Asia* (ed., et al), The East-West Centre, Honolulu, 1992.

Wieger, L. *A History of the Religious Belief and Philosophical Opinions in China*, Arno Press Inc, New York, 1969.

Wright, Arthur (ed.) *Confucianism and Chinese Civilisation*, Stanford University Press, Stanford, 1959.

Yang, C. K. *Religion in Chinese Society*, Cambridge University Press, 1961.

II. CHRISTIANITY

The Holy Bible New International Version, Hodder and Stoughton, 1984.

Badham, Paul 'The Meaning of the Resurrection of Jesus', in *The Resurrection of Jesus Christ*, ed, by Paul Avis, Darton, Longman and Todd Ltd, London, 1993.

Baelz, P. R. *Ethics and Belief*, Sheldon, 1977.

Barclay, William *Ethics in a Permissive Society*, Collins, London, 1971.

Barth, Karl *Church Dogmatics*, T. & T. Clark, Edinburgh, 1956–1977.

Bowker, John *The Sense of God – Sociological, Anthropological and Psychological Approaches to the Origin of the Sense of God*, Clarendon Press, Oxford, 1973.

Brandon, S. G. F *Man and His Destiny in the Great Religions*, Manchester University Press, Manchester, 1962.

Brown, Collin (ed.) *The New International Dictionary of New Testament Theology*, The Paternoster Press, Exeter, 1976.

Bultmann, Rudolf *The History of the Synoptic Tradition*, Blackwell, Oxford, 1963.

Burnaby, John   *Amor Dei – A Study of the Religion of St. Augustine*, Hodder & Stoughton, London, 1938.

Calvin, John   *Institutes of the Christian Religion*, Presbyterian Board of Christian Education, Philadelphia, 1936.

D'Arcy, M. C   *The Mind and Heart of Love*, Meridian Books, New York, 1959.

Furnish, Paul   *The Love Command in the New Testament*, SCM Press, London, 1973.

Gene, Outka   *Agape: An Ethical Analysis*, Yale University Press, 1972.

Gill, Robin   *A Textbook of Christian Ethics*, T. & T. Clark, Edinburgh, 1985.

Kierkegaard, Søren   *Works of Love*, trans. by Howard and Edna Hong, Collins, London, 1962.

Lambert, Tony   *The Resurrection of the Chinese Church*, Hodder and Stoughton, Sevenoaks, 1991.

Macquarrie, John   *In Search of Humanity – A Theological and Philosophical Approach*, Crossroad, New York, 1982

Niebuhr, Reinhold   *The Nature and Destiny of Man – A Christian Interpretation*, 2 volumes, Nisbet & Co., London, 1941 and 1943.

Nygren, Anders   *Agape and Eros – A Study of the Christian Idea of Love*, trans. by A. G. Herbert, SPCK, London, 1932.

Quell, Gottfried and Stauffer, Ethelbert   *Love*, trans. by J. R. Coates, Adam and Charles Black, London, 1933.

Richardson, Alan (ed.)   *A Theological Word Book of the Bible*, SCM Press, London, 1957.

Snaith, Norman H.   *The Distinctive Ideas of the Old Testament*, The Epworth Press, London, 1944.

Tillich, Paul   *Dynamics of Faith*, Harper & Row, New York, 1957.

White, R. E. O.   *Biblical Ethics*, The Paternoster Press, Exeter, 1979.

Williams, Daniel Day   *The Spirit and the Forms and Love*, Harper & Row, New York, 1968.

III.   COMPARATIVE STUDY OF RELIGIONS

Ching, Julia   *Confucianism and Christianity: A Comparative Study*, Kodansha International, Tokyo, 1977.

Eliade, Mircea   *Patterns in Comparative Religion*, Meridian Books, Cleveland, 1963.

Gernet, Jacques   *China and the Christian Impact – A Conflict of Cultures*, translated by Janet Lloyd, Cambridge University Press, 1985.

Hodgson, Marshall   *The Venture of Islam*, University of Chicago Press, Chicago, 1974.

James, E. O.   *Comparative Religion-An Introductory and Historical Study*, Methuen & Co., London, 1961.

Kraemer, Hendrik   *Christian Message in a Non-Christian World*, Kregel Publications, Grand Rapids, 1956.

Küng, Hans   *Global Responsibility*, SCM Press, London, 1991.

Küng, Hans and Ching, Julia   *Christianity and Chinese Religions*, Doubleday and Collins Publishers, 1989.

Little, David and Twiss, Sumner B.   *Comparative Religious Ethics*, Harper & Row, San Francisco, 1978.

Mungello, David E.   *Leibniz and Confucianism: The Search for Accord*, The University Press of Hawaii, Honolulu, 1977.

Rowley, H. H.   *Prophecy and Religion in Ancient China and Israel*, Athlone Press, London, 1956.

Rule, Paul A.   *Kung-tzu or Confucianism? – The Jesuit Interpretation of Confucianism*, Allen & Unwin, Sidney, 1986.

Sharpe, Eric J.   *Comparative Religion – A History*, Duckworth, London, 1975.

Smart, Ninian   *The World's Religions: Old Traditions and Modern Transformations*, Cambridge University Press, 1989.

Tillich, Paul   *Christianity and the Encounter of World Religions*, Columbia University Press, New York, 1963.

Whaling, Frank   'Jen and Love', in *Confucian-Christian Encounters in Historical and Contemporary Perspective*, ed. by Peter K. H. Lee, *Religions in Dialogue*, vol. 5, The Edwin Mellen Press, Lampeter, 1991.

Weber, Max   *The Sociology of Religion*, trans. by Ephraim Fischoff, Methuen, London, 1965.

Young, John D.   *Confucianism and Christianity: the First Encounter*, Hong Kong University Press, Hong Kong, 1983.

Index

Printed and bound by CPI Group (UK) Ltd, Croydon, CR0 4YY

09/06/2025

14685823-0002